One World Women's Movement

One World Women's Movement

CHILLA BULBECK

PLUTO  PRESS

First published 1988 by Pluto Press
11-21 Northdown Street, London N1 9BN

Distributed in the USA by Unwin Hyman Inc.
8 Winchester Place, Winchester
MA 01890, USA

Typesetting: Ransom Typesetting Services,
Woburn Sands, Bucks

Printed and bound in the United Kingdom by
Billing & Sons Ltd, Worcester

British Library Cataloguing in Publication Data

Bulbeck, Chilla
  One world women's movement.
  1. Feminism related to racism 2. Racism
  related to feminism
  I. Title
  305.4'2

ISBN 1-85305-014-8

Contents

Acknowledgements

This book grew out of a course I wrote for Griffith University's School of Humanities' Part Time Programme. I thank the School for allowing me to use parts of that text, and my colleagues in the programme who made suggestions for the course, in particular Stephen Garton. Janice Mitchell cheerfully and accurately corrected the text many times and guided me through the complexities of communicating by computer disk and fax with the publishers. My special thanks go to Judith Allen who through comments on an earlier draft and many discussions over the course of writing this book has generously shared her knowledge, insight and friendship.

For my female friends

Preface

This is not primarily a book about the position of women across the globe. Rather it is an analysis of the debates between feminists in different cultures, debates heightened by the recently passed United Nations Decade for Women (1975–85). As Ashworth (1985: 93) remarks, there will probably not be another such Decade. It thus seems timely to reflect upon the gains in global communication achieved by this Decade, and to respond, if it is not deemed an impertinence given my own limited (white, western middle-class) experience, to the voices of other women in other countries.

While women of colour in the United States, Britain and Australia have been analysing their differences with white feminism since the early 1970s, it is only more recently that white feminists have engaged in the debate, not only with their sisters at home but also abroad. A suitable academic legacy of the Decade for Women would be the routine integration of issues that concern non-white non-western women in women's studies courses. Systematic attention to both the historical and contemporary experiences of these women may lead feminism to rewrite not only its own theory, but also its history and its politics.

This book brings together the three strands of the debate that form the basis of an analysis of the arguments made by non-western feminists: the arguments within western feminism concerning the potential for a global feminism, analyses by women of colour concerning the racism of white western feminists and their ignorance of the specific experiences of women of colour, and the debates between third world women and white western feminists over whether feminism is a 'luxury' in countries where a large proportion of the population, both male and female, does not have adequate food, shelter or health care.

Note on Capitalizations

Readers of the literature surveyed in this book will notice that terms such as 'Black women', 'women of Colour' and 'Third World women' often appear with initial capitals. Such writers, writing about themselves, sometimes also describe 'white women'. It seems inconsistent, a sign of the not coming of age of the category, to capitalize one term – for example women of Colour – and not its complementary term – white women. It is also the case that some more recent texts do not capitalize 'colour', perhaps suggesting a more widespread use of the term in discourse. In this book then, 'women of colour', 'black women' and 'third world women' will not be Germanicized, although 'Aboriginal women' will be, as this term fits more closely with Asian women, Australian women, and is still universally capitalized by Aboriginal writers.

1

Introduction

> The war against unwanted population growth in developing countries has taken a new turn with the unveiling of the latest weapon, the soap opera. No, the Americans have not embargoed Dallas and Dynasty until birth rates decline. Rather, the Washington-based Population Institute is encouraging developing nations to produce their own soap operas featuring such themes as family planning, continuing education, the emancipation of women and the like. (Picard, 1986: 3)

This quotation points to a number of debates that have emerged between white western feminists and other feminists during the United Nations Decade for Women (1975–85). First, the opening sentence informs us that population growth, or at least some of it, is 'unwanted'. Western feminists have for almost a century fought for contraceptive freedom. First wave feminists identified the debilitating effects of long years of childbearing on women in the nineteenth and early twentieth centuries. Besides often adopting for themselves chastity or spinsterhood, they advocated for working-class women access to contraceptive devices such as the cap and the condom. Women in the post-Second World War period, or 'second wave' of feminism as it is sometimes called, fought for 'abortion on demand'. However, many women – for instance blacks and Puerto Ricans in the United States, and women in third world countries – have had birth control forced on them – sterilizations performed without their knowledge or Depo-Provera administered without concern for its risks to health and long-term fecundity.

Secondly the article suggests that a cultural form and its technology developed in the west is suitable for transfer to the third world. Werner Fornos, president of the Washington-based Population Institute, reports plans to bring soap opera technology to Pakistan, Bangladesh, Thailand, Indonesia, the Philippines, Brazil, Kenya, Nigeria, Egypt, Zaire and Turkey, following its success as a birth-control measure in Mexico and India. Fornos is quick to deny the charge of cultural imperialism, which he admits the export of 'Dallas' or 'The Waltons' would be. His proposal is different because 'native genius' will develop

1

and produce the soap operas in each targeted country. However, he does argue for the universal appeal of the cultural form: 'people are incurable romantics. Television is a reflection of people's fantasies, and we want them to see that the key to the better life is a better education, a lower birth rate and the equality of women' (quoted in Picard, 1986: 3). Thus the universal appeal of soap operas and romance is claimed for people the world over. Similarly, western women's political strategies – education, lower birth rates and 'equality' (whatever that might mean) – are assumed to be appropriate for women of the third world.

This book does not seek to analyse in any great detail the position of women in the third world or of women of colour in western nations. Such a task, if it were not to force countries into categories that ignore the historical specificity of women's diverse experiences, would require many volumes. Rather, the book seeks to address the debate that has emerged between white western feminists and women of colour on appropriate political strategies for women in the third world or in oppressed ethnic and racial groups in the west. This debate has gained momentum at the forums provided by the United Nations Decade for Women. The clashes with non-western feminists have left many white feminists puzzled and hurt. That they have, on the whole, responded with attempts to understand and make space for non-western women's concerns is an optimistic sign for global feminism. On the other hand, even with the greatest will in the world, it may be impossible to bridge the different political orientations of women across the planet.

The 100-year sweep of development that brought the western feminist movement to its present position was largely the result of white middle-class educated women. Quite naturally their concerns have reflected their experiences and their perceptions of oppression. However, they have often claimed to speak for all women. As will be discussed in Chapter 2, western feminists who argue that patriarchal structures are a feature of almost all (if not all) societies, consider that the political means of white western feminism should also be those of women of colour and women in the third world. The issues of western feminism – campaigns around sexuality or control of women's bodies, the right to work and be rewarded for it and the right to enter the public political arena – are assumed to be the major concerns of all women.

Sometimes the misunderstanding between women in the west and women of colour is based on a difference of orientation that can easily be resolved once western women become aware of the needs and experiences of other women. For example, Picard, in the quotation above, stresses family planning, by which he means birth control. Western women have campaigned around access to abortion but the translation of this issue into a third world setting often raises the spectre of eugenics for these women. This problem disappears if western women's concern for abortion rights is reconstituted as a concern for women's control over their own reproductive strategies: in this way both the concerns of western and third world women can be expressed.

Other differences do not present such easy resolutions. White western women are accused of being privileged in relation to both men and women of colour and third world men and women. Whether or not this privilege is seen as an effect of racism or imperialism, it has provoked considerable debate between feminists. I will explore some of these debates in Chapter 3 focusing on women of colour in the western nations, and in Chapter 4, focusing on women in the third world.

A further argument is that white western feminists themselves are racist and imperialist, that they have attempted to speak for all women without seeking to understand the differences in position and concerns of women throughout the world. Non-western women argue that their traditional practices, for example veiling or infibulation, are measured against the template of western women's concepts of liberation, and without any understanding of the social context of such practices. Black women in the United States argue that their history, a history of slavery, has produced very different experiences for black women. This experience survives today in terms of greater responsibility for the economic support of families and sexual stereotypes that sharply differentiate white and black women. The ignorance of white feminism of this different history is another aspect of the debate explored in the book.

One of my key objectives will be to disentangle the project of feminist politics from other political campaigns, based around race, or class, or national liberation, for example. It may be that women of colour see national liberation or black liberation as more pressing than women's liberation. To these third world women, often struggling for national independence, and sometimes against forces backed by, for example, the United States, women in the west may seem 'imperialist aggressors', indistinguishable from their governments. However, one needs to consider whether such race- or class-based struggles can indeed bring about the changes in the position of women for which western feminists have struggled. Chapter 4 focuses on this issue by considering some of the struggles of third world women in both 'women's' forums (like the United Nations Decade for Women) and in national political forums, like socialist or other national liberation struggles.

The debates in this book underscore the question of what a single world women's movement might mean: a universal and nationally undifferentiated women's political movement? An opposition to men of all countries by women of all countries? A loose alliance of women in different countries struggling for different goals? There are no hard and fast answers to the questions 'Is there a global feminism?' and 'Can there be?'

However, the book does develop two arguments that suggest the conceptual, if not practical, possibility of a global feminism. First, patriarchal structures are universal on the planet; there is no society where women are not subordinate to men at least in some respects. Thus at least some *structural* conditions for a single world women's movement exist. Secondly, one must be careful not to confuse women's struggles with other political struggles. It is not the place of feminist analysis to decry national liberation struggles or struggles to end racism. But it *is* the role of feminist analysis to ask whether these are women's struggles, whether there are some aspects of women's subordinate position that cannot be changed through these struggles. To the extent that national liberation struggles are not feminist struggles, many of the disputes between white western feminists and other feminists evaporate. They become not battles over an appropriate women's movement, but battles over the correct political strategy. Of course as long as women – in both the west and elsewhere – put non-gender-based struggles ahead of the women's movement, the possibilities for a unified global feminism are remote. However, the contemporary matrix of struggles in which women are engaged does not deny the dream of a global feminism.

A Short History of the Women's Movement

The debates in this book should be set in the context of western feminism's theory and history. Often women of colour and the third world assume that western feminism is a unitary movement, that it is concerned only with raising the status of middle-class white women (for example, it is argued, through affirmative action programmes) or deals only with 'lifestyle issues' like the freedom of sexual choice. Such attacks, often also made by white feminists working within a marxist tradition, must be analysed. Just as western feminists have no doubt misread the concerns of third world feminists or women of colour, so too it is possible that the political strategies of some white western feminists have been misread.

Until recently, the women's movement was seen as two waves with long inactive troughs in between. On the crest of the first wave, and during the first two decades of this century, the suffragists won the vote for white women in most western countries. The second wave, postwar feminism, reputedly erupted from almost nothing like a bushfire in the late 1960s. Its major concerns were the double standard and thus sexual libertarianism for women as well as men, and the right to paid work and equal rewards for it as an escape from household drudgery.

This simple reading of the history, even the recent history, of western feminism has over the last five years undergone a series of challenges (for example, Jeffreys, 1985; Rendall, 1985). The rereading of first wave feminism is no doubt a reflection of the growing complexity of contemporary western feminism as it struggles over the perennial question: 'equal' or 'different'?

While the suffrage movement gathered the energies of many feminists around a single issue, the fact of that struggle should not blot out the activities that preceded or followed it. Perhaps the campaign for the vote is the remembered legacy because it can so easily be inscribed within male-dominated political history. Thus Mary Wollstonecraft is read as merely demanding an *extension* of the rights of men to women, rights to education for rational thought or participation in public life. But virtually no feminist thinker has ever been, nor can she be, that simple-minded.

For Wollstonecraft, as for other feminists who wrote after her, the starting-point was women's position. The dependence of women on men for their livelihood, Cicely Hamilton's famous appellation of 'Marriage as a Trade', meant that no analysis of the rights of women could fail to take account of their position in relation to men. The rights of men, on the other hand, could be asserted in relation to the rights of other men.

Demands for the right to a profession, which preoccupied Schreiner, Hamilton and Woolf, could not be merely the marxist-inspired demands for a right to fulfilment in labour. Feminist demands for access to the workforce grew out of an assessment of women's presumed trade – marriage – and the effects on women of the monopsonic control of this trade by men. As long as women had little choice in their trade, they were forced to accept the conditions imposed by their employers (husbands) in that trade – no wages, self-effacement, violent domestic lives and so on.

From the first, then, the rights of women were refracted not merely through political claims but also through domestic analyses. And from the first too, the long debate about equal or different emerged. The period before the suffrage movement saw feminist campaigns that were premised on woman's difference – woman's moral superiority. This was part of the dominant culture – 'the Angel in the House'. It was thus comparatively easy for women to use their presumed virtue as a leave pass to go beyond the house – to the slums, to the settlement houses, to the social purity campaigns. However, in this fulfilment of their specific mission, women learned organizational skills and battled with men to establish their own space for public politics: 'women's sphere'. It was the definition of 'women's sphere' and female purity that gave women the moral conviction to fight against the Contagious Diseases Act, to battle against child and female sexual abuse and to join the temperance movement, the largest women's movement of the time.

This adaptation of the ideology of female virtue encouraged women to develop a feminism, a sense of women's shared humanity, that later allowed and provoked them to struggle for 'women's rights', demands that were measured against the privileges of men. If Berg's (1979: 267–9) analysis is correct, while women operated within 'women's sphere', they accepted and emphasized the community of all women – black, Indian and immigrant. It was only with the entry into the male sphere of demands for the vote, that some of the suffragists turned their backs on feminism, compromising the rights of some women to promote those of others.

The first wave feminists had little difficulty then with the notion 'equal yet different'; for them this did not smack of the apartheid overtones of 'separate but equal'. They negotiated the rights they felt all human beings should share while constantly asserting that when women rather than men exercised these rights – to employment, to an education, to vote – they would do so to different effect: be their goal peace, equality, the elevation of motherhood or of chastity.

Postwar feminists were initially reluctant to embrace the feminist past of moral purity campaigns or belief in the spiritual superiority of women. Instead, the feminism of the late 1960s was premised on the right to sexual expression, the right to enter the higher echelons of the workforce and the right to participate in public life. Very quickly, however, these rights that seemed to be merely an extension to women of the rights men in contemporary western society already had – 'liberal feminist' demands as they were sometimes called – were recast to take account of the unique position and experiences of women.

To take a simple example, rights to free sexual expression for women required access not only to a different evaluation by men of the 'loose' woman but also to contraceptive freedom and abortions. In time, some feminists argued that the template of genital gratification could not be lifted from men's bodies and laid on women's bodies. Partly because of their erotic experiences of childbirth and childraising, partly because of the different relations girls and boys had to their mothers, women's sexuality and pleasure were more polymorphous than men's. What began as a demand to erase the double standard, became an acceptance of sexual difference. Similarly, demands for equal access to careers and jobs for women required a negotiation of women's role in childbearing and raising. Thus equal employment opportunity required maternity leave, childcare facilities and the sharing of childraising obligations by fathers. For women to achieve the same access as men to jobs, their different social and biological positions had to be proclaimed and negotiated.

As these effects were worked through, for example in unions and business houses hostile to 'peripheral' women's issues, and thought through, for instance in women's studies courses and consciousness-raising groups, western feminism began to splinter into almost irreconcilable camps. Some feminists remained committed to containing the demands of women within the demands of workers. They focused on the needs of working-class women, and asserted that women's liberation would follow from the transformation of class relations and the access of all people to the rewards of labour. Others rebelled at what they saw as the 'biologism' of 'radical' feminists, fearing that the assertion of difference would lead to the ghettoization of apartheid. It was after all, they claimed, women's difference that was used by conservative political polemics to argue for women's relegation to family responsibilities. Some feminists, then, concentrated on erasing the differences between men and women by seeking equality before the law, access to political decision-making, and in extreme formulations, such as Shulamith Firestone's, freedom from natural reproduction. They sought to submerge the private role of woman in the public man she could become.

Other feminists, and they were to become an increasing irritant to the minimalists (those who eschewed women's irreducible difference), began to locate their analyses increasingly around sexuality, or the specificity of women's bodies and their social construction and political manipulation. Sexuality is a shorthand term for all those issues that specifically and almost exclusively affect women; practices which deprive women of control of their bodies and put them in the service of men, either particular men or men in general. Sexuality issues include rape and other forms of sexual violence, incest, pornography and other sado-masochistic representations of the female body in the full gamut of the media, compulsory heterosexuality, gynaecological practices and so on. The feminists exploring sexuality were not satisfied merely with carving out a place in cultural representations and everyday social life for the specifics of women's oppression. They went further to read the effects of the marking of sexual difference in access to jobs, the law, self-determination. They attempted to explain the conundrums that feminists wrestled with in other political discourses. The sexual division of labour cannot be explained by marxism any more than the inequality of women before the law can be explained by liberalism. In seeking to explore these issues, analyses of sexuality forced so-called marxist feminists and liberal feminists to re-evaluate and reshape the political discourses within which they worked.

Thus Liz Gross (1986) identifies a kind of reverse transformation to that of first wave feminism. Where nineteenth-century feminism began with women's difference from men and culminated in the struggle for equality with men over the vote, postwar feminism began with demands for equality and is now entering a phase of demanding 'automony': 'a space where women write, read and think as *women*' (Gross, 1986: 204). The space is new and small and difficult to define but for these feminists it is a space that should grow, both discursively and politically, as women practise their autonomy.

While autonomy does not necessarily mean separatism, it does imply that in some respects at least women will 'go it alone'. Whatever women choose to do politically with their autonomous space, the identification of specifically female 'oppression of women by men marks postwar western feminism apart from earlier feminist formulations and apart from other contemporary political positions' (Allen, 1987: 84).

Western feminism's preoccupation with oppression poses two dilemmas for non-western women. It asserts that the oppression of women cannot be eradicated by other political struggles, that this oppression must be attacked on its own grounds by a women's movement. It thus places women first, and while not placing men necessarily in opposition to women, places their interests and demands outside the space of its own political activity. Secondly, although analyses of sexuality and oppression have sought to explain workplace sex-segmentation, unequal access to education and other material goods, recent focus has been on issues that other political movements have neglected: the representation of the body in pornography and films, the phallocentric nature of western knowledges, the violence to and invasion of women's bodies in the family, in workplaces and on the streets; control of women's bodies by the medical, scientific and legal professions. These two strands of contemporary feminist analysis – its focus on women to the exclusion of men, and its recent reorientation away from economic welfare to physical and psychic welfare – troubles women of colour and the third world. These women often claim that the most pressing concern for them – and their menfolk – is economic security, freedom from starvation or poverty. In contrast, issues concerning the representation of women in advertisements or films, or even in terms of access to contraception or freedom from infibulation, seem remote concerns.

Perhaps they are – and that is certainly for non-western women to judge. But the concerns of western feminism are neither solely those of middle-class women, nor are they merely trivial 'lifestyle' issues. To claim that they are reflects the same priorities by which male-dominated discourses have distinguished the public sphere and the personal sphere, the events of the nation and the shape of everyday life. By refusing to focus on the personal, male-dominated discourse persists in seeing the subordination of women in families or social life as 'natural', and therefore unchangeable. Of course there is no clear separation of the public and the private, but it has been the success of feminist movements to reveal the everyday and the personal as a site of political power and therefore a necessary site for political struggle – 'the personal is political'.

Whether these experiences and strategies are in any way useful to non-western feminists must be for non-western women to judge. However, according to some feminists, it is the universal existence of patriarchal structures that provides the basis for a universal women's movement. It is these arguments, concerning the prevalence of patriarchal structures, that the next chapter explores.

2

Global Patriarchy

Sexuality is to feminism what work is to marxism: that which is most one's own, yet most taken away. (MacKinnon, 1982: 1)

The View from the West

First-wave feminists were not unaware of women of colour. The battle for the vote in the United States split the suffragists over whether or not a choice had to be made between women and negroes. These two terms, 'women' and 'negroes', indicate that when some American suffragists chose to campaign for women, particularly following the Civil War and the defection of negro men from their campaign, they chose to campaign for white women, to the exclusion of negro women. Olive Schreiner, born in Southern Africa, left the Women's Enfranchisement League, established in Cape Town in 1908, because the League refused to allow coloured women to vote inside the movement (Graves, in Schreiner: 1978: 'Preface'). These early struggles, where white and coloured women lived in the same country but not together, have a contemporary legacy, as Chapter 3 explores.

Neither did first-wave feminists discuss the position of white women in their own societies without also reflecting, at least in passing, on the position of women in other places or times. Cicely Hamilton (1981: 73) and Schreiner (1978: Ch. 1) described women's role in traditional societies as more comprehensive, active, independent and valued. Both noted the effects of colonization on the devaluation of women's position in these countries (Hamilton, 1981: 73; Schreiner, 1978: 200), an argument that I will be taking up in Chapter 4. Virginia Woolf (1977: 45–7) explained English women's attachment to 'our splendid Empire' as a product, not so much of ethnocentrism or imperialist attitudes, as of their economic dependence on men and their narrow boring lives in private houses. Certainly to many of their male contemporaries, these women were not part of the public political empire. Lord Curzon, former Viceroy of India, argued that hundreds of millions of subjects would lose respect for the Imperial Government if they learned it was put into office by the votes of women (Sachs, 1978: 37).

First-wave feminists also recognized class differences in the position of women:

> The really hard labour of housework and rearing children is done in those households where the wages of subsistence are lowest; and the women who receive most money from their husbands are precisely those who pass on the typical duties of a wife and mother to other persons – housekeepers, cooks, nurses and governesses. Excellence in the trade is no guarantee of reward. (Hamilton, 1981: 67)

Nevertheless it was the idleness of married life, the denial of women's access to intellectual pursuits, and the position of daughters of educated men which primarily concerned Hamilton, Schreiner and Woolf. Woolf, however (1977: 77), also recognized the claim of people of colour to equal access to education and employment opportunities:

> You shall swear that you will do all in your power to insist that any women who enter any profession shall in no way hinder any other human being whether man or woman, white or black, provided that he or she is qualified to enter that profession.

Whether all black women have the same access to education and other social rewards and privileges as the daughters of educated men, and whether white western women have done 'all in their power' to make this so are two of the key questions posed in this book.

In 1984 Robin Morgan published a collection of essays from 70 countries called *Sisterhood is Global*. A desire to compile a global feminist anthology grew out of *Sisterhood is Powerful* (1970), the first anthology of writings from the United States' women's movement. Fourteen years later *Sisterhood is Global* was published. Contributors had freedom of choice concerning the means by which they exemplified the position of women in their countries. They chose social analyses, anecdotes, fables or poems, while Morgan's research team compiled a statistical summary (including a 'Gynography' of marriage, contraception, incest, sexual harassment, traditional/cultural practices and other women-oriented statistics), Herstory (of female historical actors) and Mythography (women in myths and legends) for each country. The result was akin to a women's world encyclopedia.

Morgan introduces the collection with a discussion of the possibilities of planetary feminism. She notes the now famous United Nations figures on women's contribution to and share of the world's productive resources. Women are responsible for two-thirds of all working hours and yet receive only one-tenth of world income and own less than 1 per cent of world property. She further notes that women have less access to education, significant sole responsibility for raising families, limited access to birth control but more than their share of poverty and starvation (Morgan, 1984: 1–2). For Morgan (1984: 8) reproductive freedom is the key to women's liberation: 'the centrality of a *woman's right to choose* ... [childbearing] is inextricable from every other issue facing women.' Women's 'biological materialism' allows the double standards in marriage and divorce, and is the base of violence against women – rape, sexual harassment, the traffic in women, religious practices such as suttee and female circumcision or the customs of dowry and child marriage. Without the choice not to be defined and rewarded primarily as 'reproducers', and reproducers for particular husbands, women have little chance of escaping these practices.

Morgan (1984: 4) identifies continuities between 'patriarchy's vast and varied set of rules that define not only a woman's physical appearance but her physical reality itself', from purdah to pornography, from genital mutilation to cosmetic plastic surgery, from the veil to the dictates of fashion. Whether enclosed or exposed, women are reduced to a limited role, and one often based on their primary identification as sexual beings.

Thus women share a fundamentally similar position. Nevertheless they are politically divided. Morgan attributes this to a patriarchal plot to separate women along lines of class, race, caste; to call feminism in the third world a 'neocolonialist plot', in the west communist, and in the USSR imperialist (Morgan, 1984: 19 and 4). She (1984: 23) suggests that national liberation struggles have not freed women, a claim that will be investigated in Chapter 4. Against this, Morgan offers the true internationalism of peace and disarmament. Women must eschew male produced definitions of politics – right, left and centre (Morgan, 1984: 25–6). Women's own revolution will be based on 'power *to*, not power *over*' (Morgan, 1984: 30), the search for the self (Morgan, 1984: 36) through using women's position and resources in positive ways. Morgan suggests that some such positive mechanisms are using segregation as a power base, endorsing the pluralism of feminisms as healthy, seeking to unite thought with feeling and theory with action (Morgan, 1984: 31, 32, 37).

Despite this empowering vision, Morgan (1984: 26) admits the gulf separating women, but also notes the attempts to bridge this gulf. The gulf of class: 'a time when the women sitting on the sofas would join hands with the women kneeling washing the floor' (Morgan, 1984: 19). The gulf of apartheid: 'the black and white contributors from South

Africa strain toward each other across the abyss' (Morgan, 1984: 19), but they do not, and cannot, join hands.

In identifying the gulf, Morgan implicitly recognizes the difficult questions for global feminism. Can women achieve alliances across classes and nations in a world still characterized by poverty and imperialism? Can women find 'selves' that are empowering in a world still marked by racism and ethnocentrism? In other words, should women fight male power and its effects – sexual violence, lack of control by women over their own bodies – before they fight specific localized battles around class or nation: union-based battles to improve wages for men *and* women, national liberation struggles for men *and* women of that nation? Can global feminism grow in a world marked by other inequalities or should western feminists focus on cleaning up their own house, and free the women's movement of racism and ethnocentrism?

The major cause for women's oppression, according to Morgan, is biological materialism, the identification of women with reproduction and male sexual pleasure. From this stems women's unequal access to paid work, education and the public political sphere. Two well-known explanations for this universal condition have been proposed by Sherry Ortner (1974) and Gayle Rubin (1975); as such they seek to identify structural bases for the global incidence of patriarchal practices. Ortner and Rubin drew on anthropologists' analyses of the position of women in traditional societies in their formulations. The subsequent critiques of universal 'patriarchy', largely by marxist feminists seeking to integrate patriarchy with capitalism in the explanation of women's oppression, shifted the focus to women in western societies. Following the failure of marxist feminists to theorize this integration, analyses moved into what Judith Allen (1987: 33–4) calls the 'adjectival mode', discussions of the specific instances of patriarchal structures across a wide range of social sites. The debate in western feminism concerning the 'transhistorical' 'universal' nature of women's oppression has its resonances in the critiques of western feminism by women of colour and third world women.

Women, Nature and Exchange

Not only in every contemporary society are women on average poorer, less likely to be found in leadership positions and more likely to be bodily oppressed, but also there is no hard unarguable evidence that any known society has exhibited the reverse of patriarchy: subjugation and economic oppression of men by women. Matriarchy, or rule by women, is either a rare or non-existent phenomenon. Matriarchy should not be confused with matrilineality – tracing a person's descent through the mother. Nor should it be confused with loose usage of 'matriarchy', usually by male commentators, to describe 'mum-centred' family life (matrifocality is the term here – see Tanner, 1974).

The global incidence of patriarchy (Harding, 1986: 658) is also evidenced by 'crimes against women', called by Kathleen Barry 'female sexual slavery' and by Mary Daly, the 'sado-ritual syndrome'. Both of these authors detail the almost inexplicable but extraordinarily widespread and systematic violence of men against women. Barry (1979) discusses the coercion of women as the means of men's sexual gratification, whether through the slave trade of white, Asian or African women, through prostitution, or through marriage. She argues that whether marriage is arranged without a woman's consent or with her consent, most women face lack of real choices.

Barry (1979: 254) asks 'why do men do these things to women?' She answers 'because, in part, there is nothing to stop them' (1979: 202, 258). While boys learn to express uncontrollable sex drives, girls learn to be passive, and to seek validation through men. So needful of this validation are women that they internalize the values of the colonizer, performing infibulations, procuring prostitutes for their pimps, allowing husbands to force incest on their daughters. Barry (1979: 203) stresses the universal existence of female sexual slavery: western women's position is not 'culturally unique'.

The International Tribunal of Crimes Against Women, a kind of alternative to the United Nations International Women's Year Conference in Mexico in 1975, invited women from around the world to give 'personal testimony' (this being favoured over abstract theoretical debates) on 'all man-made forms of women's oppression', even where these were not officially recognized as crimes. Forced motherhood, compulsory sterilization, compulsory heterosexuality, persecution of non-virgins and unmarried mothers, incarceration in mental asylums, torture, wife-battering, sexual objectification through prostitution and pornography were among the crimes to which women testified. Universality of women's condition was the watchword: an international tribunal allowed participants to 'recognize our common interests as women' (Russell and van de Van, 1976: xv).

The Sado-Ritual Syndrome

Mary Daly (1978) argues that footbinding, suttee, female circumcision, gynaecology, and witch-burning are all warp and weft of the same cloth of the 'sado-ritual syndrome'. White women may rebel at the equation of female circumcision in Africa and gynaecological practices in the

United States as lessons in bearing pain, or of suttee's blaming the victim with American men's claims that they are worked to death by parasitic women. White women may well know which sado-rituals they would choose. But this may be because we embrace and accept the familiar, because white women's ethnocentrism fails to discern the meaning of western rituals.

When *Gyn/Ecology* was published, Daly was accused of ethnocentrism and racism, of raking over the coals of exotic anti-woman rituals and neglecting the sins of her own menfolk. This is manifestly unfair, given her treatment of American gynaecology and psychiatry. Perhaps more pertinent is Audre Lorde's (1981: 96) (a black feminist from the United States) claim that while Daly uses African examples of genital mutilation, she does not use African goddesses or African instances of women's 'old traditions of power and strength' in her final chapters. These chapters, in which Daly uses largely European examples, discuss 'gyn-ecology' or the possibility of a woman-centred environment. Lorde's criticism introduces a recurring theme in the debate between white feminists and women of colour – the ignorance white feminists display of the traditions and concerns of women of colour. Lorde makes a significant point: the ignorance is partial – we know of infibulation but we do not know of Afrekete, the black goddess.

The Origins of Patriarchy

It cannot be seriously argued that women on average are in a better economic, political or social position than men in any country in the world. None the less patriarchy has become something of a dirty word among feminist scholars. This is not because some feminists question women's subordinate status in society, but because the patriarchy debate was developed mainly by marxist feminists for specific purposes. They sought either to explain women's oppression in terms of class oppression or to integrate patriarchy and capitalism in their analysis of female oppression. Such systemic explanations have fallen out of favour, given their failure to achieve theoretical fulfilment and the consequent concern with the multiplicity of sites and processes of women's oppression. None the less, a review of the debate is useful because some of the issues – for example class as opposed to gender as the basic oppression – resonate in the arguments by women of colour that race is the basic oppression. The starting-point will be explanations of the origins of patriarchy, a product of this early enthusiasm for global explanations of women's oppression.

It should be remembered that reasons for the appearance, as opposed to the persistence, of phenomena are not always the same. Thus answers to 'What is the basis for women's oppression?' may not be the same as those to the question 'Why does it continue?' For these reasons even if explanations of the origins of patriarchy may not seem to 'fit' or describe the functioning of patriarchy in contemporary capitalist societies, that is not proof of their lack of utility.

Most explanations for the origins of patriarchy focus on the one undisputed difference between all men and most women – women bear children. An early investigation of this problem was provided by Frederick Engels. Engels published *The Origin of the Family, Private Property and the State* in 1884, using data gathered by the anthropologist Lewis Henry Morgan. Engels argued that childbearing created the first division of labour. This sexual division of labour only led to an inequitable distribution of resources between men and women when societies developed the capacity to produce significant surpluses. Engels argued that men wished to pass such surpluses to their biological sons, so they developed the institution of monogamous marriage to control women's reproductive freedom. Engels never questioned why men should desire patrilineage, thus revealing his unquestioned acceptance of at least this custom of his time. Explanations based on Engels' formulation are sometimes favoured by commentators working within a marxist framework, being analogous to the explanation of class exploitation based on unequal access to the means of production.

Other writers have suggested that men in traditional societies were either afraid or envious of women's power over birth. Mary O'Brien (1981), Azizah Al-Hibri (1981) and Marilyn French (1985) focus on how men have dealt with this envy. O'Brien discusses the compensation of erecting a spiritual and then intellectual world. Al-Hibri adds to this the compensation through production and the control of technology – as Freud observed 'with every tool man is perfecting his own organs' (quoted in Al-Hibri, 1981: 173). Al-Hibri (1981: 175) argues that the female 'was planted deeply into the cycle of life and the womb of nature. Thus she had no reason to feel cut off, frustrated or shortchanged.' The male however had to gain compensatory control of production and culture: 'It would hardly have been acceptable for him if women reproduced and also produced, while men only produced.' However, in many African societies, for example, women both produce *and* reproduce.

French suggests that before the rise of patriarchy, societies were not based on control of some members by others. However, once some individuals (men) sought such power as compensation for childlessness, then it was easy to subjugate others who did not. Furthermore, once males discovered their paternity, they sought to control females to ensure that offspring were their own.

Daly argues that because women have the power to give life, men seek a compensating power, to cause death. She (1978: 69–72) links boundary violation – rape of women – to rape of life itself, in mother-miming and necrophilia. Susan Brownmiller (1975: 13) suggests that the cause of patriarchy lies in male and female physiology: 'man's structural capacity to rape and woman's corresponding structural vulnerability'. Elaine Morgan (1972) explores a fascinating hypothesis that at a certain stage of evolution men could only have intercourse with women by raping them, and so the practice persists.

Ortner (1974: 71) argues that because of their natural procreative function and the subsequent care of small children, women are seen as being closer to nature than men. Boy children pass out of the natural world of women into the cultural world of men through their initiation rites. Because societies value cultural activities over natural activities, they value men over women. However Ortner's analysis suffers from a circularity in that the measure of the universal second-class status of women is also the proof of it. Women's second-class status is proven if women are represented in cultural ideologies as devalued and defiled or alternatively if women are excluded from the 'realm in which the highest powers of society are felt to reside'. But we are not told who identifies the realm in which the 'highest powers' reside. Men, compared with women, as many female anthropologists have discovered, often provide different answers to this question. Furthermore, Ortner suggests that cultural representations of women are sometimes in contradiction to their observable activities and status, without explaining this contradiction.

A final criticism is Ortner's (1974: 86) 'bet each way'. She attempts to use the same analysis both to explain women identified with culture, that is women apparently at the top of the symbolic scale, and women identified with nature, or apparently at the bottom of the symbolic scale. Thus she suggests that even if women are identified with culture, as in Nazi Germany or European courtly love, this is but an inversion of the usual identification. The only explanation she gives for this inversion is another bet each way, that women 'stand at both the bottom and the top of the scales of human modes of relating' (Ortner, 1974: 85). Given that there are only women and men in this dichotomization, Ortner is attempting to explain every possible combination: women at the top, women at the bottom; woman is to nature, woman is to culture. The only situation not covered by Ortner's analysis is where men and women are not differentiated in terms of ideologies, activities or status. As Popper (1963) argues in the context of a critique of Freud and Marx, there is no possible empirical refutation of such a hypothesis, unless one further enquires as to how and why the inversion from the usual relationship occurs. Whether one considers empirical refutation necessary is another matter.

These criticisms aside, Ortner's essay made a significant contribution, in that it first elaborated the woman/nature and man/culture dichotomies as both predicated on women's child-bearing functions and as socially constructed. Ortner's analysis has provoked considerable subsequent analysis and argument, most of it critical, and her classification is now treated as far too simplistic in the face of social diversity. In some societies the categories of nature and culture do not seem to exist. For example gypsy culture contrasts the clean gypsy world with the outside 'Gorgio' world, although it is women who mediate with this foreign world. In some societies the acculturated are not men, but married couples for instance. In other societies men are identified with a nature they have mastered, for example the Gimi of Papua New Guinea who associate women with the imprisoning culture of the enclosure (French, 1985: 109–11). French (1985) has, however, recently attempted to salvage some of Ortner's arguments.

Ortner stresses that women are closer to nature than men, not that they *are* nature. Women thus perform a mediating role between the fearful but devalued world of nature and the cultural, and controlling, world of religion, ritual, politics. French (1985: 104) reworks Ortner's analysis to suggest that 'what patriarchy finds appalling is that which ties men to women and thus to nature'. French (1985: 111–12) reformulates Ortner's position to argue:

Clearly, men perceive women as the Other. But women's otherness is of a particular kind: women stand between men and whatever elements of experience they disconnect themselves from, renounce, or fear. Whether it is wildness or uncleanness, the divine or the civilized, women are held responsible for men's relation with the alien realm. This sense of women's not-quite-human status may be a consequence of the old notion that women were part of nature and men marginal within it. It may also be related to the fact that men are defined by their relations to females, as Gayle Rubin points out. However much men may transcend necessity or the unclean, the animal or the earthly, they are related to each other through their inevitable tie to the female body – to mother or wife. Only in institutional life can men pass power directly to other men without the intervention of a woman. Institutional life therefore has great meaning to men, and is often perceived as a truer home than the familial home ... Patriarchy is an extreme attempt to create a man's world.

The Exchange of Women

Gayle Rubin's (1975) attempted explanation of women's oppression, as based on the 'traffic in women', derives from reformulations of the 'masters' of social science: Marx the political economist, Mauss and Lévi-Strauss the anthropologists, and Freud and Lacan the psychoanalysts.

Rubin (1975: 163) rejects marxist explanations of patriarchy: 'no analysis of the reproduction of labor power under capitalism can explain foot-binding, chastity belts, or any of the incredible array of Byzantine, fetishized indignities, let alone the more ordinary ones ... inflicted upon women.' Instead, she turns to Lévi-Strauss and Freud for the beginnings of an answer. Patriarchy is the shorthand term for the political economy of 'sex, gender and procreation' (Rubin, 1975: 166): 'Sex is sex, but what counts as sex is ... culturally determined and obtained' just as economic activity is (Rubin, 1975: 165–6).

The 'traffic in women' Rubin argues, is based on the kinship system, the organizational matrix in which women are exchanged by men. Marcel Mauss, a student of Emile Durkheim, argued that the exchange of gifts between groups cemented social relations between them. Claude Lévi-Strauss adapted this notion of gift exchange to an analysis of women as gifts, indeed the 'most precious of gifts' because this exchange produces long-term relations of kinship (Rubin, 1975: 173). Rubin seeks to rework these analyses, initially by pointing to the obfuscations of Lévi-Strauss's analysis.

The exchange of women binds individuals into 'in-law' relations with their accompanying obligations, relationships in which women are vitally necessary as the coinage of exchange (the giving of one's daughter so that one's son can receive a wife for example). But, despite his protestations, Lévi-Strauss treats women as mere signs or commodities in this exchange. Women are exchanged by men and no thought is given by Lévi-Strauss as to what women's status before and after exchange is, or how such a system of exchange may affect the division of labour, or constrain female sexuality in society, or the relative power of men and women.

According to Rubin (1975: 201) Lévi-Strauss's blindness to 'one of the greatest rip-offs of all time' is partially explained by the work of Sigmund Freud, and Jacques Lacan's development of Freud's work. Again Rubin does not merely accept Freud's argument that 'anatomy is destiny', that one (a boy) either has a penis or one (a girl) lacks it but desires it.

Neither does she completely accept Lacan's redefinition of anatomical difference as a basis for symbolic classification of men and women, the non-castrated and the castrated. What is of prime concern to Rubin is how the meaning of 'castrated' and 'non-castrated' relates to power differences between men and women. Thus to have a penis is to be a male, is to 'have rights in women which women do not have in themselves' (Rubin, 1975: 191). It is to be, in terms of Lévi-Strauss's analysis, the giver of the gifts of women. To put it very crudely, penis envy is not about physiological 'lacks' but about the social power relations that go with biological differences.

But why do women accept this state of affairs? Rubin (1975: 192–8) poignantly describes the repressed pain that accompanies the young girl's education in her destined sex role. Once the girl comprehends the sexual system and her place in it, she must repress the discovery that she is the loser, in order to survive in adult society. She will be 'exchanged' not 'exchanger'; she must reorganize her early homosexual attachment to her mother; she will never get the phallus, it only 'passes through her', and that by the 'joy of pain' of defloration and childbirth.

That is the bad news. The good news is 'the organisation of sex and gender once had functions other than itself – it organized society. Now it only organizes and reproduces itself' (Rubin, 1975: 199); now we can escape it. Rubin suggests that traditional societies are organized around gender relations and these determine economic relations, political relations and social relations. In contemporary western society, however, only the ideas about sexuality, the subordination of women to men, or the ideal of chastity for women, survive. They do not form the basis of our politics, our educational systems or our economy. Because Rubin argues that the Oedipal complex had its beginnings in the kinship system, she assumes, somewhat unguardedly perhaps, that this will be resolved by equal parenting and allowing people choice in their sexual preferences (Rubin, 1975: 199). Such a statement does a disservice both to the complexities of post-Freudian psychoanalysis and the intractability of the sexual division of labour and compulsory heterosexuality in contemporary society.

This stark contrast between traditional societies, where the oppression of women is an inevitable component of the social fabric, and western societies, where the emancipation of men from the ties of kinship and pre-capitalist economic organization also provides the grounds for the emancipation of women, makes Rubin an easy target for accusations of ethnocentrism. Such analyses ignore both the vastly different positions of women in non-western societies (Carby, 1982: 220) and the fact that in a variety of ways women in some third world countries are more autonomous or powerful than western women.

One clear example of the higher status of women in some traditional societies, and one to which even Rubin alludes, is the case of cross-gender females, females who take on the role of men. This not only suggests that some women in traditional societies may acquire the status of men, but would seem to undermine her analysis of women as always exchanged. Rubin (1975: 182) skirts the problem by arguing that in all societies a person must be a man or woman, but cannot be a little of each and that the social construction of gender is more significant than its biological manifestation. According to Nancy Hartsock (1985: 298) this statement, while unobjectionable in itself, 'serves to underline the abstract and qualityless character of the symbols that constitute the kinship system' in Rubin's analysis. In failing to negotiate the specific material conditions for cross-gender classifications and in failing to consider the value of women's labour as a further reason for her value as a gift in exchange, Rubin falls into Lévi-Strauss's error whereby 'the signs themselves seem to speak through persons' (Hartsock, 1985: 296). Much of Hartsock's critique is based on an assumption that a marxist materialist based argument is inherently superior to one which locates women's oppression 'in the purely social and even intellectual realm of ideology' (Hartsock, 1985: 299). This argument may be unconvincing to those who are not marxists. However, Rubin's neglect of the sexual economics of kinship systems, for example the extent to which women perform labour that is appropriated by their husbands, does leave a gap in her analysis – both as to the specifics of women's condition in different societies and as to some of the ways women can negotiate or resist their expected roles.

Both Ortner and Rubin rely on data from pre-industrial societies for their theories. Rubin additionally attempts to resolve the apparent inadequacy of marxism to explain women's oppression, and supplements economic analysis with psychoanalytic explanations. Similar resolutions have been attempted by marxist feminists in the 'partriachy debate', a debate which focused not on traditional but capitalist societies. From the mid-1970s, the 'patriarchy debate' erupted in the United States, Britain and Australia. According to Lydia Sargent (1981: xiii–xviii), the debate grew out of the experiences of women in anti-capitalist and anti-imperialist left-wing movements. Women found themselves relegated to the role of nurturers, secretaries, cleaners or sex partners, who were required to leave the 'real business' of politics to the men. When women attempted to discuss the internal division of labour in the movement, they were told that the most important political struggles concerned imperialist aggression in the third world or capitalist exploitation at home. Women began to come together in separate groups to examine their own oppression through consciousness-raising and other strategies captured by the slogan 'the personal is political'.

Marxist or socialist feminists thus became feminists who 'went to twice as many meetings'; denoting the theoretical dilemma as to whether sex oppression or class oppression was primary. According to the terminology of this time, marxist feminists accepted the primacy of class struggle, of women struggling as workers, while socialist feminists attempted to combine patriarchy and class oppression (Sargent, 1981: xxi). New tools were needed, it was felt, to theorize patriarchy; psychology, psychoanalysis, the notion of a cultural domain, were among those used. In this sense Rubin's analysis fed into the patriarchy debate.

The first contribution to the debate was a collection of articles edited by Annette Kuhn and Ann Marie Wolpe (1978). The term patriarchy was to become a *theoretical* concept with the same status as capitalism. This was to be achieved through a rigorous structuralist account of sex oppression, which explained both its basis and its varying forms, but which was to be distinguished from mere concrete description. This project derived from the Althusserian promotion of Theory as opposed to empiricism (Kuhn and Wolpe, 1978: 5). Similarly Sally Alexander and Barbara Taylor (1981: 80) argued that a theory was necessary rather than 'a welter of dissociated and contradictory "facts". Nor can women's own testimony about their relations with men be taken as unproblematic'. Kuhn and Wolpe (1978: 8) sought to link the analysis of patriarchy to the analysis of modes of production: the 'subordination of women is to be analysed historically in terms of the relation of women to modes of production and reproduction.' Reproduction became a much-discussed term, covering both the necessity (for capitalism) to reproduce the workforce and women's particular biological, economic and social role in this. For example McDonough and Harrison (1978: 28) argued that human reproduction must be studied to understand the specific nature of women's oppression. However the 'social relations of human reproduction ... are class-specific relations' (McDonough and Harrison, 1978: 34). As marxists do, McDonough and Harrison (1978: 36) identified women's lack of access to the means of production as crucial to their subordination.

Analyses of reproduction focused on the family as a site of women's oppression, and this brought attention to the possibility that not only capital but also individual husbands were beneficiaries of women's reproductive work. Kuhn (1978) explained this in terms of the separation of home and work under capitalist industrial expansion. She suggested that domestic labour was 'at the heart of both class and sex oppression' (Kuhn, 1978: 57), but tried to add a psychic or ideological dimension to marxist categories of class exploitation. The family is the 'privileged place of the operation of ideology' (Kuhn, 1978: 66) while the 'notion of patriarchy does indeed unite property relations and psychic relations' – the 'rule of the father' means property is expropriated by men (Kuhn, 1978: 65).

A year after the British collection of essays was released, a collection from the United States revealed similar concerns – the value of using the marxist method to assess patriarchy (Eisenstein, 1979a: 6–7); the need to explain both the why and how of patriarchy (Eisenstein 1979b: 43); the requirement to link patriarchy with changing modes of production to avoid falling into the trap of ahistoricism (Eisenstein, 1979b: 44); and the importance of production and reproduction, the sexual division of labour and the family to understanding patriarchy (Eisenstein, 1979a: 16–17; 1979b: 47). Zillah Eisenstein explicitly attempted to salvage patriarchy from its ahistorical fate or its separation from the dynamics of class oppression at the hands of radical feminists (Eisenstein, 1979a: 20; 1979b: 44). Unfortunately, as Eisenstein (1979a: 5) admits, patriarchy predates and postdates capitalism and it is hard for radical feminists, despite these warnings from marxist feminists, not to see it as a universal phenomenon. The marxist feminists' response was that, while patriarchy may be a universal phenomenon, it must be 'periodized' and 'historicized' in the same way that the universal category mode of production has been. However, not only must the changing forms of patriarchy be identified and explained, these must be linked to changes in the relations of production.

The Psychoanalytic Link

Marxist feminist critiques could thus be criticized for 'giving patriarchy no history *of its own*, that is, for making it the effect of another history, that of forms of organisation of private property' (Adlam, 1979: 84). If patriarchy was to have its own history, it (apparently) needed its own explanation, and psychoanalysis seemed a likely contender, given the 'ideological' domain in which the family operated. The task of psychoanalysis was necessary to formulate explanations of patriarchy which escaped the charges of biologism and essentialism, while also articulating the explanation of patriarchy to marxist theory. Nevertheless, psychoanalytic accounts tended to 'relegate' patriarchy to the 'less important' superstructural sphere of ideology. Juliet Mitchell's formulation in *Feminism and Psycho-Analysis* was seen to produce a transhistorical account (Adlam, 1979: 85.) Furthermore, Diana Adlam (1979: 93–9) argues that psychoanalysis contains no necessary implication of domination and subordination; it merely refers to sexual difference. Additionally, the unwary (often feminist) analyst confuses the categories of masculine and feminine with concrete men and women. Psychoanalysis thus cannot explain how sexual difference becomes an antagonism between the sexes whereby men's interests are served and women's denied, and it is this which feminism wishes to understand.

There was in fact among feminists a deep suspicion of psychoanalytic explanations; not only as a result of possibly crude readings of Freud's 'biology is destiny' which suggested oppression could not be escaped. It was also the case that Freud and the later psychoanalysts were not concerned to explain women's oppression, and this concentration on 'sexual difference' or 'instances of representation', as Allen (1983: 101–2) describes 'the m/f line', served to neglect the position of concrete women as the subjects of politics as well as analysis. Thus Rosalind Coward (1981: 102) notes that feminism is a politics about being a woman, not a category. The danger for feminism when it seeks to rework the categories of other discourses whose interest is merely in difference, is that this is a deflection from the task of explaining domination and subordination. This may apply equally to psychoanalysis as it does to marxist discussions of the division of labour (see for example, Kuhn, 1978: 53–4). Thus Heidi Hartmann (1981: 15–16) identifies as the material base of patriarchy men's control over women's labour power, the ability to exclude women from access to essential productive resources and the control of women's sexuality. Already, however, Hartmann is in trouble with her analysis. The division of labour by sex and sex inequality is the 'universal solution' to biological reproduction but she can see no necessity for this sex inequality. Biology becomes the basis for patriarchy, while empirical examples evidence what theory cannot explain: the existence of patriarchy.

Almost as soon as the term came into use, 'patriarchy' came under heavy attack. It was considered to have too many possible meanings: for example the power of the male household head over women and younger men, the rule of men, an institutional structure of male domination, an ideology that arose out of the exchange of women between kinship groups (McDonough and Harrison, 1978: 12; Rowbotham, 1981: 72; Barrett, 1980: 16). This criticism aside, and it is not a very significant criticism if an agreed definition of patriarchy or even several discourse-specific definitions can be constructed, patriarchy presented a number of other problems. Marxist feminists recoiled with horror at the 'biological fatalism' which seemed to arise from explanations of women's position based on their role in reproduction (Phillips, 1981: 93). Secondly the (apparent) empirical fact of the universality of patriarchy seemed to imply that it was essential to social organization, and thus could not be overcome, while diverting attention from the varying ways in which patriarchy operated in different societies. Thirdly the continued quest to articulate class and gender focused marxist feminist attention on particular issues, to the exclusion of others. The final decision about which explanation of women's oppression was most significant led some feminists to accept a divorce from marxism, while others continued to work to save the putative child of the marriage – patriarchy. All these issues are revealed in the following statement by Sheila Rowbotham (1981: 72–3):

> the word 'patriarchy' presents problems of its own. It implies a universal and historical form of oppression which returns us to biology – and thus it obscures the need to recognise not only biological difference, but also the multiplicity of ways in which societies have defined gender. By focussing upon the bearing and rearing of children ... it suggests there is a single determining course of women's subordination. This either produces a kind of feminist base-superstructure model to contend with the more blinkered visions of marxism, or it rushes us off on the misty quest for the original moment of male supremacy.

Defenders of patriarchy, as well as other feminists, have consistently pointed out that sex and gender (or femininity or whatever its cultural representation) are completely different issues. The anatomical woman is constantly and continuously reorganized in terms of the representation and policing of her sexuality (Coward, 1981: 104). Attempts to salvage women from biological determinism led some feminists into the now prolific work in the area of cultural representation – the path lay variously through psychoanalysis, structural anthropology (Rubin, 1975; Alexander and Taylor, 1981: 79) or cultural politics and Gramsci (Coward, 1981: 106).

However, without a specifically feminist viewpoint, such analyses did not explain why men control women, why reproduction is constructed as a curse rather than a blessing, why women as other/different is also inferior. Secondly, although such analysts eschew biologism, representations of sexuality are constructed, however tenuously, on the base of biological sex differences. Oppression may be 'constructed diffusely' in 'representational practices' and there may be 'historical changes in the construction of sexual identity' (Coward, 1983: 272, 279), but these are claimed to have their basis in biological sexual differences. It is the position of women that feminists seek to explore and change. But women, it seems, share only three possible things – their biological bodies, the representations of those bodies as not their own, and oppression on the basis of gender. All of these bases for defining women as a political category have associated problems; because all three explanations may lead to the conclusion that what is desirable about women derives from their biology, the interactions between their bodies and their understanding of the world, or their oppression; singular and unhelpful explanations of an enormous variety of experiences and structures across the globe.

The relationship between feminist and biological women continues to plague both the theory and politics of feminism. Thus Adlam (1979: 101) argues that Prime Minister Margaret Thatcher is accorded the status of 'honorary man' to retain the purity of women as potential feminists, while working-class conservatism is never seen as misguided socialism. Adlam's analogy loses some of its force however, given a long marxist tradition of attempting to explain working-class conservatism as false consciousness. The same attempts at essentialization (of class category instead of biological category) with appropriate political responses (Lenin's 'class instinct' for example) are in play here.

Western feminists may recoil from biologistic arguments, not only because of the fear that biology cannot be escaped, but also because of the low esteem accorded to nature in western society. Perhaps we have sought to escape biology, to seek 'equality' with men, because so little power and status derive from childbirth and child-rearing in the west. However, in some societies, as we shall see below, women derive considerable power from their unique role in reproduction. Indeed, and possibly partly as a response to such cross-cultural comparisons, some western feminists have questioned whether female biology is an undesirable destiny. Two vastly different analyses are those of the neo-maternalists and the French feminists. There has been a resurgence of interest in the specificities of the female body and its relation both to women's material circumstances and to a variety of representational practices:

we stress that humans are *embodied* creatures – not Cartesian minds that happen to be located in biological matter in motion. Female embodiment is different from male embodiment. Therefore we want to know the implications for social relations and intellectual life of that different embodiment. Menstruation, vaginal penetration, lesbian sexual practices, birthing, nursing, and menopause are bodily experiences men cannot have. (Harding, 1986: 661)

On the other hand, as Flax (1987: 638) points out, men have bodies too. The task should not be to identify women with bodies/nature but to resurrect the significance of embodiment in all forms of theory construction, social understanding and the policing of women by men in society.

Even though the domination of women by men appears to exist everywhere, marxist feminists wished to save it from the sin of universalism. Thus the origins of patriarchy, as well as explanations for its continuance and the modalities of its transformation, were sought. Firestone is reprimanded because she explained male 'dominance in a supposed logic of biological reproduction. This has paved the way for a consideration of patriarchy that tends to stress male supremacy as male control over women's fertility, without a case being made as to why and how men acquired this control' (Barrett, 1980: 12). Patriarchy has been stubbornly resistant to a convincing explanation both of its origins and its persistence. Given the inexplicability (to me at least) of some of the regular forms of violence done by men to women, I wonder whether women from their own experience or even an informed reading of male knowledges may ever discover the 'reasons' for patriarchy. On the other hand, as Allen (1983: 100) notes, the objection to patriarchy's universalism (after all it is a more or less universal phenomenon) often derives from the unsuccessful attempts by marxist feminists to periodize women's oppression with class oppression (see Allen's (1983: 100–1) discussion of Barrett, 1980). For some 'radical' or 'cultural' feminists the need to explain patriarchy's origins is not a pressing concern; attention should be given to exploring its specific manifestations, and possible remedies.

Patriarchy and Capitalism

The various attempts to integrate patriarchy and capitalism have generally focused on the changing relations between capitalist production and the family under capitalism, using concepts like reproduction, the sexual division of labour and domestic labour as the linking mechanism.

As Michèle Barrett (1980: 249) argues, the household of dependent wife and children and the accompanying ideology of women's dependence 'is not the only possible form of efficient reproduction of labour power under capitalist relations of production. It is the product of historical struggles between men and women.' Johanna Brennar and Maria Ramas (1984), in a critique of Barrett's thesis, suggest that capitalism actually has no interest in reproduction; that it was the logic of the sexual division of labour which recommended to women that they withdraw from the labour force in order to meet their childcare obligations. This then led to their lower pay through lower workforce attachments and greater desperation for jobs which fitted their childcare obligations. This argument is not borne out by the now well-documented resistance of male unions and management to the equal participation of women in higher-paid, higher-skilled or otherwise better rewarded jobs. See for example, Game and Pringle (1983) for Australia; Walby (1986: 244) and Cockburn (1983) for Britain.

Indeed Ann Game and Rosemary Pringle's case studies reveal an uneasy tension between the effects of patriarchy and capitalism. It would appear to be in management's interests to employ as many women as possible, given that they are cheaper, yet management on the whole accepts the gender organization of jobs. Sometimes however, male workers are punished by being given women's jobs, or capitalists seek to replace men with cheaper women. Thus capitalists as profit-makers and as men asserting dominance over women have contradictory interests. As Barrett (1980: 27) remarks, a marxist framework does not explain why particular categories of workers – women, black and migrant workers – should be paid lower wages. Ideology provides the motif for an answer: the relations of production are grounded in a 'deeply ideological division of labour' (Barrett, 1980: 40). As Sheila Rowbotham (1985: 60–1) summarizes the conceptual tactics in the patriarchy debate:

> But in making these obvious connections, feminists tended to succumb to dominant versions of marxism, in which material life narrowed into struggle at the point of production. Even in opposition, the equivalent blinkered regard focused on the family. It either became a factory in which the products happened to be human or even more oppressively a kind of Hobbesian sweatshop based entirely on coercion and violence or for the more Leninist inclined, there were laborious attempts to insert domestic activity into the existing body of marxist thought with the ponderous arithmetic of surplus value.

Catharine MacKinnon (1982: 11–12), from a different perspective, criticizes marxist feminists' use of the family as the 'single form of confinement' which is '*presumed* [to be] the crucible of women's determination'. The marxist 'meaning of production, the elevation of productive relations, is punned into an analysis of biological reproduction'. In covering both biological reproduction and relations within the family and social reproduction and relations with the workplace (Beechey, 1979: 78), the deployment of the term reproduction failed to answer Barrett's question: why *this* family form? What is the connection (if any) between the requirements that reproduce the capitalist system (or any system) and the particular forms of gender oppression and the division of labour which exist in western families?

The debates around the domestic mode of production have similarly 'shown signs of diminishing returns for some time' although from the first its 'profitability was highly questionable' (Lockwood, 1986: 17). Again it could not be discovered whether women serviced primarily their husbands or capital, why it was *women* who performed domestic labour, or the value of that labour. For example, Lise Vogel (1983: 155) argues that the private reproduction of domestic labour takes more labour than the socialization of these tasks would (see also Walby, 1986: 53–4). On the very same page Vogel acknowledges the extremely high costs (and therefore barriers to socialization) of some forms of domestic labour – for example 'child-rearing and household maintenance'.

In focusing on some things, marxist feminists ignored others. This is inevitable:

> clearly, there is a relationship between how and what a theory sees: is there a marxist method without class? a feminist method without sex? method in this sense organizes the apprehension of truth; it determines what counts as evidence and defines what is taken as verification. (MacKinnon, 1982: 13)

Marxist feminists focused on those aspects of women's subordination that appeared most susceptible to an integration with marxist analysis – the division of labour, reproduction, domestic labour. In this task of reconciliation marxist feminists were not spectacularly successful. According to Judith Allen (1983: 92) this is because marxism is a phallocentric discourse (like many others). It is not willing (is theoretically incapable perhaps) of accepting that 'women's oppression ... is distinct from the exploitation of labour' (Allen, 1983: 95). Thus the issues repressed from the pages of the patriarchy debate are 'sexual violence' (Phillips, 1981: 93), such as infibulation, clitoridectomy, hysterectomy, involuntary sterilization (Ehrlich, 1981: 125); rape, which 'can be theorised in many ways that do not involve analysis of its possible role in the maximising of the surplus value of capital' (Allen, 1983: 95); 'homophobia, monogamous heterosexual marriage or masculine feelings of superiority' (Ehrlich, 1981: 118); analysis of state population policies, abortion and so forth, which must recognize that 'the subject at stake is the intensely political struggle over the control, issue and duties of *women's bodies*' (Allen, 1983: 104).

Sometimes this so-called 'radical' feminist critique of marxist feminism is seen as an attempt to give primacy to 'patriarchal sex oppression' and hence to see the elimination of this as necessarily prior to the elimination of class- and race-based oppression (Sargent, 1981: xx). This is certainly not Allen's (1983) argument. These feminists are often as happy to assert the *autonomy* of gender-based oppression. Their irritation at being labelled 'radical' feminists suggests that the need to establish the 'final cause of women's oppression' (Adlam, 1979: 90) is a product of the theoretical labour which attempts to force the marriage of marxism and feminism. The marriage may be possible as long as women are seen primarily as workers or as serving the interests of capital, as long as it is the relationship of women to the exploitative capitalist system that is at issue. But 'women as women, across class distinctions and apart from nature, were simply unthinkable to Luxemburg, as to most marxists' (MacKinnon, 1982: 7). In other words, when women are being oppressed and the only apparent beneficiaries are men – for example, bodily exploitation – marxist feminists literally do not know what to say. At times the major response appears to be anger at radical feminism's construction of a separatist politics based on analyses of 'men's violence' and greed (Segal, 1987: xiii, 17, 48).

There are two interrelated reasons for silence on this issue. First the theoretical categories of marxism do not explain the systematic control of women's bodies, sexuality, self-esteem in a wide variety of cultural settings. Secondly, there are political implications, and these are very similar to the dilemmas women of colour and third world women confront.

'The Personal is Political'
'The personal is political' was a feminist slogan which came to stand for a number of characteristics of feminist analysis and practice. First it sought to interrogate a space that was deemed private, natural and cosy by arguing that this too was a space of power and violence: to '*know* the *politics* of women's situation is to know women's personal lives' (MacKinnon, 1982: 21). Secondly, in the practice of consciousness-raising, feminism sought an integration of theory and experience. Thus MacKinnon (1982: 15) argues that it was not Freud or Lacan who taught feminists about sexuality but feminist politics around issues such as 'abortion, birth control, sterilization abuse, domestic battery, rape, incest, lesbianism, sexual harassment, prostitution, female sexual slavery, and pornography'. The practice of consciousness-raising opposes

the scientificity of materialism and its focus on a 'reality outside thought' with the notion that 'women's intimate experience of sexual objectification ... is definitive of and synonomous with women's lives as gender female' (MacKinnon, 1982: 21 and 29).

Thirdly, 'the personal is political' denotes that oppression is both internally and externally imposed:

> Because marxists tend to conceive of powerlessness, first and last, as concrete and externally imposed, they believe that it must be concretely and externally undone to be changed. Women's powerlessness has been found through consciousness-raising to be both internalized and externally imposed. (MacKinnon, 1982: 6)

Finally however, personal politics focused on the practices of men as something other than capitalists. Personal politics generated strategies of opposition to, so it appeared, men as a category; for example in the politics of separatism. Such political oppositions made many marxist feminists nervous. Rowbotham (1981: 74) argues that while the working class can do without the capitalist, 'a biological male person is a more delicate matter altogether', some aspects of male–female relationships being based on 'varying degrees of mutual aid'. Barrett (1980: 13) warns of the 'dangers' for women of reassertion of 'separate spheres'. Jenny Bourne (1983: 12) distinguishes between socialist feminism's focus on a 'system of patriarchy (or whatever)' and radical feminism's focus on 'individualised sexism of particular men'. Because some women *have* seen men as 'the enemy' (and no doubt for a series of other reasons to do with self-preservation, sexuality and so on), they became separatists. Marxist feminists see this as 'no strategy at all for it can never change things' (Barrett, 1980: 4). What they mean by 'things' is *capitalist* things, because as Allen (1983: 96) points out:

> it seems almost too obvious to observe that whatever else it is, separatism is a strategy that does change, absolutely, the relations between men and women. It challenges the ready accessibility to women for men, rejects phallocratic masculinity and offers men women's indifference.

The real problem, at least for some marxist feminists, is that class as a category of exploitation must take precedence over gender. Working-class men, who are also exploited, must not be thrown to the wolves as oppressors, because this denies their experience of subordination. Similarly 'reformist' 'bourgeois' campaigns around equity

in family law, equality of employment opportunity or lesbian visibility
must not take precedence over struggles to liberate working-class women,
preferably through the mechanism of a revolution (see for example,
Allen's (1987) commentary on Ann Curthoys; and Bourne, 1983: 18). Thus
Vogel (1983: 167–8) warns that separation of women and men into
private and public spheres may mean that feminists 'overlook the
fundamental distinction between the working class and other sections of
society' and misapply their energy to 'bourgeois women's' goals of equal
rights within capitalist society.

Sylvia Walby's (1986) assessment is one of the most recent attempts to
incorporate some of the findings of radical feminism concerning the
'state and male violence and sexuality' (Walby, 1986: 50–1) into a
marxist analysis. She nevertheless asserts that under capitalism
'patriarchal relations in paid work are of central importance to the
maintenance of the system', although other relations have 'a certain
degree of autonomy and significance'. Thus Walby (1986: 62–5) details
'institutionalized violence', 'the legal violence of the patriarchal
state', the support of the patriarchal state for male violence against
women; she even accepts that violence among men is 'endemic' and
against women 'widespread'. Nevertheless, male violence only
'contingently supports patriarchal relations'. Rather the 'battering of
women by the men that they live with cannot be understood without an
understanding of the reasons why it is so difficult for women to escape
from these situations' (Walby, 1986: 65). Male violence is explained by
women's acceptance of it, and that acceptance is based on economic
necessity. Even Walby (1986: 65) rapidly retreats from the implications
of this statement:

> Thus violence against women by the men they live with is primarily
> to be explained by the patriarchal structures which lock them into
> relationships in which they may have little power, *and secondly, by
> the general culture of aggression among men.* (italics mine)

However in accepting that men may be authors in some way of their
violence, Walby does not explain why they do this to women. (Indeed
her analysis almost amounts to the argument that 'like Everest, it is
because women are there.')

Similarly, discussions of sexuality receive short shrift in Walby's
(1986: 66–9) hands. While 'certain forms of sexuality are crucial for
patriarchal relations, in particular ... the institutionalization of
heterosexuality', feminists have failed to establish that sexuality is
the 'basis of patriarchy rather than merely one of its necessary

conditions. Such feminists underestimate the significance of material factors outside of marriage.' This is mere assertion, as is Walby's claim ('I consider' – Walby, 1986: 69) that the sexual divisions in paid employment are the most significant cause of gender relations. Walby's arguments owe more to her felt necessity to marry patriarchy and capitalism than to any logical, systematic analysis of either theories or facts about women's oppression.

In the same year that Walby's book was published, the patriarchy debate, somewhat belatedly one might argue, graced the pages of a book on stratification theory. David Lockwood (1986: 18–19) gives 'patriarchy' short shrift, arguing that no weight of evidence on the 'imbricated nature of patriarchal domination' will substitute for 'decomposing the idea of patriarchal domination itself'. Women as a potential stratification category suffer various problems: '*it is fairly clear* that in itself, sex or gender is a relatively insignificant basis of status-group formation; the status a woman inherits or acquires from a man is more important than any she shares with women in general'; gender relations are interpersonal and dyadic – and 'macrosocial deference has very little to do with the relations between the sexes.' As a result 'patriarchy has not proved to be a concept that entails any radical revision of conventional stratification theory, whose purpose is to explain variations in the degree of class and status formation' (Lockwood, 1986: 20–3, italics mine). As Christine Delphy and Diane Leonard (1986: 61) point out, the straitjacket of stratification theory, focusing on public hierarchies, may be as responsible for Lockwood's conclusion as the failures of the concept of patriarchy: 'Sociologists have still not recognized that "the family" is a particular form of *social* relationship. It is not an organic whole: *it is a hierarchical system*.'

Socialist and Cultural Feminism

According to Michèle Barrett (in Connolly et al., 1986: 15), the demise of socialist feminism in the 1980s has given way to cultural and radical feminism, feminist peace initiatives and the demands of black feminists. Beatrix Campbell (in Connolly et al., 1986: 16) suggests that the peace movement 'drew on a culture of femininity and radicalized it'. Anne Phillips (in Connolly et al., 1986: 29), however, is concerned both about single-issue women's politics, and 'a new kind of respectable feminism which defines its politics around women and does not connect with any other political concerns'. Perhaps respectable is another word for bourgeois, and this complaint is yet another complaint against a feminism which will not connect itself to class issues.

It would be tempting to argue that the bankruptcy of the patriarchy debate has contributed to this shift. Interestingly in this 1986 'round table' discussion by 'socialist feminists', in which the above viewpoints were expressed, some still hold to the old views that patriarchy and marxism need to be integrated, that theory and practice must go together and that patriarchy is merely 'a description' (Angela Weir in Connolly et al., 1986: 19). Phillips, on the other hand, argues that she is no longer a marxist because she does not accept its 'totalizing explanation of the world' (in Connolly et al., 1986: 19). Barrett (in Connolly et al., 1986: 18–19) summarizes the patriarchy debate, both defending patriarchy as 'a concept developed with considerable sophistication' but saying 'Marxism and feminism are different theories trying to explain different things and nobody has satisfactorily reconciled them.'

On the other hand, Lynne Segal's (1987) recent angry attack on cultural feminists argues for the resurrection of socialist feminism. From the premise that the only conceivable political action is 'collective', based around 'party politics', 'trade unions' and the 'state' (Segal, 1987: 206, 231, 244), Segal deplores the disintegration of feminism into the 'political is personal' and a separatism which constructs the enemy as man and attempts to repress the differences between women. Much of the book is devoted to a defence of men, or at least some men, and of women who seek heterosexual relations with them. Feminists who repudiate men do so in an attempt to escape 'infantile and unconscious entanglements' (Segal, 1987: 15). Many women have not been sexually assaulted, and some women 'do not feel sexually oppressed by men – they may even desire sex with men' (Segal, 1987: 36). With a quite misplaced attribution of biological essentialism to cultural feminists, Segal (1987: 73) wonders how something as 'fragile as men's genital equipment' can be an 'instrument to dominate and control'. Indeed, it is not all men who are the enemy, just 'white, middle-class, heterosexual and able-bodied' men (Segal, 1987: 29). Politically sound men have learned the lessons of feminism: 'Few men on the left fail to pay the women's movement due respect' (Segal, 1987: 39). Due respect apparently amounts to lip-service, as Segal admits these men do not share in childcare or housework (Segal, 1987: 40). They also seek to reduce feminism to an individual struggle which can be distinguished from the more significant class struggle (Segal, 1987: 211–12). Like Walby, Segal is attempting to reconcile the irreconcilable, the complete array of feminist projects and class politics. It is this pursuit of the holy grail which peppers her book with contradictions and qualifications. She accepts the facts of women's oppression but cannot see her way clear to give struggles against it an autonomous political space.

The same procedures are deployed by the marxist feminists, the contributors to the magazine *m/f*, and Lockwood: feminism is to be measured against the concepts and theory of the 'master discourse'. It is almost always found wanting and therefore is required to 'shape up or ship out' (Allen, 1983: 102). This stubborn blindness to the autonomy of feminist analysis is premised, according to Allen, on a very real concern that feminism cannot be made to toe the line, cannot be subsumed under the categories of whichever master discourse its theoretical servants purvey. A discourse that has not mastered feminism may therefore seem to lose its claims to totalizing explanations. Despite the fact that feminism could perhaps lay the greatest claim to being a totalizing discourse, given the universality of patriarchal practices, it has not attempted to colonize other discourses, but rather to borrow from and transform them in the service of its own ends. Feminism certainly criticizes other knowledges for their neglect of the 'woman question' or their attempt to subsume this question under other 'more significant' issues. But the flexibility and openness of feminist theory (perhaps born of the subordinate status of women, who must thus pay attention both to men and to themselves in the interests of self-preservation – see Kappeler, 1986: 212–19; Segal, 1987: 148), has allowed it to respond to a variety of criticisms: for example from marxist feminists, from women of colour and the third world. In the process, cultural feminism, at least, may transform but not reject its goal, to analyse the oppression of women.

Race, Gender or Class?

Central to the debate between marxist feminists or women of colour and cultural feminists is whether more things divide or unite women. It is not that cultural feminists argue that women are all in the same position. Thus MacKinnon (1982: 9) argues that while women in capitalist countries are valued in terms of their 'merit' by male standards, in socialist countries they are valued only in their capacity as workers: 'Feminists do not argue that it means the same to women to be on the bottom in a feudal regime, a capitalist regime, and a socialist regime; the commonality argued is that, despite real changes, bottom is bottom.' 'Bottom is bottom' for women, *in relation to men*. Against this Gloria Joseph (1981: 100–1) criticizes Hartmann's definition of patriarchy by arguing that 'all white women have ultimate power over black men' and 'that there is more solidarity between white males and females than between white males and black males'; for Joseph race differences take precedence over gender differences. Some theorists (for example, Walby, 1986: 50; Anthias and Yuval-Davis, 1983; Segal, 1987) have argued for an integration of race, gender and class in the explanation of women's oppression. Barrett (1984: 128) argues that white feminists must now admit their 'own ethnic specificity' while not ignoring the 'differences made by ethnicity and racism to both the empirical situation and discussion and the mode of analysis'. But what are these differences? For some it is a 'simultaneity' of class exploitation and race and sex oppression (Gail in Carmen et al., 1984: 60). For others it is the multi-dimensional approach of social stratification analysis, gender, race, class and so on, seen as independent and cross-cutting. For others, the interaction of these must be addressed – colonial plantation labour in the expansion of capitalism for example (Crompton and Mann, 1986: 5). Contributors to feminist journals now assert that we must take race, gender and class differences seriously. However there are few attempts to analyse the interconnections of these categories. Perhaps the first move must be a widespread understanding on the part of white western feminists that when we say 'women', we often mean 'women like ourselves'. To stop and think every time the category woman is used, as we now stop before writing 'man' or 'he', is the first, but not insignificant, step in rewriting feminism; either to be contained within its proper limits as white middle-class feminism or to be expanded through the possibilities of a global feminism.

Thus, while feminists should avoid the sterile debate over which is *most* oppressive – race, class or gender systems (a debate we will return to below) – we must also remain sensitive to the fact that women have different experiences and therefore different political priorities. We should not attempt the mechanical coupling and subordination of one discourse to another in our explanation of the position of women of colour. But neither should we neglect the specificity and autonomy of gender-based oppression, revealed according to Allen (1987: 53–4) by the movement of patriarchy into its 'adjectival phase' where it has been joined by a host of other adjectives – 'phallocentric', 'phallocratic', 'phallologocentric', 'androcentric', 'masculinist'.

Patriarchy has been a useful word to denote the widespread experience of exploitation, despite the fact that attempts to unravel its operation have not been successful:

Gail: Why I can't call myself a 'lesbian feminist' because to me it is a whole concept that says you subsume everything to patriarchy

Carmen: It depends on what patriarchy means ...

Gail: It depends on what capitalism means ... (Carmen et al., 1984: 66)

Just so. Let us turn our attention then to the 'oppression of women', which points to the same widespread experience as does the notion 'patriarchy', but which has not been held up to the light of marxist theory, and thus found wanting.

Hierarchies of Patriarchy

Some writers have sought to categorize groups of societies according to different levels of female oppression. Such analyses are rarely proposed by anthropologists, sensitive to the uniqueness of each culture, but are often based on anthropological field work. Some of the variables that have been considered are whether women in traditional societies work, whether they may do so in the capitalist sector of such societies, and whether kinship organizations are patrilocal or matrilocal – whether the bride goes to live with her husband's family or vice versa. These factors are explored briefly below.

There has long been a debate as to whether this planet has ever seen societies that, if not matriarchal, at least accorded women high status. French (1985) explores the warmth of the perhaps mythical matriarchal past when violence, slaughter and hate were not the order of the day. Morgan's (1984) collection reveals that almost every country has a mythography of powerful and/or benevolent goddesses. Not all these goddesses were creators; some, like the oft-mentioned Amazons, were fighters. The warrior women Sigyns of Iran could not take a husband until they had killed three male enemies (Morgan, 1984: 330). On the other hand, Anne Cameron (1983) relates Canadian Indian stories of the Original Women, who found men incomplete and dull and preferred each other's company. There are still some extant gathering, hunting and horticultural societies which perhaps suggest that these myths reflect an earlier time when women had greater status and power (French, 1985: 56–63).

Factors in Women's Status in Third World Societies
Work
As French indicates, these societies were usually hunting and gathering societies. Such societies sometimes changed into horticultural, or crop-planting, societies. According to Ester Boserup (1970) it was the transition from horticulture to agriculture, from hoe to plough farming, that marked one significant change in the status of women. Boserup's (1970) analysis of the effects of the replacement of the hoe with the plough on women's labour suggests that in plough-based economies (for example, much of India), women of status are freed from agricultural labour while in hoe-based economies (for example, much of Africa),

women remain key agricultural producers. In west Africa particularly, women are also traders (Cutrafelli, 1983: 9,299). This activity allows African women to accumulate surpluses, form co-operatives, congregate together, travel away from their homes and sometimes exert considerable political influence.

Boserup (1970: 186–90) argues that women's agricultural participation increases the likelihood that they will be traders which then increases their access to western-style jobs. However, the links are by no means certain. While women in many south and east Asian countries are economically very active in the capitalist sector, in Africa it is deemed inappropriate for women to work for men who are not their husbands. In South America, women have low rural participation rates but quite high workforce participation rates in the towns. In some Arab countries women have access to the professions and sub-professions of medicine and education because seclusion means that men cannot teach girls or examine their bodies. In many Chinese cultures women are encouraged to participate in the workforce but also to hand all their earnings over to a mother or mother-in-law (Johnson, 1984: 83). Many women escape this obligation by leaving home, for example to live in a dormitory (Kung, 1984: 112).

Conversely, remaining on the land may also be a route to economic independence. Some African women who remained when their husbands went to the cities to work grew crops on their husbands' land, traded and invested. They were thus able to repay the bride-price and leave their husbands (Obbo, 1980: 148, 154). In these instances, attempts by various African leaders to protect traditional culture by confining women to their villages rebounds against them.

Thus it seems that without access to economic independence, women seem less able to change the conditions of their life if they so wish. However, one should not too hastily agree with the marxist proposition that labour is the route to emancipation. First, as suggested above, women already do a majority of the world's work. Such work provides women with little power unless they also control the products of that labour. Second, for many women, as much as their husbands, escape from toil to the domestic sphere is seen as freedom and increased status. Thus in Muslim and Hindu societies only wealthy families can afford to seclude their wives, but many women prefer seclusion (Sharma, 1980: 127). Being 'immured in a cage' has attractions over the 'degradation of impoverishment and backbreaking work' (Jeffery, 1979: 174). Various writers report similar attitudes in South East Asia (Robinson, 1983: 124), in rural Malay societies (Barnard, 1983: 138), and in Puerto Rico (Safa, 1980: 107).

Participation in both traditional and capitalist paid labour may be at the cost of marriage and a family, as Maria Cutrufelli (1983: 71) argues for African women. In Bali, for example, women who choose to be midwives, herbalists and traditional masseuses must often remain spinsters because of various taboos. This status is considered a bleak one: in Balinese temples childless women are pictured 'being suckled by caterpillars and subject to other hell torments' (Connor, 1983: 66).

Access to trading activities as well as much capitalist sector work requires freedom of movement and permission to mix in wider society. Sometimes attempts are made to restrict women's freedom of movement. As noted above, African women are encouraged to remain in rural villages to protect traditional culture (Obbo, 1982: 149). The freedom of movement of women in Muslim cultures is severely circumscribed. Secluded women can only leave home for a few hours and ideally should be accompanied by a male at all times. There are two aspects to seclusion. On the one hand, women are denied access to the world of work and politics. On the other hand, women have considerable control over their own women's community, with its festivals, ideologies and information networks (for example, concerning potential marriage partners). In this community, power often devolves on older women who are mothers of sons (Jeffery, 1979: 171–3; French, 1985: 256).

Bride-price and Dowry

Another key indicator of women's status, itself linked to economic activity and mobility, is the system of exchange of women – whether women attract a bride-price or cost a dowry. Patricia Jeffery (1979: 25), following Boserup, argues that in the transition from hoe culture to a more settled plough culture, women came to be valued not for their productive capacities but for their reproductive capacities. Thus women were secluded to prevent misalliances, and instead of a bride-wealth being paid *for* the woman, a dowry was paid *with* the woman. Ursula Sharma (1980: 142) suggests that the dowry is a compensation paid to the husband's family for the woman's financial dependence on the husband, although she stresses its size is also a status symbol.

On the other hand, in some societies where women can pay off their bride-wealth, for example in Africa, they can annul the marriage. Where Moroccan wives are taken without payment of a bride-wealth, they have the right to remain with their own kin (Maher, 1981: 79). Conversely, in societies, such as India, where women bring dowries, they seem far more susceptible to immolation where the dowries are deemed insufficient. It should be noted that the contributors to Manushi (1983: 204) attribute the contemporary burning of Indian wives to consumerism, that is to western, not Hindu values. Sankar (1984: 239) discusses a traditional Chinese silk-growing community where girls belonged to girls' houses, customarily resisted marriage, and could choose spinsterhood by joining a sisterhood, with a ceremony similar to the marriage ceremony. One of the key arguments daughters used against their families to resist marriage was that they were productive workers and could not be spared from their fathers' silk growing enterprise.

Bride-price and dowry, then, are related to whether women are seen as productive labourers or not. Women who are productive labourers seem to have more opportunities to escape the marriage system or to reverse the marital relationship. Women who come with a dowry as reproducers have far fewer chances of escape.

Bride-service, in which the husband pays gifts of labour to his wife's family, appears to give women even more marital independence. Bride-service is seen as proof of fitness to be a husband (rather than payment for a wife), which must be continually reinforced or the woman can choose to leave her husband. In bride-service cultures the groom is not in debt to his elders (who will supply the bride-price in other cultures) while women often resist marriage, as they have the same access to products of the hunt (provided by their male blood relations) whether single or married. Men seek marriage as this gives them access to the products of their wives' labour (Collier and Rosaldo, 1981).

A further explanation for the varying position of women in traditional societies is based on whether the system is patrilineal or matrilineal. According to Cutrufelli (1983: 53–69), in patrilineal systems women have no inheritance rights, they are not consulted over community decisions, polygamy and private property ownership are favoured. All this is in contrast to matrilineal systems, where, if they are also matrilocal, polygamy cannot be practised because men would be unable to control their scattered wives. Nancy Tanner (1974) argues that it is not matrilineality or matrilocality but matrifocality – the elevation of the mother–child and sibling relationship over the conjugal relationship – that determines the greater status of women. Matrilocality means that place of residence promotes strong ties between women and with the kin of their family of origin.

The line of argument here, then, is that women will tend to have less power where they have little access to the rewards of labour, where they are secluded, where they are given with a dowry and where they go to live with the husband's family.

Networks

Perhaps the most interesting classification of patriarchal societies is provided by Lisa Leghorn and Catherine Parker (1981). They base women's power on their ability to form and develop networks, identifying three types of societies. In societies where women have minimal power, they have little access to resources and little freedom in reproduction. There is low valuation of their capacities to reproduce, much violence against women, denial by men of female values and little sharing of experiences with other women. In societies where women have token power, they have varying access to resources, there are mixed messages on the value of reproduction, female values are denied and women have some freedom to create networks. In societies where women have negotiating power their resources are often different from men's, women have enough economic independence and leverage to bargain, there is high valuation of reproductive work, men have dealt with their fear and awe of women by ritualizing it, and women have some freedom to create networks (Leghorn and Parker, 1981: 29, 278).

These three types of societies do not conform to third world, capitalist and socialist, although Leghorn and Parker suggest that the western impact reduces women's power in negotiating power societies while increasing it in minimal power societies. Sometimes the benefits which follow colonisation flow principally to middle-class women, because of the reproduction of western societies' class stratification.

Anthropologists can rarely be accused of ethnocentrism. The early founders of the discipline, Bronislaw Malinowski and A.R. Radcliffe-Brown, insisted on the particularity of each society and the importance of discovering the function for that society of practices that had previously been seen as titillating or offensive to a white audience. Today, some feminists like Mary Daly are accused of being ethnocentric when they describe different social practices as manifestations of the universal oppression of women. Are these feminists ethnocentric in the way Malinowski and Radcliffe-Brown accused their forebears of being?

By western feminists' standards, women in some societies *do* have more power than they have in other societies. Although many anthropologists may rebel at the classifications attempted by writers such as Boserup, there do seem to be some general explanations for these differences – whether women have access to productive labour and the fruits of that labour, whether they are seen primarily as reproducers and as a result are often secluded, whether they have access to networks with other women – for example, if they trade, if the society is matrilocal, even if they go to common wells to collect water.

However, Leghorn and Parker's focus on women's networks points to the ethnocentrism among many western feminists in their assessment of other cultures. Until recently there has been a strong tendency to focus on 'equality' of women and men in the west (for example, access to higher paid jobs or election to government). Advocates of such a programme would perhaps dismiss the 'separate but equal' attitude of many non-western women. The argument that women have their own spheres, for example, in the secluded household or in their role as reproducers, which give them a power, a negotiating power over men, has sometimes been discounted by western feminists.

Fay Gale argues that the title of her edited collection *We are Bosses Ourselves* reflects the opinion of Australian Aboriginal women that they have more power than white Australian women because they have their own responsibilities and communities within wider Aboriginal society. Some anthropologists go so far as to say that such resources give women equal power with men in negotiating power societies. Whether this is the case, or the result of the long tradition of cultural relativism or anti-ethnocentrism in anthropology, cannot be decided without a measure of what equality for women means. Thus feminists often disagree over how to measure equality.

Most western feminists do not deny differences in status, power and cultural valuations between women of different cultures. But overall the cultural feminists conclude that despite these marked differences there is a generalized and overriding oppression of women; that is, whatever their power or avenues for resistance or escape, women are always less powerful than men in economic and cultural terms: 'bottom is bottom' as MacKinnon (1982: 9) puts it. It is this that produces the basis, according to these feminists, for a global feminism.

Women's Studies in International Perspective – Statistical Indicators

Another means of exploring, at least in a shorthand way, the diverse experiences of women around the world is through comparative statistics. As part of the UN Decade of Women, *The New Internationalist* compiled 'A World Report' of women (Davis et al., 1985). Analysis of the figures and tables in the 'World Report' suggests that women in developing countries seem to be worse off than those in developed countries. For instance women in the third world participate less in the paid labour force (Figure 5: 31), are more likely to become teenage mothers (Figures 8 and 9: 58–9), less likely to receive schooling (Table 4: 71), more likely to have their children die (Figure 10: 86), less likely to have access to contraception. However, there are some anomalies. A greater percentage of women in Venezuela are bosses than in Germany (Table 2: 36); women receive the lowest wages compared with men in Japan, not Burma, El Salvador or Kenya; more countries in Africa, Asia and Oceania have equal opportunity in employment legislation than in Western Europe and North America (*New Internationalist* , No.145, August 1985: 10).

Furthermore, the choice of variables for evaluation may be questioned; they seem to be based on the issues western feminists see as crucial to women's subordination. Should all women desire greater use of contraception, given that eugenics is a specific concern of women of colour and third world women? The large amount of unpaid agricultural work of women in developing countries is not represented in data on the paid labour force, while some third world women see work as drudgery not liberation. Education is represented in the west as a means to better paid jobs, and as a correlate of reduced birth rates but is this mechanism of upward mobility desired by all women? Equal rights legislation is very much a product of the efforts of liberal feminists in the west. Not only is the legislation often no indication of real civil rights (compare the Constitution of the USSR or the United States with the practices in those countries for example), but also this type of legislation may be an inappropriate means for enhancing the position of women in third world countries.

In Chapter 4 these issues will be analysed in terms of the debate between women of the 'western' and 'third' worlds. Western mechanisms for achieving equality – access to paid labour, education, legal rights, contraceptive freedom – pervade the analyses of western women and the plans produced by the United Nations Decade for Women. While such projects are not always rejected by the women for whom they are designed, there is some debate as to whether these are the best, or only, mechanisms of liberation.

The figures in the World Report do not distinguish different racial, ethnic or religious groups in each country when assessing the position of women. As Chapter 3 explains, women of colour assert that such considerations are essential. When western feminists demand equality, they are implicitly demanding equality not with men of colour or working-class men but with white middle-class men. Thus tables in *The New Internationalist* (No. 140, March 1985: 10–11) suggest that for all the indicators chosen, coloured people in Australia, Canada, the United Kingdom, New Zealand and the United States have fewer resources than whites – they are more likely to be unemployed, have inadequate housing, little or inappropriate education, their life expectancy is lower while infant mortality rates are two and three times higher than the national average. Aborigines in Australia earn on average half the income of whites, as do Puerto Ricans in the United States, while coloured immigrants to Britain earn significantly less than white workers. In South Africa earnings of black Africans are less than 5 per cent of white earnings in the mining sector while infant mortality rates are six times higher for blacks than whites (van Vuuren, 1979: Table E, Chapter 8).

Such figures do not give comparisons between white and coloured men and women, comparisons rarely produced in the statistical literature, but Tables 1–4 do. For an analysis of the relationship between race and gender, South Africa, the United States, Australia and United Kingdom have been chosen. Tables for the United States reveal that white males are advantaged over all other groups on every variable except life expectancy. Black women tend to be at the other end of the scale. However, a greater percentage of black women than black men are in the managerial and professional occupations (Table 1).

Table 1   Occupations by Race and Sex: Civilian Workforce (USA)

	White Male No.	%	White Female No.	%	Black Male No.	%	Black Female No.	%
Managerial & professional	(13,420)	27.5	(9,587)	24.6	(599)	13.0	(786)	16.2
Technical, sales, adminis- trative	(10,414)	21.3	(18,166)	46.6	(752)	16.3	(1,762)	36.4
Service occupations	(4,429)	9.1	(6,740)	17.3	(955)	20.7	(1,500)	31.0
Precision production	(10,490)	21.5	(870)	2.2	(682)	14.8	(98)	2.0
Operators, fabricators, labourers	(10,106)	20.7	(3,620)	9.3	(1,618)	35.1	(693)	14.3
Total (000's)	(48,859)	100	(38,983)	100	(4,606)	100	(4,839)	100

Note: excludes farming, forestry, fishing
Source: United States Department of Commerce, Bureau of the Census, Statistical Abstract of the United States, 1985, Washington, p. 401

Black and white women's college enrolment rates are closer than are the rates for men, though the gap grew between 1970 and 1983 (Table 4). Table 2 shows that the average earnings of black men were in 1974 higher than for white women in the north and west of the United States, although not for the whole country. Table 3 reveals that in 1981, black women earned on average 60 per cent of black men's earnings who earned 66 per cent of white men's earnings, while white women earned only 44 per cent of white men's earnings. The results for year-round full-time workers reveal the same ordering but the wage differentials are lower. Since 1947 the gap between white women and white men has widened (0.472 to 0.437, with its lowest point in 1966), while for the other groups the gap has closed. Thus black women and white women now earn on average almost the same wages (0.919 compared with 0.538 in 1948).

Table 2   Median Income of Persons 14 Years Old and Over by Race and Sex 1974 (USA)

	United States	*South*	*North and West*
White men	12,434	11,508	12,782
Black men	8,705	7,411	10,491
White women	8,794	7,988	9,161
Black women	5,370	4,306	6,874
Ratio:			
Black men to white men	0.70	0.64	0.82
Black women to white women	0.61	0.54	0.75
Black men to white women	0.99	0.93	1.15

Source: National Institute of Education, Conference on Education and Occupational Needs of Black Women, held December 1975, vol. 2, Washington, 1978, Statistical Appendix compiled by E.C. Lee, p. 259

As French (1985: 465) argues, the near equality is at the expense of a growing gap between male and female earnings. In 1980, 70 per cent of those below the poverty line were white. So while blacks were over-represented (30 per cent of the poor but only 12 per cent of the total population), the bulk of those in poverty were white. Phyllis Palmer (1983: 154) argues that this growing feminization of poverty may provide grounds for drawing black women and white women together over struggles to improve state pensions and services and women's wages. However while in 1981, 12 per cent of white households were headed by women, 42 per cent of black households were (Palmer, 1983: 161), and the fact that white male incomes remain higher than black male incomes means that economic dependence for white women is still likely to give them a higher standard of living than such dependence gives black women. On the other hand, Palmer (1983: 163) and Sylvia Hewlett (1987: Part Two) point to the alienation of both working-class white women and black women from a white women's movement which focuses on intra-family power or access to the professions.

Table 3   Mean Income Ratios for White and Non-white Men and Women and Year-round, Full–time Workers 14 Years and Older, 1948–81

	All Persons				YRFT Workers			
	WW/WM	BW/BM	BM/WM	BW/WW	WW/WM	BW/BM	BM/WM	BW/WW
1948	.472	.479	.530	.538				
1949	.478	.511	.508	.543				
1950	.444	.454	.520	.531				
1951	.441	.432	.526	.515				
1952	.457	.449	.540	.531				
1953	.449	.515	.533	.612				
1954	.449	.498	.532	.591				
1955	.437	.456	.530	.554	.605	.630	.548	.571
1956	.420	.483	.525	.603	.579	.641	.540	.598
1957	.424	.476	.538	.605	.579	.628	.561	.610
1958	.420	.484	.538	.620	.582	.633	.569	.618
1959	.406	.511	.520	.654	.572	.662	.542	.627
1960	.403	.488	.551	.667	.554	.639	.602	.694
1961	.403	.512	.543	.688	.546	.662	.579	.702
1962	.402	.510	.531	.675	.550	.645	.557	.653
1963	.400	.487	.566	.689	.559	.594	.607	.645
1964	.408	.501	.597	.734	.559	.645	.628	.724
1965	.397	.518	.563	.734	.540	.647	.588	.705
1966	.395	.531	.576	.775	.536	.658	.594	.728
1967	.404	.537	.601	.800	.548	.661	.628	.758
1968	.406	.534	.612	.804	.540	.658	.635	.775
1969	.401	.551	.602	.828	.549	.710	.637	.824
1970	.406	.581	.617	.882	.561	.726	.661	.856
1971	.413	.579	.626	.880	.556	.729	.672	.882
1972	.402	.599	.625	.931	.545	.729	.666	.892
1973	.399	.554	.642	.891	.542	.680	.686	.862
1974	.411	.570	.664	.920	.550	.707	.729	.938
1975	.420	.604	.652	.938	.552	.719	.720	.938
1976	.424	.608	.648	.930	.561	.729	.713	.928
1977	.427	.600	.652	.918	.553	.728	.716	.942
1978	.414	.591	.669	.956	.558	.711	.742	.944
1979	.408	.581	.667	.952	.563	.726	.733	.944
1980	.427	.608	.666	.948	.587	.716	.746	.911
1981	.437	.606	.663	.919	.590	.726	.729	.897

WM = white men, WW = white women, BM = non-white men, and BW = non-white women
Source: Randy Albelda '"Nice Work If You Can Get It" Segmentation of White and Black Women Workers in the Post-War Period', *Review of Radical Political Economics*, 1985, vol. 7, no. 3, p. 73

Table 4   Per cent High School Graduates as College Enrolment of Persons 18-24 Years Old, by Sex and Race 1960, 1970, 1983 (USA)

	All Persons			Male			Female		
	Total	White	Black	Total	White	Black	Total	White	Black
1960	23.7	24.2	18.4	30.3	31.1	20.8	17.8	17.9	16.5
1970	32.7	33.2	26.0	41.2	42.3	28.7	25.8	25.6	24.1
1983	32.5	32.9	27.0	35.0	35.4	27.5	30.3	30.6	26.7

Source: As for Table 1, p. 149

Table 5   Economic Status of Economically Active by Ethnic Origin and Sex, 1983 (UK)

	Employees		Self-employed	Out of Employment
	Full-time	Part-time		
White males	73.0	2.3	11.3	11.6
West Indian & Guyanese males	62.0	2.1	2.5	27.6
Indian sub-continent males	60.5	1.3	14.6	21.5
All ethnic origin males	72.2	2.3	11.3	12.1
White females	46.3	34.9	5.2	10.1
West Indian & Guyanese females	56.0	18.8	1.0	18.0
Indian sub-continent females	50.3	13.3	10.6	21.6
All ethnic origin females	46.4	34.0	5.2	10.4

Source: Central Statistical Office, *Social Trends* 15, 1985 Edition, Government Statistical Office, HMSO, London, 1985, p. 61

Michèle Barrett and Mary McIntosh (1985: 31) report results for West Indian women in Britain that confirm the data in Table 5. The average earnings of West Indian women were £4 a week higher than for white women and £8 a week higher than for Asian women. Barrett and McIntosh suggest that a higher percentage of lower earning older white women partially explains the low earnings of white women. French (1985: 465) attributes black women's relatively high earnings in the United States to a tradition of work and a greater sense of independence.

For example, in 1920 39 per cent of black women compared with 17 per cent of white women worked (Giddings, 1985: 196). However, in so far as it can be determined, similar results do not apply for South Africa and Australia. Table 6 shows that Aboriginal and Torres Strait Islander women are considerably less likely than all women or the total population to earn over $8,000 p.a. and much more likely not to go to school than white women (Table 7). Nevertheless, as with black women in the United States, Aboriginal women are more likely to have professional, technical etc. jobs than the total Australian population or Aboriginal and Torres Strait Islander males (Table 8). Meredith Burgmann (1984: 32) reports a Brisbane survey which revealed that 38 per cent of Aboriginal women had been educated to Grade 10 or higher compared with only 9 per cent of Aboriginal men in 1974, that 63 per cent of Aborigines in tertiary education were female and that 46 per cent of women were in white collar jobs compared with 7 per cent of men. In New South Wales in 1981 Aboriginal women were less likely to be unemployed than Aboriginal men. For South Africa, while there is an enormous discrepancy in university attendance between whites and blacks, the differential which occurs between white men and women is greater than between black men and women (Table 9).

Table 6   Per cent Of Occupational Group Earning Over A$8,000 by Sex and Race (Australia)

	Total Australian Population	All Women	Aboriginal and Torres Strait Islander Women
Professional & technical	83.4	72.1	40.7
Clerical	70.7	61.4	50.2
Service, sport & recreation	64.8	32.4	29.0

Source: Department of Employment and Industrial Relations, Women's Bureau, *Aboriginal Women's Training and Employment Opportunities*, AGPS, Canberra, 1985, p.19; Australian Bureau of Statistics, *Cross-classified Characteristics of Persons and Dwellings*, 1981 Census, AGPS, Canberra, pp. 50–1

Table 7 Age Left School by Gender/Aboriginal (Torres Strait Islanders)/Total Population, 1981 (Australia)

Left School	Males	%	Females	%	Total	%	Males	%	Females	%	Total	%
12 or less	1,802	4.0	1,540	3.2	3,342	3.6	149,411	2.8	155,307	2.8	304,718	2.8
13	1,977	4.4	1,684	3.6	3,661	4.0	173,116	3.2	160,007	2.9	333,123	3.1
14	6,771	15.1	6,618	14.1	13,389	14.6	978,611	18.1	1,057,667	19.1	2,036,278	18.6
15	11,776	26.2	12,491	26.6	24,267	26.4	1,260,211	23.3	1,430,545	25.9	2,690,753	24.6
16	7,246	16.1	8,631	18.4	15,877	17.3	1,032,740	19.1	1,084,885	19.7	2,117,625	19.4
17	2,496	5.5	3,028	6.5	5,524	6.0	697,251	12.9	702,921	12.7	1,400,172	12.8
18	1,039	2.3	1,068	2.3	2,107	2.3	429,549	7.9	325,882	5.9	755,431	6.9
19 and over	427	0.95	333	0.7	760	0.8	163,248	3.0	84,077	1.5	247,325	2.3
Did not go to School	4,878	10.86	4,933	10.5	9,811	10.7	38,618	0.7	46,949	0.9	88,267	0.8
Still at School	2,478	5.5	2,667	5.6	5,145	5.6	232,737	4.3	229,752	4.2	462,489	4.2
Not stated	4,030	8.97	3,901	8.3	7,931	8.6	239,437	4.4	243,808	4.4	483,245	4.4
Total	44,920		46,900		91,820	100	5,394,929	100	5,524,497		10,919,426	100

Source: As for Table 6, p. 24

Table 8   Occupational Distribution of the Employed Aboriginal and Torres Strait Islanders and Total Australian Population Census 1981 (% total employed)

	Aboriginal/TSI Male	Aboriginal/TSI Female	Total Population Male	Total Population Female	All Australia
Professional, technicians, etc.	4.0	12.6	11.7	17.0	13.6
Administrative, etc.	1.0	0.7	7.4	1.9	5.3
Clerical workers	3.6	16.4	8.3	31.9	17.1
Sales workers	1.6	5.1	6.8	11.5	8.5
Farmers, fishermen, etc.	16.7	1.8	7.6	4.4	6.4
Miners, quarrymen	1.6	0.1	0.9	0.0	0.6
Transport and communications	6.6	1.4	6.6	1.7	4.8
Production process workers, labourers etc.	44.5	8.3	39.5	9.0	28.1
Service, sport recreation	5.3	25.6	5.2	13.7	8.4
Armed forces	0.9	0.1	1.5	0.2	1.0
Other inadequately described or not stated	14.2	27.8	4.5	8.9	6.1
Total	100.0	100.0	100.0	100.0	100.0

Source: As for Table 6: Department of Employment and Industrial Relations, p. 21

Thus women of colour in the United States and the United Kingdom seem to suffer less relative deprivation, compared with both white males and white females, than they do in Australia and South Africa. This may be explicable in terms of their greater integration into capitalist society in the United Kingdom and the United States, itself a result of their non-indigenous status.

Table 9   University Attendance as Percentage of Population 20–4 Years of Age, 1983 (South Africa)

	%
White Males	42.99
White Females	26.99
Black Males	0.98
Black Females	0.78
Coloured Persons	1.09

Source: Compiled from data in *South Africa 1985*, Department of Foreign Affairs, Government Printer, Pretoria, 1985, pp. 27, 32, 695, 712–13, 718

These tables provide a caution in their interpretation. Should we accept that women are disadvantaged compared with men and compare black and white women? Or should we focus on the fact that compared with white men, both black and white women are disadvantaged (and avert our gaze from discrepancies between them)? Or should we argue that race is the key discriminator and compare the relative deprivation of white women compared with black women and of white men compared with black men? Thus Tables 1 and 4 show that *vis-à-vis* men of the same colour, black women are better placed than white women. On the other hand, French focuses on the growing gap in earnings in the United States between all women and white men. To which Bell Hooks (1981: 147) argues that attention to the growing similarity of earnings between white and black women suppresses that fact that black women's wages are merely approaching the 'set norm', the wage levels white women have enjoyed for so long.

Eugenics or Contraception?

Mention was made of third world women's ambivalent attitudes to contraception. These attitudes are shared by some women of colour in western societies. Some Aboriginal women in Australia see family planning as a 'deliberate attempt to limit the size of the Aboriginal population' (quoted in Burgmann, 1984: 42); while Gwen Deemal-Hall reported at the ANZAAS (Australia and New Zealand Association for the Advancement of Science) Conference in Townsville in September 1987 that Depo-Provera was being given to Aboriginal girls as young as 13 (Black Women's Action newsletter, September 1987: 4). Amina Mama (1984: 30) suggests that in Britain the National Health Service places pressure on black women to have abortions and use the pill. French (1985: 465) suggests that in the United States black women are three times as likely as white women to suffer unnecessary sterilization; while Angela Davis (1981: 204) argues that 80 per cent of the deaths due to illegal abortions in New York in the 1970s were deaths of black and Puerto Rican women. This very quotation points to the contradictions for black women in relation to contraceptive choice. It would appear that some black women desire safe abortions (Radl, 1983: 40; Hooks, 1981: 74). However, Davis (1981: 205) argues that women of colour resort to abortion, not so much as an expression of reproductive choice, but because of their 'miserable social conditions'. Rather than free abortions, these women need jobs, higher wages, better schools.

Furthermore, while first wave feminists' advocacy of 'voluntary motherhood' was a vision 'rigidly bound to the lifestyle' of the middle-class woman (Davis, 1981: 208), the birth control movement which arose out of it soon became racist and eugenicist. Thus to many women of colour 'abortion is murder, family planning is genocide' (Radl, 1983: 40). The early feminists – Marie Stopes, Josephine Butler, Christabel Pankhurst and Margaret Sanger – have been accused of eugenicist tendencies (Amos and Parmar, 1984: 13; Davis, 1981: 212); whether because they endorsed the dominant eugenicist ideology of the time, or compromised with it in order to expand their services, as Margaret Sanger seems to have done (Petchesky, 1986: 93).

Women of colour (as well as white feminists) have fought to have the dangerous contraceptive Depo-Provera taken off third world markets (Amos and Parmar, 1984: 12; Bryan, Dadze and Scafe, 1985: 103), and to expose and combat sterilization abuse (Smith, 1983: xxxv). White women's fight for contraceptive freedom can only mean, according to some writers, that more coloured women will be guinea pigs to test the new drugs before white women are exposed to them (Bryan et al., 1985: 105; OWAAD, 1981: 146).

Arguments of this sort will be met throughout the succeeding pages so it is worth spending a little time unpacking the implications of such statements. There is considerable evidence that women of all nations and colour want access to safe contraceptive measures. In fact a survey of 350 ancient and pre-industrial societies revealed that abortion was practised in all of them (cited in Petchesky, 1986: 1–2). Surely then Bryan et al. are not arguing that white women should resist medical advances in the area of contraception. However this is the implication of the statement that coloured women will be 'guinea pigs' for the new drugs. By putting the problem in the way that the authors do, they suggest that the interests of western women and other women are diametrically opposed. The different responses to contraception policies by women of colour and white feminists are in part a result of the differential impact of state policies on these two groups of women. Rosalind Petchesky (1986: 130) identifies population control as state-based eugenicist policies to control the reproduction of the working classes, usually with forced sterilization rather than abortion. She contrasts this with birth control, the rights of women to choose the form and incidence of their own childbearing. Because population policies were and are directed at expanding the white middle-class population and reducing the population of black people, the experience of birth control (or lack of it) is quite different for these two groups of women.

However, by putting the issue in another way, by focusing on birth control, feminists can argue for women's common interests: that women of all colours should resist the testing, introduction and use of dangerous contraceptives while affirming the rights of women to choose both to have and not to have children. Nevertheless statements concerning common feminist goals often suppress the differential impact of class, race and imperialism on women. Thus it *is* more likely that women of colour and in the third world will be exposed to dangerous drugs. On the other hand, they are by no means the only such women, as the incidents of the Dalkon Shield and thalidomide indicate. Furthermore, Bryan et al.'s argument ignores the fact that western feminists have also campaigned to take Depo-Provera off third world markets.

In a detailed review of the incidence of abortion across class and race lines, Petchesky (1986: 148–61) points out that abortion is more often chosen by white middle-class women because they are more likely to have alternative career choices. Thus during the 1970s, while the enrolment of black women in colleges increased by more than twice that of white women, there was a concurrent rise in abortions among black women. Petchesky argues that abortion should be available to all women who want it: young girls who choose to carry a child to term are more likely to get less education, remain poorly paid or unemployed and have more babies. When high schools allowed pregnant girls to remain in education, it was black girls who most benefited from this change in policy. In 1979 76 per cent of white teenage mothers dropped out of high school, usually to marry a boy, while only 19 per cent of comparable black teenage mothers did, relying instead on their own mothers and kin to help them with childcare. This points to the significance of race-based analyses in explaining the differential impact of abortion and other state policies on white and black women. Petchesky concludes that poor women most often sought abortions out of necessity rather than desire; her argument being that a 'right' to choose must be backed up by economic and other infrastructural support whatever the choice a woman makes. Poor women often cannot choose, cannot exercise the right, because they have no means to support their child.

Thus a complex of factors differentially determine the experiences of women along class and race lines as a result of changing state policies. Neither of the feminist slogans and the campaigns around them – 'Abortion on Demand' or 'A Woman's Right to Choose' – have captured all these vicissitudes. Nevertheless Petchesky (1986: 161) concludes 'this does not contradict the fact that the rise in legal abortions coincides with major gains for women as a whole, gains that affect most women, but differentially, in a society structured on class and race divisions'.

This chapter has provided an overview of both the argument that patriarchy is a universal phenomenon and the counterpoint argument that, while this may be so, women are not equally placed *vis-à-vis* each other or in relation to men in each country. Some anthropological arguments for these differences have been introduced – women's access to rewards for work, their mobility and their significance as costing a dowry or earning a bride-price. Finally, analysis of statistics on the global position of women suggests that white western women are better placed on the whole than other women, at least in terms of the variables analysed. The effects of this placement on the politics of women of colour and the third world, and on the consequential debates around the project of a unified world women's movement will be the tasks of the remaining chapters.

3

Race and Gender

Canada was built on the backs of strong women: the Europeans who colonized it and the native Indians who resisted that colonization. (Nemiroff, 1984: 109)

The statistics analysed above confirmed the lower economic and political status of coloured people. When the data was analysed in terms of both colour and gender, however, it was clear that, on the whole, black women are the worst off and that occasionally black men are in a better position than white women. Given these two facts, it is by no means certain that the position of coloured women can be better explained by racism than sexism. None the less, and quite understandably, since both forms of oppression seem to operate, women of colour have questioned whether their allegiance should be to their 'black brothers' or their 'white sisters'. Why they should construct the analysis in terms of this stark opposition and the answers they give to the question will be explored here.

In this book 'black' or 'women of colour' is used to describe women who so identify themselves. Thus Pat O'Shane (1976: 33) argues that the alternative to accepting an Aborigine's self-definition as Aboriginal is white-imposed definitions of 'half-caste', 'quarter-caste' and so on. Or as Marilyn Frye (1983: 115) says, it is an aspect of white supremacy to decide who may or may not be a member of the club: white-washing women of colour (refusing their identity) is just as insulting as excluding them because of their colour. Jeanie Bell (in Coleman and Bell, 1986: 75) argues that white Australians are 'freaked out' by 'very fair' Aborigines who define themselves as Aboriginal. Fear by whites of the growing numbers of self-defined Aborigines produces attempts to restrict entry into the 'club' of non-whites. The problem of having one's Aboriginality defined by others has also been experienced by Pat Eatock (1987: 28) – in her case a blood-sister who was 'passing' for white and started a rumour that Pat Eatock was not an Aboriginal. The salience of the rumour, however, was that white women were treating Eatock more 'tolerantly' because she was Aboriginal. Elizabeth Williams (1987: 72) has also been regarded by other Aborigines as 'quarter-caste' or 'half-caste'.

Jessie Fauset (1928) in *Plumball* explores the 'betrayal' of her family, her community and ultimately her 'self', by an American woman of colour who passes as white.

For both women of colour and white women, the significance of Aboriginality can take many forms – accredit one to speak for other Aboriginal people (both on white and black stages), forgive one one's excesses, condemn another to the same definition as Aboriginal. Which of these are 'racist' and which are not is difficult to determine.

Self-definition also allows one to avoid the thorny problem of whether there are 'real' (read biological) racial differences and focuses attention on the social construction and negotiation of those differences. As O'Shane's comment indicates, these social constructions are not necessarily shared by white and coloured women. How many white people would spontaneously hit on the following definition of 'black'?

When we use the term 'Black', we use it as a political term. It doesn't describe skin colour, it defines our situation here in Britain. We're here as a result of British imperialism, and our continual oppression in Britain is the result of British racism. (The Organisation of Women of Asian and African Descent (OWAARD), quoted in Bryan, Dadze and Scafe, 1985: 170)

Racism in common usage means prejudice, and assumed superiority, by white people over coloured people. However, women of colour argue that racism also has structural correlates: less access to economic resources; discriminatory laws and police practices based on race or nationality; more brutal treatment of coloured women's bodies; cultural stereotypes of coloured people which maintain ignorance, justify lower status and different treatment (for example by medical or welfare institutions) and perpetuate neglect.

A History of Racism

Many women of colour, for example in the United States, Britain, Australia and South Africa, claim that racism is more important than sexism in defining their situation. It was white colonization of the globe which produced a slave-based economy (the United States), apartheid (South Africa), invasion (Australia), imperialism (Britain). This condition both connects and divides women: '*history* has divided the empire of women against itself' (Spillers, 1984: 79). It is a history which saw some women as partners of conquerors, controllers and exploiters and other women as conquered, controlled and exploited. This division was quickly imbued with notions of colour and racism.

Hooks (1981: 38), in a memorable image, quotes an eyewitness account from the days of slavery: while the negro slave is being brutally whipped in the yard the white daughters of her torturer watch from an upstairs window. Hooks argues that white women learned two things by such experiences. First, fear due to the cruelty of their husbands/fathers but secondly that they had a higher status than the black slaves, and were thus the 'most immediate beneficiaries' of slavery. White women were the immediate beneficiaries of slavery because it 'created a new status for the white female' (Hooks, 1981: 153), above that of coloured people. As a result, white women and women of colour were necessarily at odds with one another (Hooks, 1981: 154). When Hooks (1984: 74), in a later book discusses the 'negative impact of sexism on male personhood', she suggests that when poor and working-class men attack or abuse women, they are not the beneficiaries. Rather 'the ruling-class male power structure that promotes his sexist abuse of women reaps the real material benefits and privileges from his actions', because it deflects him from attacking sexism and capitalism. Given that Adrienne Rich (1984: 282) argues that slaveowners' wives were powerless before their cruel husbands, and that working-class indentured white women were also treated like slaves when masters occasionally forced their black slaves to rape them, surely white women benefited as little from their status above the slaves as men of colour benefit from their occasional status above white women.

According to both Hooks (1981) and Davis (1981), the history of slavery lies at the heart of contemporary race oppression. Both these authors have recovered that history of brutality to and resistance by women of colour in the ante-bellum period. Davis (1981: 18–19) goes so far as to argue that the black family under slavery was egalitarian, because the labour of both adult members was equally necessary. However, women of colour were anguished to see their men 'degraded' as this meant their sons would not have 'an example of a strong black man in front of them' (Davis, quoting Genovese, 1981: 19). Hooks (1981: 20) responds that this concern with the 'feminization of coloured men' reveals a belief that 'the worst thing that can happen to a man is that he can be made to assume the social status of women.' Instead, she focuses on the 'masculinization' of women, through their participation in field labour, in a situation where 'only debased women worked in fields' (Hooks, 1981: 2).

Out of the slave experience and its rereading by white society grew two stereotypes concerning the woman of colour, first that she was a strong matriarch, and secondly that she was sexually permissive. Hooks and Davis explore the ramifications of these stereotypes in terms of the contemporary position and treatment of black women, for example in their relations with black men and in their treatment as rape victims. Black women writers also trace the racism of contemporary feminism to the abolitionist and suffrage movements.

The suffrage movement is one of the few narratives from first wave feminism that has not been totally lost to the memory of succeeding generations of women (Spender, 1982: 4). The racism of this movement in the United States has been subjected to heated attack by black feminists. One such instance is Susan B. Anthony's request that Frederick Douglass (a black man supporting their campaign) not sit on the stage with suffragists in the southern states because she 'did not want anything to get in the way of bringing the southern white women into the suffrage association' (Davis, 1981: 111). Elizabeth Cady Stanton was absolutely opposed to black male suffrage as this would 'render black men superior' (Davis, 1981: 73). Douglass's daughter was prevented from attending classes with white girls by the female abolitionist principal (Davis, 1981: 59). On the other hand Ellen Dubois (1978: 68–9) suggests that Frances Gage declared herself for the 'cause of women, without regard to colour', that Anthony and Stanton did speak publicly in the cause of black women, while Olympia Brown said the black woman 'needed the ballot more than anyone in the world'.

Again it is a difference of emphasis that influences these accounts – Davis refers to the white suffragists' views of black *male* suffrage and black men while Dubois refers to their statements concerning black *women*. Furthermore, Hooks (1981: 90) admits that Douglass 'clearly believed it was more appropriate and fitting that men be given the right to vote', and that certainly he, and other supporters of votes for women, did not oppose sexism.

The uneasy alliance of white women and blacks fell apart when the suffragists claimed the right to vote on the basis of education. While this was a 'fundamental betrayal of democracy' (Davis, 1981: 116), it was also a betrayal of both white and black women so excluded: it was not racist *per se* (Rich, 1984: 286–7). Thus one could argue that it was classist – an attempt to advance the position of white and black middle-class women at the expense of working-class women. One should remember, however, the argument of the British suffragists, when they split with the male labour movement. It did not matter what criterion was used (for example, hair colour would be just as acceptable) as long as *some* women got the vote. Against this it must be accepted that the criterion of education would have given the vote to more white women, just as the criterion of black hair would have favoured coloured women.

The choice of criterion may be significant, and probably was. The leaders of the movement – white and middle class – no doubt chose criteria that favoured women such as themselves. Indeed, histories of the suffrage movement often render black women invisible, as the following extract indicates:

> When black people are talked about the focus tends to be on black men; and when women are talked about the focus tends to be on white women. No where [sic] is this more evident than in the vast body of feminist literature ... A case in point is the following passage describing white female reactions to white male support of black male suffrage in the nineteenth century taken from William O'Neill's book *Everyone Was Brave*:
>
>> Their shocked disbelief that men would so humiliate them by supporting votes for Negroes but not for women demonstrated the limits of their sympathy for black men, even as it drove these former allies further apart.
>
> This passage fails to accurately register the sexual and racial differentiation which together make for the exclusion of black women. In the statement, 'their shocked disbelief that men should so humiliate them by supporting votes for Negroes but not for women', the word men in fact refers only to white men, the word Negroes refers only to black men, and the word women refers only to white women. The racial and sexual specificity of what is being referred to is conveniently left unacknowledged or even deliberately suppressed. (Hooks, 1981: 7)

This, despite the fact that one of the most famous women of the period was Sojourner Truth, who responded to men's taunts at a suffragists' meeting with her famous speech: 'Aint I a woman?' (It should be noted that Hooks' example of 'feminist literature' quoted above is actually William O'Neill, although in a later paragraph she attacks Berg's *The Remembered Gate*.)

Interestingly, as Hooks (1981: 3) herself suggests, white men in giving the vote to negro men, revealed that their 'sexism ... was at that brief moment in American history greater than their racism'. Why or how this happened is not interrogated, and elsewhere Hooks (1981: 122) argues that 'American society is one in which racial imperialism supersedes sexual imperialism.'

Hooks (1981) and Davis (1981) use their exploration of black women's history to uncover their forgotten story – 'no other group in America has so had their identity socialized out of existence as have black women' (Hooks, 1981: 7). Black women's history is also deployed to expose the manifold instances of white women's racism, not only in the suffrage movement, but also in the segregation of the women's clubs (Hooks, 1981: 129), the reinforcement of race-based divisions of labour at work (Hooks, 1981: 135), the endorsement of the myth of the black male rapist (Davis, 1981: 187), the advocacy of birth control to eliminate the negro race (Davis, 1981: 212).

Neither women of colour nor white feminists deny the incidence of racism among contemporary and earlier white feminists. The debate concerns how the racism of white women is interpreted and whether countervailing incidences are presented. Thus Rich (1984: 281) suggests that 'Women did not create the power relationship between master and slave, nor the mythologies used to justify the domination of men over women'; rather in the history of slavery and racism, white women have been 'impressed into its service' (Rich, 1984: 282). Rich goes on to argue that women of colour too have been pressed into the service of 'masculine civilization' – African women who perform clitoridectomies and Chinese women who bound their daughters' feet. Hooks (1981: 124) has little sympathy with this argument, claiming that 'sexist discrimination has *prevented* white women from assuming the dominant role in the perpetuation of white racial imperialism but it has not prevented white women from absorbing, supporting, and advocating racist ideology or acting individually as racist oppressors' (italics mine). Thus while Rich sees women as having little choice in the matter of supporting racist practices, Hooks suggests that if they had the choice, they would have been more racist.

While Hooks and Davis focus almost exclusively on racism in white women's history, Rich (1984: 284) presents examples of 'our white foresisters' who have been 'disloyal to civilization'. Hooks (1981: 125) replies (to an earlier version of Rich's paper) that there is little historical support for Rich's argument that 'white women as a collective group' were disloyal to civilization, and further that their motivations for reform were only due to 'religious sentiment'; they 'attacked slavery not racism'. Rich was not, on the whole, describing 'collective' disloyalty, and she did describe white women who endorsed racist stereotypes but opposed the brutal treatment of negroes as 'disloyal to civilization'. Hooks focuses on racism rather than (patriarchal) civilization, and so imposes a more stringent criterion of disloyalty. (Who was not, is not, racist in some respects at least, in a society where race relations are of great significance?)

The Strong Black Women – The Passive White Woman

Today a far greater percentage of black American households than white are female-headed. This has been offered as proof of the 'strong black matriarch' but also, to some white observers, of the pathological nature of black family forms. Women of colour reveal ambivalent responses to this stereotype of the strong black woman. Hooks (1981: 6) argues that the 'tendency to romanticize the black female experience' ignores 'the reality that to be strong in the face of oppression is not the same as overcoming oppression'. Dianne Sadoff (1985) offers a reconciliation of the image of the black matriarch and the fact that the strength of these women was a response to 'poverty, urbanization and oppression' (Sadoff, 1985: 11) rather than a characteristic to be unconditionally celebrated:

> With terrible irony, this mystification originates in white resentment of the slave woman's seeming power through her sexual relationship with the master, when that relationship signifies instead her status as a chattel. Forced to submit for survival, the black slave woman could yet resist her oppression because the dominant culture failed to define her as stereotypically 'feminine' ... her ironic freedom from the restraints of submissive white southern ladyhood allowed her to fight both alongside of and apart from the black man. Thus the black (slave) mother represents the contemporary black woman's double history of enslavement and survival. (Sadoff, 1985: 10)

Defined as woman and not as female, the black slave woman escaped certain prescriptions – but her escape and her response were premised on a more brutal treatment from white men. The treatment made her resourceful but it did not give her power over the master.

Of Betty Friedan's advocacy of paid labour as a path out of oppression, Hooks (1981: 134, 145) says that for millions of women paid work is a drudgery that they would cheerfully forgo. Hooks suggests that often women of colour took on the backbreaking jobs happily relinquished by men (for example, in tobacco factories). Again, Hooks contrasts this with white feminists' campaigns for access to men's jobs, which she (1981: 145) denounces with: 'Like all good capitalists, they proclaimed work as the key to liberation.'

On the other hand, Davis (1981: 231) applauds the 'assertiveness and self-reliance' of black women who work outside the home, while Hooks (1984: 102–4) herself later argues that women must struggle to attribute value to all the work women do, whether paid or unpaid: women 'need to know that they create their humanity through participation in work'

(Hooks, 1984: 104). As the previous chapter argued, cross-culturally women who both labour and control the products of their labour seem to have more choices than those who do not, however much they may wish to live in the 'gilded cage' of the white home-bound housewife.

Other arguments have been made about the greater strength of women in non-western cultures. Both Catherine Berndt (1983) and Diane Bell (1983: 255; 1983) argue for the high status of women in traditional Aboriginal societies – for example, the jilimi (all women groups). Paule Marshall in *Praisesong for the Widow* (1983) explores a black woman's escape from materialist luxury to revival of her cultural roots. Others search for 'a natural' or holistic way of life for black people, in contrast with the culture imposed by white 'civilization' through slavery and colonialism (Brown, 1983: 82).

Both O'Shane and Bobbi Sykes (quoted in Burgmann, 1984: 28) express concern for their Aboriginal menfolk emasculated and driven to drink by the dominance of Aboriginal women in the community. This concern is similar to Davis' and Hooks' anxiety over the plight of black American men. As one Aboriginal woman Burgmann (1984: 42) interviewed said, 'The white woman is still higher on the ladder than the black man.' Employment statistics discussed in Chapter 2 support this claim. Sykes (reported in Black Women's Action Group Newsletter, September 1987: 3) attributes the better position of Aboriginal women to the greater fear in the general community of Aboriginal men achieving power and status.

The early role of the slave woman as domestic servant in the white household persists today with many women of colour working as domestics in white people's households (see Tables 1 and 9 above). According to Hooks (1981: 155), the person who directly benefits from a servant's work is the white woman, because she is relieved of her household chores. Against this Rich (1984: 297) argues that the role of women of colour as housekeepers and childminders in many white women's houses contributed to the 'infantilism' of the white wife and mother. The contemporary variant of this situation is Davis' (1981: 96) claim that liberating work for white women will be earned at the cost of black women becoming their housekeepers. Thus Hazel Carby (1982: 218) suggests that coloured women were allowed to emigrate to Britain in order to perform domestic and other service work, while white women returned to the workforce in higher status jobs. Hooks (1984: 97) argues that even affirmative action programmes are mechanisms by which white women displace black women and men. These suggestions can be compared with Morgan's (1984: 19) statement that global feminism means the woman sitting on the sofa will join hands with the woman kneeling and washing the floor. Hooks and Davis argue that this is not possible. The woman on the sofa participates in the exploitation of the woman scrubbing the floor.

Several few analyses of representational effects of the interaction of race and gender have been attempted, most often in the United States, where race is a more persistent element of perhaps even white women's identities. Palmer (1983) offers a possible explanation of the 'benefits' white women derived from the slavery and subsequent imagery of black women. She 'suggests that the widespread dichotomization in the images of women, as 'good' and 'bad', or 'virgin' and 'whore', also divided white women and black women in American society. The white woman, increasingly freed from domestic and paid manual labour, became constructed as the virgin with a 'mission of social improvement'. The black woman came to represent 'sexuality, prowess, mysterious power' (Palmer, 1983: 158) (see also Kaplan, 1986: Chapter 7 for a similar argument). However Palmer notes that, while many white women have drawn comfort from this image and refused to associate with black women because they felt superior to them, 'their privilege is not power, and it is based on accepting the image of goodness, which is powerlessness.' Indeed another construction of the image of white women (by the black woman doris davenport) is 'powerless, spineless, and invisible' (Palmer, 1983: 159).

The second impact of the slave experience was the distinction between women of colour who were (and still are) deemed to be sexually permissive, and white women who became desexualized. Hooks (1981: 31) argues that the desexualization of white women was imposed upon them by white men. Barbara Berg (1979) suggests it was advocated by white women as a mechanism for securing some respite from childbirth and legitimating a 'women's sphere' of influence. Slave women were seen as sexually available by their masters, who either raped or seduced them, depending on the extent of resistance. According to Hooks (1981: 36, 154) this produced 'hostility and rage' in the white wives whose husbands preferred another woman. Rich (1984: 292) says, with a different nuance, that white women were 'forced into impotent jealousy'. According to Davis (1981: 173), this early experience persists in the treatment of women of colour today as promiscuous, and thus reinforces police refusal to believe women of colour's charges of rape, to the point where police officers often commit a second rape on the complainants.

Davis (1981: 172, 199) argues that rape laws were originally introduced to protect upper-class men's wives and daughters, and rapists of these are still more zealously prosecuted. According to Davis and Hooks, white feminists also mete out different 'sentences' in their analyses of black and white rapists.

White feminists' treatment of black male sexuality has attracted considerable heat from black feminists. According to Jacquelyn Hall (1983: 345) and Davis (1981: 187–9), lynching was justified as a means of protecting white women from sexual assault by black men, and such justification secured widespread acceptance of lynching. Davis makes this claim despite her own admission that the majority of lynchings did not involve accusations of sexual assault (Davis, 1981: 187). Davis (1981: 194) argues that women were active members of lynch mobs. Children were given a public holiday in Paris, Texas 1893 to attend the torture and burning of a black man accused of raping a five-year-old white girl (Giddings, 1984: 89), incidents like this reaffirming for children the rightness of violence against coloured people. Davis (1981: 190) argues that lynching had an added advantage to the white ruling class in that it defused white workers' hostilities to their employers through the elaboration of a racist solidarity.

Valerie Amos and Pratibhar Parmar (1984: 14) report a contemporary variant of lynching in male vigilante groups formed in Britain. 'Reclaim the Night' marches were held by white women as protests against women's exposure to sexual assault at night. A number of white men responded to these marches by forming vigilante groups which beat up black men as their contribution to securing safety for white women at night. Amos and Parmar do not assert that the women marching asked for this form of male 'protection'. It is thus difficult to see why the marchers should be blamed for the male vigilantes' racism and interpretation of a women's political campaign, unless one argues, as some women of colour do, that white women must weigh up all the possible race-based hostilities their campaign may evoke before undertaking any action.

Hooks (1981: 53) argues that the rape of one white woman is considered equal to the rape of thousands of black women. Thus the rape of black women under slavery is passed off by Susan Brownmiller (1975) as an 'institutionalized' crime of slavery, which allows Brownmiller to ignore the continued raping of women of colour after abolition up to the present day; an absence in Brownmiller's analysis that Hooks additionally attributes to the widespread belief that black women are sexually promiscuous. While Brownmiller does not devote a later chapter exclusively to the rape of black women in contemporary America, she does not ignore its continued prevalence (for example see Brownmiller, 1975: 338).

Davis (1981: 172ff) attacks Brownmiller for her endorsement and perpetuation of the myth of the male black rapist. Thus Brownmiller (1975) argues that black men commit rapes because they do not have access to 'legitimate' expressions of male sexuality. Furthermore, argues Davis, Brownmiller's description of the murder of Emmett Till, suggests that this adolescent black boy (who *merely* whistled at a white woman) 'was as implicated in the possession of women as any rapist'. Of the Scottsboro Nine, innocent boys falsely accused of rape, Brownmiller expresses 'contempt' by describing them as 'pathetic, semi-literate[s]'. In contrast, she excuses the women's perjury because they were 'confused and fearful' when cornered by a posse of white men. Joseph (1981: 100) instead argues that

> a vagrant, thieving white woman can be vindicated, even lionized by crying 'rape' or 'assault' if the accused is Black ... the white woman has the ultimate power because the judicial system is racist, the executive system is racist, and the legislative system is racist.

Davis' reading of Brownmiller refuses the latter's major point, that both black men and white women were the victims of white men in these two crimes. Brownmiller (1975: 215, 234, 369) makes it clear that black men convicted of raping white women were many more times as likely to receive the maximum penalty, and that they could also be victimized by false accusations and lynching in ways that white men obviously were not. However, Brownmiller, unlike Davis, does not seek to exculpate the black rapist, to maintain her earlier political belief that all blacks were innocent and all white women who accused them were 'crying rape'. On the Scottsboro Nine case she tries to explain why two 'po' white trash' (Brownmiller, 1975: 230) women may feel threatened by an armed possee of 45 men, or being held in prison until the trial, or even weak enough to be tempted by a 'dignity of a sort' in claiming to be rape victims (Brownmiller, 1975: 231). Her description of these women is no less flattering than that of the black boys. Brownmiller's assertion is that a jury of white men convicted the boys, that it was white men who engineered the charges and that both 'black men and white women [were] movable pawns' (Brownmiller, 1975: 233).

On the Emmett Till case Brownmiller (1975: 245) asserts its 'sheer outrageousness, for indefensible overkill with community support'. Brownmiller and Davis part company, not over the excessiveness of the retribution, but concerning whether it is only white men who treat women as property (Davis' position) or whether black men are also happy to do so if they can get away with it (Brownmiller's position). In attacking Brownmiller for exposing the tortured but nevertheless consistently anti-woman discussions around interracial rape, Davis ignores, and so does not confront, Brownmiller's argument that white men are the key powerholders. Davis, in trying to redeem black men and accuse white women, almost loses sight of what both she and Brownmiller would no doubt agree is the main agent of oppression – white men. Davis is really arguing that white women must keep silent about rape by black men; especially as the vast majority of rapes are committed by white men (Davis, 1981: 199), and are also unreported. This is no doubt true, if only because most men in the United States are white. But in seeking to protect the black male rapist, Davis also ignores the black victims of rape (some of whom no doubt are raped by black men): black women are three times more likely to be raped, assaulted or murdered than white women (French, 1984: 465).

Shulamith Firestone (1972: 106–20) is also attacked: for her identification of black people with children, and her argument that black men seek revenge on their fathers (white men), by having sexual relations with their mothers (white women) (Davis, 1981: 181). While Firestone's analogies may be questioned as unconvincing, it seems to be a misreading to suggest that black women and men are like 'children' in anything other than the political and economic power they have in white-dominated patriarchal society. Moreover, Brownmiller (1975: 248–51) documents an admittedly small number of black men who do see rape of white women as part of their revenge on white men. The rapist Eldridge Cleaver said 'I was very resentful over the historical fact of how the white man has used the black woman. I felt I was getting revenge.' The poet Le Roi Jones penned 'Come up, black dada nihilisims. Rape the white girls. Rape their fathers.'

Firestone attacks, or attempts to explain, the less than perfect behaviour of all the actors (white and black) in the 'racial family'. Furthermore, she only offers in passing that the black man 'may lust after the white woman' (Firestone, 1972: 108). When Firestone (1972: 115) next mentions interracial sexual relations, she blames white and black men equally. Firestone thus does not appear to add much fuel to the 'myth of the black male rapist'.

Davis (1981: 23–4) argues that focusing on the black man's 'uncontrollable desire for sexual relations with white women' results in 'the old racist sophistry of blaming the victim' (the black male rapist). As feminists do not usually see men as victims, Davis' argument requires some consideration. Women of colour argue that black men are victims because the effects of racism exclude these men from the jobs that would enable them to live up to society's image of masculinity. This leaves them emotionally scarred (Hooks, 1984: 73). However, it could be argued that class position rather than race *per se* is the reason for these black men's emotional scarring. Few white feminists excuse working-class male rapists because unemployment has left them emotionally scarred. That black feminists endorse such an argument is perhaps testimony to the stronger links between black men and women, links that themselves may be a result of shared oppression on the basis of race.

It may also be a reflection of the belief that the real oppressor lies outside the black community, in the state's policing of black people. Thus Aimée Sands asks for a 'new side' for feminism which supports both the black man who claims he has been framed as a rapist and the white female victim (quoted in Bourne, 1983: 14). Because (or if) the male has been framed, Bourne (1983: 14) can argue that black people and women can unite in their opposition to the racist state which will both convict the black man and often refuse protection to a white victim. But what if he did commit the rape? Can feminists 'find a way of fighting the violence from men on the streets without at the same time enhancing state racism against black people' (Bourne, 1983: 14)? One strategy Bourne (1983: 18) approves is a refusal to protest male violence in districts where many black people 'happen' to live, because such marches give credence to racist stereotypes. Liza Newby (1987: 115) makes a similar argument about white Australian feminists' campaigns for punitive sanctions against rape. Such sanctions fall most heavily on disadvantaged minority men and poor men; the feminist campaign thus disaffects women in these groups. Feminists, then, are asked to be silent about certain issues of real relevance to women because to speak out would both play into the hands of racists and drive a wedge between women of colour and white women.

Evidence suggests that black men also assault and rape black women, but here their victims receive even less protection from the law than white women do. Both in Australia (Bligh, 1983: 101) and Britain (Bryan et al., 1985: 214) black women do not report rape or sexual assault because they know that white stereotypes of 'gin', 'easy lay', 'promiscuous', will mean that police often ignore their complaints. Furthermore, 'no black woman's going to grass up a black man to the police' (Bryan et al., 1985: 217).

Instead the support of female kin often fills the gap. One battered wife reports that her mother came round and 'told him that if he didn't leave right that minute, she'd kill him, and she meant it too' (quoted in Bryan et al., 1985: 217). Sometimes female kin are not available, either because the immigrant is alone in a foreign land, or because the perpetuator of violence is a father rather than a husband. Daughters claiming incest-rapes are less often believed than wives claiming battery.

Joan Riley presents a fictional account of such a situation for a young girl, Hyacinth. Her stepmother has left, warning her only indirectly of her fate – that her father's violence will be replaced by sexual assault. She cannot tell the doctor her father hit her – 'her father had warned her about white people – how they hated black people, how they would trick them and kill them' (Riley, 1985: 30). Neither can she call the police when she runs away from his attempt to rape her:

> She knew that she did not need money to phone the police, just had to dial 999; but the thought of doing that frightened her almost as much as going back.
> 'They don't like neaga here.' The words came back to her, echoing in her head every time she tried to build up the courage to make the call. Instead, she stayed where she was, looking longingly at the phone booth a few yards away. (Riley, 1985: 64)

Thus women of colour accept that they also suffer from sexual oppression, but they are less likely to trust or receive the protection of the law than white women.

'Hierarchies of Oppression'

Slavery is the legacy of racism, but the legacy persists, it is argued, in the white feminist movement and society as a whole. Both Davis (1981: 126) and Hooks (1981: 33) strenuously object to the first wave feminists' analogy between slavery and their condition as dependent wives. Hooks suggests that there was little similarity in the day-to-day lives of slaves and white women, and that white women were 'simply appropriating the horror of the slave experience to enhance their own cause' (Hooks, 1981: 126). In other words, Davis and Hooks argue that even though negro men and women and white women could share a common platform for the vote, at least for a time, the kind of slavery blacks suffered was far more oppressive than that of white women in their 'gilded cages'. Furthermore, contemporary white feminists would not have to use the metaphor of slavery if they really were poor and downtrodden; nor would they need a theory to inform them if they were 'truly oppressed' as it would be quite obvious (Hooks, 1981: 142; 1984: 10). Catherine Stimpson (quoted in Gardner, 1985: 84) agrees that such comparisons avoid making feminism's 'protest clear and irrefutable'. Women of colour's refusal to equate slavery with the position of housebound women is a result of a 'hierachies of oppression' argument, often found either explicitly or implicitly in the writings by women of colour.

One of the key contentions of women of colour is that there is a 'hierarchy of oppression' with white men at the top, followed by white women, then black men, with women of colour at the bottom. While Rich (1984: 289) argues that the 'fruitless game of "hierarchies of oppression" has the savor of medieval theology' and ignores the 'central fact of male gynephobia and violence against all women', Hooks (1984: 4) asserts the very opposite. Class and race create a different quality of life, status, lifestyle, and these differences 'take precedence over the common experience women share'. White middle- and upper-class women repress these differences in order to co-opt women of colour to a movement which seeks only to improve the position of privileged white women in patriarchal structures – the colleges, the higher echelons of the labour market. By equating their position with either coloured people or women as a whole, but not elaborating the differences, white middle-class women have secured privileges from white men. Hooks (1981: 145) contends these men would be less willing to yield if they had been aware of white middle-class women's superior position in relation to working-class women and men (Hooks, 1981: 145).

The meaning given to 'oppression' by these different writers goes some way towards explaining the debates concerning hierarchies of oppression. Hooks (1984: 5) defines oppression as the absence of choices, a definition also adopted by Frye (1983: 2). However, unlike Frye, Hooks believes that 'some women are able to use their class, race and education privilege to effectively resist sexist oppression' (Hooks, 1981: 145). So, for Hooks (1981: 195) race, class and imperialist oppression are more oppressive than sex-based oppression. But nowhere in her analysis does Hooks separate the effects of race and class. In the upshot, white feminists are attacked because they are 'upper and middle class women' who are not interested in the conditions of poor women, be they white, yellow or black (Hooks, 1981: 145). This would seem to indicate that Hooks sees class as more significant than race. Nevertheless, Hooks uses the terms race *and* class, she does not subordinate one to the other; and neither does she interrogate the relations between them.

Sometimes Hooks (1986: 132) seems to deny the hierarchies of oppression argument, suggesting that feminists should avoid 'pitting one struggle against the other'. Nevertheless, because in the West 'the philosophical foundations of racist and sexist ideology are similar' (Hooks, 1986: 131), women must actively 'resist racist oppression' (Hooks, 1980: 133). It is clear that race or class oppression is more significant than gender oppression when Hooks (1986: 132) explains that even 'the most politically naive person' can see that the 'white supremicist state' will respond to white women's demands before it responds to those of 'black people'. A '[r]adical movement to end racism is far more threatening than a women's movement shaped to meet the class needs of upwardly mobile white women'. It is the radical nature of the anti-racist movement and conversely the bourgeois nature of the women's movement which makes the analysis 'obvious'.

When Alice Walker (1984: 57–8) compares her childhood house in a state of decay with the well-preserved house of Flannery O'Connor (another writer from the south of the United States but white) saying 'it all comes back to houses', is she making a comment about race or class? As was noted in Chapter 2, black women are in all classes – 'I am a lesbian woman of color whose children eat regularly because I work in a university' (Lorde, 1984: 132) – as are black men. On the other hand, would it be colour-blindness to ignore the fact that particular ethnic or racial groups are concentrated in particular types of jobs, just as it is sex-blindness to ignore the concentration of women in certain jobs? In a country like South Africa, where economic divisions are buttressed by an extensive network of racist legislation, such colour-blindness is impossible.

A way out of this impasse may seem to be to distinguish, as far as possible, the structures of oppression based on race, sex, class and imperialism. However, attempts at distinguishing causes of oppression quickly come up against the interrelated nature of these oppressions. Thus class divisions may seem most appropriate to explaining different workforce positions, but class is overlaid by gender and race distinctions that deem certain groups as more suitable for particular jobs – white women in clerical work, women of colour in domestic service. Arrest rates for Aborigines, gaoled at 23 times the rate of other Australians, have been explained not as an effect of racist discrimination, but purely as the result of greater poverty, family breakdown and unemployment among Aborigines. These factors produce the same arrest rates among Aborigines and whites (a study by Faye Gayle, reported in *Australian*, 31 August 1987: 3). One could retort that racism produces the enormous incidence of poverty and unemployment among Australian Aborigines, 23 times the rate of whites. Against this, both Jenny Bourne (1983: 3) and Gloria Joseph (1981: 103) argue that racial differences and antagonisms are not primarily due to economic exploitation. Furthermore, as the patriarchy debate reveals, even though working women can be defined by their class position, marxist analyses of capitalism do not explain why women and migrants have the lowest workforce positions. Race and gender operate independently of class. Similarly white working-class men will align themselves with management to exclude both women and black workers from the better jobs.

Alternatively, and just as bad in the eyes of women of colour, is the appropriation of a struggle by female workers of colour to a class-based strategy and explanation (for example, the Grunwick strike in Britain: Bhavnani and Coulson, 1986: 88; Bourne, 1983: 9). Anthias and Yuval-Davis (1983) argue that 'sisterhood' is impossible: *'every* feminist struggle has a specific *ethnic* (as well as class) context.' They attempt to work beyond the 'triple oppression' of race, gender and class which defines women of colour, to 'the study of the intersection of these divisions' (Anthias and Yuval-Davis, 1983: 63). Ethnic phenomena divide people into different collectivities and communities. Upon these divisions are based exclusion/inclusion practices and relations of dominance and subordination. A structural analysis thus reveals that 'there can be no unitary category of "women"' (Anthias and Yuval-Davis, 1983: 71). The conclusion would seem to be that class, race and gender effects cannot be separated when exploring the lives of women of colour. It may be only because of their priveleged position, their ability to ignore their whiteness just as men can ignore their maleness, that allows some white western feminists to argue for the conceptual possibility – at least – of sex oppression distinguished from race oppression.

Racism: The Heaviest Oppression?
Britain
Racism is seen as providing the key to explanations of different social evaluations and treatment of women of colour and white women, for example the stereotype of the woman of colour as promiscuous or as strong. This has effects in the differential treatment of women, for example by law enforcement agencies. The British state is analysed as not only capitalist but also specifically racist, a site for differential treatment of people based solely on their nationality.

Amos and Parmar (1984: 15) argue that the Contagious Diseases Act of 1868 in India sought to control the (Indian) prostitutes but not the (white British) soldiers who used them. But the very same Act was applied in Britain to (white) prostitutes, thus allowing a reading on the basis of sexist oppression rather than racism. On the other hand there *is* contemporary legislation specifically directed against people of colour, for example the 1971 British Immigration Act and the 1981 Nationality Act (see Parmer, 1982: 245). This legislation separates families, or prevents them from uniting; it thus makes white feminists' claims about the oppressive nature of the nuclear family sound hollow in the ears of deported wives.

In 1985 successful appeals against the sexual discrimination in British legislation which made the immigration of fiancés relatively easy in comparison to fiancées were made to the European Court of Human Rights. The legislation was changed so that the same tight restrictions applying to women were extended to men. Thus 'under the rhetoric of creating "equality" between women and men, the state develops further racist practices' (Bhavnani and Coulson, 1986: 85). The state has differential, racist strategies for different ethnic groups; as Petchesky (1986) explores in relation to population policies. The British state has also developed ideologies and practices associating black people with crime, deviance and disorder which then 'justifies' coercive policing. In 1985 police raids led to the shooting of black mothers in London, one of them fatally (Bhavnani and Coulson, 1986: 88, 84). The state evaluates black homes and mothers negatively (i.e. in relation to white middle-class homes) and so a higher proportion of black children are in care. Black people seem more likely to be admitted as psychiatric patients, on the basis of 'black-specific' categories of mental illness feeding off cultural stereotypes, for example 'religious mania' among West Indians or 'marital psychosis' among young Asian women. The treatment of black patients focuses on electroconvulsive treatment, drugs and other physical interventions while that of whites is more likely to include therapy and counselling. The Mental Health Act allows deportation of any in-patient who does not have the right of abode (Mama, 1984: 30–2).

Because of these practices, black women react vehemently against white feminists who, in their campaigns against male violence, march 'through black areas ... calling for greater policing' (Bhavnani and Coulson, 1986: 82). For black people there is no such thing as police protection. Instead, the family is often a 'basis for solidarity' (Bhavnani and Coulson, 1986: 89), not the anti-social institution some white feminists claim. In fact the British state does treat family types differently – it supports the white nuclear family but disrupts the black family.

For many women of colour racism is the key factor of oppression because, they argue, this is the basis of the violence they most often suffer:

> I think if you're a Black woman, you've got to begin with racism. It's not a choice, it's a necessity ... What's the point of taking on male violence if you haven't dealt with State violence? ... or rape, when you can see Black people's bodies and lands being raped every day by the system? (quoted in Bryan et al., 1985: 174)

South Africa

In South Africa the legal prohibitions of apartheid may make it almost impossible for black and white women to work together, and similarly impossible for black women to define themselves primarily by anything other than race. 'You can only hit back as a black because you are virtually isolated' (Winnie Mandela in Lipman, 1984: 137), even though some may wish this were not so (Annie Silinga in Lipman, 1984: 51). Sheena Duncan, National President of the (all-white) Black Sash organization says:

> White women have more rights than black men, so it's a[n] ... uneven kind of thing ... but they're [black women] not feminists ... a woman said to me that the oppression of black people had so emasculated black men that she didn't feel any desire or even right to put any further pressure on her husband ... she saw the greater oppression as the oppression of the whole people. (quoted in Lipman, 1984: 133–4)

Judy Kimble and Elaine Unterhalter (1982) trace the history of women's involvement in the African National Congress (ANC) of South Africa, their continued commitment to 'a principled unity in action' because 'In our country white racism and apartheid coupled with economic exploitation have degraded the African women more than any male prejudices' (quoting Nhlapo). (Note here the translation of gender-based oppression into 'prejudices'.) Women in the ANC were encouraged to agitate for abolition of pass laws, better wages and houses and the development of family life. Generally, this opposition was based on women's role as 'wives and mothers' (Kimble and Unterhalter, 1982: 26). The ANC also constructed women as enormously strong. Women have thus contributed to the ANC's struggle, and it is 'still implicit that it is primarily *through* the main struggle that women will gain their "rightful" place, although it is not clear what their rightful place is' (Kimble and Unterhalter, 1982: 31–2).

The authors also note the inappropriateness of white feminist attacks on the family when South African women have suffered the destruction of normal family life by apartheid. Similarly white feminist claims for equality, when translated into equality with black men would mean continuing subjection to exploitative legislation. However, equality does have a currency in the movement – Oliver Tambo of the National Executive Council of the ANC, claiming:

> we must therefore make it possible for women to play their part in the liberation movement by regarding them as equals, and helping to

emancipate them in the home, even relieving them in their many family and household burdens so that women can be given an opportunity of being politically active. (quoted in Kimble and Unterhalter, 1982: 25)

This is an interesting speech. It reveals that equality can mean being treated as equal by one's menfolk, as well as equal treatment in relation to political structures. Secondly, the nuances of 'equal treatment' involve charitable 'helping', 'even' to the extent of taking on female-defined jobs, but only for the purpose of women's political activism.

Black South African women have indeed been politically active: resisting the pass system, holding together their settlements and communities against apartheid intervention, organising sewing and pottery co-operatives. They have also an occasions expressed their freedom as women – leaving their menfolk to avoid customs they dislike, forming separate committees to prevent the demolition of their settlements (Ellen Khuzwayo, Regina Ntongana quoted in Lipman, 1984: 20, 22, 42). White women, too, are involved in anti-apartheid activities, including attempts to improve the conditions of domestic workers (van Vuuren, 1979: 91). These women, at least, are aware of the exploitation by white women of their coloured domestic workers.

Australia
Pat O'Shane (1976) shares some of these attitudes in relation to Aboriginal women, identifying the racism of white feminists, and the priority of racism over sexism: 'Sexist attitudes did not wipe out whole tribes of our people ... racism did, and continues to do so' (O'Shane, 1976: 33). Lilla Watson (1987: 49) notes 'If you are born black in this country, from the instant of birth you are involved in the black struggle.' Elizabeth Williams (1987: 70) says 'at all times I am black first, woman second.'

Alliances with Black Men or White Women?
Neither the existence of race- or class-based oppression can explain why women, not men (in general), are raped, are the targets of domestic violence, are the objects of pornographic representation and so on. None the less, class and race *may* influence the incidence of *some* of these oppressions. Certainly class and race appear to affect the extent of prosecution of sex offenders and the treatment of the victim by law-enforcement agencies.

There seems to be a wealth of evidence that black men too have sexist attitudes and participate in gender oppression. While Davis and Hooks seek to explain (and perhaps forgive) the actions of the black rapist, black lesbians are far more aware of the sexism of black men. Perhaps the most famous example of black sexism is Stokely Carmichael's comment that there was only one position for women in the black movement: supine (see French, 1985: 463). Cheryl Clarke (1983: 198) quotes another black revolutionary who argues that 'homosexuality does not birth new warriors for liberation.' The role of lesbians in the women's movement is debated both by women of colour and white feminists. Lesbians of colour are criticised not only by black men but also by heterosexual black women. Thus Clarke (1983: 205) disapproves of Hooks' comment that separatist communities reveal a 'lifestyle choice rather than political commitment' (Hooks, 1984: 27).

Black lesbians appear more likely to realise that 'sexual politics under patriachy is as pervasive in black women's lives as are the politics of class and race' (Combahee River Collective, 1983: 213). None the less they may still reject the models of white separatism:

> Lesbian separatism 'leaves out far too much and for too many people, particularly Black men, women and children ... we do not have the misguided notion that it is their maleness, *per se* ... that makes them what they are ... [Lesbianism] ... completely denies any but the sexual sources of women's oppression, negating the facts of class and race. (Combahee River Collective, 1983: 214)

As does Pratibha Parmar (Carmen et al., 1984: 59) in Britain: 'For some of us, our sexuality doesn't mean that we have the "luxury" of organizing as lesbian separatists ... My race and class are equally important'; while Carmen (Carmen et al., 1984: 61) suggests that she once thought heterosexuality was an oppressive institution: 'but I don't anymore. It seems like a hierarchy of oppression, of sexual oppression, being more devastating than others, which I don't agree with although it is very fundamental.'

Alice Walker, in similar vein, rejects the term feminist, for her own definition of the woman of colour as womanist, a definition that emphasizes race and gender and allows black women to live with and love black men.

Women of colour often see the concerns of white feminists as trivial in comparison to the issues of race-based oppression. Debates concerning the rights of men to women's bodies, compulsory heterosexuality, rigid gender roles and the primacy of the nuclear family are a 'luxury' for black women in the face of the intense racism of the British state. Sexuality issues take second place to organizing around issues 'relating to our very survival' (Amos and Parmar, 1984: 11–12): 'discussing who you go to bed with is a privilege most of us don't have' (Bryan et al., 1985: 174). Reducing issues of sexuality to 'who you go to bed with' is a little simplistic. If Bryan et al. had not reworked sexuality issues (rape, control of women's bodies and so on) into lifestyle issues, their condemnation of the concerns of white cultural feminism would have less force. This criticism does not deny the reality of racism as a distinct and pressing issue for women of all colours, nor the desirability of race-based struggles as a first priority. What does need to be questioned is whether the concerns of feminism are merely trivial and, if not, whether they can be resolved by race-based struggles.

The American writers Hooks (1981) and Lorde (1984), unlike some British women of colour, do not describe feminist issues as 'trivial' in so many words. Instead they focus on the need to eradicate all forms of oppression:

> I am not free while any woman is unfree, even when her shackles are very different from my own. And I am not free as long as one person of colour remains chained. Nor is anyone of you. (Lorde, 1984: 133)

Women of colour often argue that the feminist movement must rework itself into a humanist movement, or at least a movement which struggles for the liberation of black men as well as all women. It seems women of colour are really arguing that feminism is not the appropriate political strategy for them, which is, rather, resistance to racism. Hooks (1981) admits in separate chapters the sexism of black men, the racism of white women, and the suppression by black women of their need to fight patriarchy in order to maintain alliances with their menfolk who do not see such struggles as significant. She advocates 'a feminist movement that has as its fundamental goal the liberation of all people' (Hooks, 1981: 13). All relationships are based on 'coercive authority', 'power and domination' whether manifested as classism, sexism, racism, imperialism (Hooks, 1984: 119). Gloria Joseph (1981: 75) also argues that 'Black women in American society have at least as much in common with black men as with white women.' Black males would have to be included in feminism's charter if 'black women are to be involved in the feminist movement' (Joseph, 1981: 98).

In their struggle against coercive authority, women must not eschew their brothers, but work together with them (Hooks, 1984: 67). Thus 'teaching women how to defend themselves against male rapists is not the same as working to change society so that men will not rape.' Rather than create refuges we should change the psyche of batterers; rather than attack heterosexuality we should have respect for the self-concept of women who want to be with men.

Despite Hooks' (for example, see 1984: 100–1, 163) apparent advocacy of economic change as the key political strategy, she actually appears to be advocating a revolution in values. Thus she stresses changing the 'behaviour patterns' associated with class (Hooks, 1984: 3) or the attitudes of male rapists and women batterers. Her notion of revolution emphasises 'cultural transformation' to eradicate 'systems of domination' (Hooks, 1984: 163).

Thus the 'hierarchies of oppression' argument has considerable political implications. By focusing on the hierarchy, women of colour draw attention to the differences between themselves and white women, arguing for the greater shared experiences of men and women of colour. By focusing on oppression, white feminists assert the significance of patriarchal oppression, gender-specific forms of oppression which do not know the boundaries of race or class.

White Feminists' Ignorance of Women of Colour
From a widespread invisibility in history, literature and feminist theory, women of colour have recently been sought out to speak on feminist platforms. To some women of colour, both the previous ignoring and the contemporary tokenising of women of colour results from a refusal to deal seriously with the specific experiences of the bulk of the world's female population. White feminists talk of women, assuming they are discussing the positions and experiences of all women, but they mean white women (Frye, 1983: 117). This is 'a deadly metonymic playfulness – a part of the universe of women speaks for the whole of it' (Spillers, 1984: 78). Coloured women are either excluded from the analysis, or if particular individuals achieve success, their colour is held up as surprising, as worthy of notice (Walker, 1983: 376). Hortense Spillers (1984: 77–8) asks why Sojourner Truth, the only coloured woman at Judy Chicago's 'Dinner Party' is presented in a totally different manner from most of the other women present. While all the dinner plates, except for Sojouner Truth's and Ethel Smythe's (a lesbian), are representations of clitorises, Sojourner Truth is represented by three faces. Truth's sexuality is erased because, according to Spillers, black female sexuality is refused, even by white feminists, and perhaps because of their fear of the birth of black children (Walker, 1984: 373–4).

Some writers have argued that the general invisibility of black women has two related causes. The dominant culture can afford to ignore them; while coloured women have not, until recently, been in institutional positions (in universities, government, the media) that will command the attention of white listeners. The situation is not dissimilar to the longstanding ignorance of white women's voices, histories, experiences. The difference is that white women have participated in ignoring coloured women.

It 'is an aspect of race privilege to have a choice – a choice between the options of hearing and not hearing. This is part of what being white gets you' (Frye, 1983: 111). In defence of white feminists, Frye asserts that they *have* chosen to hear the voices of women of colour, and that this is a hopeful sign in the struggle to overcome racism. In the United States (Lorde, 1984: 132; Woo, 1983: 143), in Australia (McDinny and Isaac, 1983: 67), in Britain (Amos and Parmar, 1984: 6), coloured women complain of white women's ignorance of their culture. Ignorance is active, it means 'to ignore' (Frye, 1983: 119), to refuse to know. As Frye (1983: 121) goes on to say 'Attention has everything to do with knowledge', in other words coloured women are not worth knowing about.

Gayatri Spivak (in Gunew and Spivak, 1986: 136–42) develops these arguments to take account both of speaking and listening positions. She points out that 100 years ago an Indian woman could not speak at all, while today a 'suspicious' reversal makes it 'only too possible' for her to speak – but to speak *as* a 'Third World person'. While she argues that speaking as some*thing* other than one's 'inviolate' self requires political consciousness, it is the card-carrying listeners, the hegemonic audience demanding that she speaks as a representative, who must be condemned.

> When *they* want to hear an Indian speaking as an Indian, a Third World woman speaking as a Third World woman, they cover over the fact of the ignorance that they are allowed to possess, into a kind of homogenization. (Gunew and Spivak, 1986: 137)

Patricia Boero (1987: 60) notes the 'tokenism' of the white Australian women's movement, treating migrant women 'as if we were all clones'.

Trinh Minh-ha (1987) makes a similar point, playing on the project of the 'Special' Third World Women's Issue of *Feminist Review*. Again and again third world women are being asked to speak, to divert their energies to overcome the ignorance of white feminists (Minh-ha, 1987: 10). But third world women are being asked to speak in a certain way:

> Now, I am not only given the permission to open up and talk, I am also encouraged to express my difference. My audience expects and demands

it; otherwise people would feel as if they have been cheated: we did not come to hear a third world member speak about the first (?) world ... the third world representative whom the modern sophisticated public ideally seeks is the *unspoiled* African, Asian or Native American, who remains more preoccupied with her/his image of the *real* native – the *truly different* – then with the issues of hegemony, racism, feminism and social change. (Minh-ha, 1987: 14)

Or as Hazel Carby says, instead of the 'cult' of black women's experience or the struggle to make women of colour 'visible', white feminists should 'challenge the use of some of the central categories and assumptions of recent mainstream feminist thought' (cited in Bourne, 1983: 17). Women of colour are not being asked to engage in debate on equal terms about the wider issues of feminist theory but to present themselves as examples of difference; and a contained difference at that, one which must not be allowed to threaten the racist assumptions and strategies of white western feminism.

White feminists have fought to make it clear that the discursive deployment of 'man' certainly did not include women although it sought to speak for the whole human race. Similarly, women of colour and third world women have exposed the use of 'woman' to its abusive neglect of their specific differences. Women of colour struggle on two fronts. First they seek to separate out the dominated groups, women of colour, third world women, from the dominant group's supposedly inclusive category of women. Secondly, they argue that the new categories 'women of colour' or 'third world women' do not denote a homogeneous entity, but that people within these categories are also different and their differences should be taken as seriously as the differences between white women. Thus Spivak (in Gunew and Spivak, 1986: 162) concludes: 'The person who *knows* has all the problems of self-hood. The person who is *known* somehow seems not to have a problematic self ... Only the dominant self can be problematic; the self of the other is authentic without a problem.'

Since white western feminists are accused of ignorance of the experiences of women of colour, does it not seem contradictory that they are also accused of ethnocentric preoccupation with practices like suttee, the veil and infibulation? Spivak's answer to questions such as this is that white women not only have a right to speak about 'Third World material', but a duty, that refusing to speak because of an 'accident of birth' allows dominant groups 'not to do any homework'. Rather white women should learn about the position of subordinate groups and at the same time develop a 'historical critique' of their position as the 'investigating person'. Thus white women must discover how their own speaking position camouflages or inflects what they 'see' when studying third world women. As a result white women and third world women will speak differently about the third world, but white women through study and self-reflection *can* earn the right to speak.

That the racism of white women has turned women of colour away from the feminist movement would appear to be a serious charge. The white women's movement has been attacked for the racism of its members as well as its theory. Pratibha Parma (in Carmen et al., 1984: 58) finds white feminists' use of 'token' women of colour to get funding 'really disgusting'. White women often look as unattractive to women of colour as is the reverse case, being described as 'juvenile', 'tasteless', 'naive and myopic' (davenport, 1983: 86–7) – indeed colourless.

However some women of colour argue that this inward-looking, 'guilty breastbeating' (Levy, 1984: 108) approach merely reduces racism to 'an interpersonal issue', 'a moral problem' (Jennett, 1987: 368). This allows a refusal to explore racism's structural correlates or, for that matter, the benefits white women derive from these racist structures. Bourne (1983) argues that while consciousness-raising may be a suitable strategy for women who experience their oppression at the hands of individual men directly and personally (although she quickly adds that men's individual sexism derives from the structural sexism of society), the same is not true of relations between black people and white people. White people benefit indirectly from the structures of racism: reducing this to an interpersonal misunderstanding plays into the hands of the conservative integrationists. It also provides an excuse not to learn about the structures of racism, 'absolves us from the responsibility of making our own judgements or shaping our own course of action and it actually suggests that white women are incapable of developing a practice that is anti-racist' (Bourne, 1983: 17). In other words, individualized responses are yet another attempt by white feminists to seek unity by evading the real issues.

Racism in the Feminist Movement Today
In their discussion of white women's racism in history, Hooks and Davis assert its continuities with racism in the feminist movement today. For example Ann Oakley (1981: 32) suggests

In America, nineteenth century feminism was born out of the realization that women as well as Negroes were oppressed, and the women's liberation movement of the 1960s and 1970s was a reaction against the sexist politics of the black rights movement.

This conveniently ignores the sexism of white new left movements, which encouraged British and American feminists to set up their own consciousness-raising groups and political campaigns. It is also an inversion of Bourne's (1983: 11) argument that the black liberation movement of the 1960s was the 'inspiration' of the women's liberation movement. Floya Anthias and Nira Yuval-Davis (1983: 71) note the earlier writings of Michèle Barrett and Elizabeth Wilson which totally ignored issues of ethnicity; later works acknowledge the earlier failure but do not compensate for it (in the same way as male writers now routinely apologize for the absence of a feminist analysis in their books). In various contributions to the patriarchy debate, a genuflection was made to race but no systematic analysis of racist structures was attempted. The desire to integrate capitalism and patriarchy was not matched by similar energy expended on the relationship between racism and patriarchy.

This failure to consider the effects of race on women's position has led white feminists to make unguarded claims. A clear example comes from the various equal rights or equal opportunity in employment campaigns. Hooks (1984: 18ff.), in an argument which Frye (1983: 125) also makes in part, points out that when white feminists demand equal rights, they are not demanding to be equal with working-class men of colour, but to participate as white men's equals in the 'white supremicist, capitalist, patriarchal class structure'. Their claims for equality ignore both the status of subordinate men and of subordinate women. Hooks explains this failure as a focus on 'liberal-individual freedom' rather than endorsement of the need to 'struggle collectively for liberation' (Hooks, 1984: 69). Elsewhere Hooks (1981: 191) describes white feminists as 'self-centred' and displaying 'narcissism, greed, and individual opportunism'. Hooks (1981: 140) suggests that white feminists' refusal to take on board the issue of racism as an issue for feminism, is not solely because of ignorance, but is also done deliberately for self-interested, political purposes.

In Australia Lilla Watson (1987: 51) suggests that when the women's movement speaks of women's liberation it means white women's liberation. However, she goes on to say 'and rightly so'. She looks forward to the day when Aboriginal women can speak of women and mean only themselves. She also believes that black women and white women will walk two roads to liberation but 'that does not mean that opportunities will not arise for us to walk down each other's road for a short time'. On the other hand, black women's liberation must be 'part and parcel of the whole liberation movement of black people' (Watson, 1987: 52). Bobbi Sykes is more adamant that the only suitable movement for black women is one which has 'built into it a means for the black community to gain *real* power and control' which 'must be available not only to black women but particularly to black men' (quoted in Jennett, 1987: 369). Obviously Sykes sees no possibility for an alliance with a feminism which focuses on the situation of women only, be they black or white; indeed the women's movement is 'obviously wasted effort for black women' (Sykes quoted in Jennett, 1987: 369). On the other hand Sykes does understand the value of using black women's organisations to gain funding available to women's groups, and which can be used as 'a conduit to our men and therefore to our community' (Black Women's Action Newsletter, September 1987: 3). Some of the benefits of white feminists' struggles have been made available to Aboriginal women, who subvert them in resourceful ways, to meet the needs of Aboriginal people as a whole. Elizabeth Williams (1987: 72) suggests that she and the women's movement have supported each other and 'the advantage has been reciprocated.' However, like Hooks, she feels that the 'women's movement should support Aboriginal issues'.

Audre Lorde (1984: 132) argues that white women have refused to recognize their differences with women of colour as potentially creative. They find it hard, after defining themselves as the oppressed group, to suddenly become the oppressor: 'She cannot see her heelprint upon another woman's face.' Or as a song has it 'Sister, your foot may be small but it's still on my neck' (quoted in Gardner, 1985: 84). Both Hooks (1981: 192) and Lorde (1984: 130) suggest that a movement that developed out of collective rage against men recoils from negotiating its internal differences and the anger these produce.

Adrienne Rich (1984: 279) repudiates a feminism that seeks 'inclusion within a white male order' or says racism is not its problem or that denies 'the histories and real differences between and among women'. Playing off sex against race is a false historical necessity produced by the identification of women with the men to whom they are attached (Rich, 1984: 286–7). Instead white women must use not merely their intellects but also 'reflection and feeling', 'personal struggle and critical theory' (Rich, 1984: 304), to develop a position that both accepts our differences and allows 'women-identification' or seeing each other as women. Failure to negotiate this dilemma means acceptance of the patriarchal command 'that the difference between us must be everything ... *that from that* difference we each must turn away; that we must also *flee from our alikeness*' (Rich, 1984: 310).

Thus white women must explore and allow their differences with women of colour, failure to do so is a social 'erasure' of differences between women (Rich, 1984: 300). Autonomy comes from strength, but separatism from fear (Smith, 1985: xi). For Joseph (1982: 106) understanding our similarities can create 'building blocks towards understanding and respect for racial and class differences'. Nevertheless, white women should be able to discuss all forms of 'male gynephobia and violence against all women', whatever their creed or colour (Rich, 1984: 289). Rich here argues that postponement of women's issues (as if they were not human issues) is part of the 'mass psychology of male supremicism' (Rich, 1984: 308).

The question Hooks' assessment of hierarchies of oppression asks, but a feminist strategy focusing on patriarchal oppression does not address, is: Can we achieve feminist objectives – the eradication of violence to women, appropriate rewards to women for their labour, women's free expression of their sexuality and reproductive powers – in a society which is still riven by class or race distinctions? Hooks argues that we cannot; Rich, and other white feminists would appear to assert that we can. In Daly's view, and possibly that of some other white feminists, it is because women's oppression is paramount: 'When will [you] understand? It is rapism that has spawned racism. It is gynocide that gives rise to genocide' (quoted in Gardner, 1985: 84).

One reason for the difference in approach is that Hooks speaks to all people of colour, advocating strategies of co-operative struggle. Rich speaks to the community of women, advocating strategies that strengthen women's solidarity and use women's political power to force changes on men. Another basis for different orientations is the project of the women's movement. Hooks suggests its goal must be to end all oppression; Rich argues that it must focus on patriarchal oppression. Thus some women of colour have turned away from the women's movement because: 'I no longer believe that feminism is a tool which can eliminate racism' (Chrystos, 1983: 69). Should it be? Certainly, all the writers discussed here would reject racism in the women's movement; that too is part of patriarchy's insistence: 'That flesh, darker or lighter than your own, encloses a foreign country ... It speaks another language. You cannot find wholeness with one whose body is formed like your own' (Rich, 1984: 309–10).

Bernice Reagon (1983) elaborates the possibilities and preconditions for different groups uniting in their political actions. She draws a distinction between family – people who are like oneself, whether in terms of colour, sexual preference, ethnicity – and those with whom one shares some political goals, but who do not have the same experiences and values as family. Although women must have a room of their own, they must also go out into the world for coalition work.

Home is a 'little barred room that is nevertheless nurturing' (Reagon, 1983: 358). The barred room, home, cannot survive however without coalition work. Coalition work requires extending the definition of 'us' and 'our' to 'include everybody you have to include in order for you to survive' (Reagon, 1984: 365). Coalition work is dangerous, undesirable, but necessary politics; it should be clearly separated from the comfort we seek 'at home'.

Reagon (1983: 358) reveals an ambivalence to the little barred rooms, calling them little micro-nations, expressions of nationalism. On the one hand, she realizes these are very exclusivist affairs, but on the other hand she recommends coalition work not for its own sake, not to produce an international movement, but in order to save the little barred room. Nevertheless, she does argue that coalition work – expanding the 'our' that makes 'our world' – is essential for survival (Reagon, 1983: 362–5). The point is that people are different in terms of their culture, race, gender, sexuality. Reagon admits difference as a basis for intimacy but not as a basis for exclusionary political struggle. Perhaps Reagon is agreeing with Rich that the point of coalition is not the 'erasure' of difference; but its acceptance. The moot question, the unanswered question, is how will the differences be represented so they are acceptable to both white women and women of colour?

The statistical indicators discussed above show that white men on average are better placed economically, educationally, occupationally, than other groups, while black women tend to be the worst off on these indicators. But variations within each category are likely to be wider than variations between the categories, just as women's average height differs from men's by several inches but variations within each sex range over several feet. White women and women of colour are found in all incomes, occupations and so on. Collectively however women of colour tend to be poorer. Should the political alliances be based on the average differences or take account of individual variations?

The Black 'Community' as a Basis for Cross-gender Solidarity

In terms of other factors, often categorized as sexuality issues, such as rape, domestic violence, harassment because of lesbian sexual preferences, stereotypical representations of women, both women of colour and white women suffer these while very few men do. When women of colour choose a political alliance with men of colour, they sometimes assert the greater significance of class-based differences over gender-based differences in determining their political alliances. They argue, however, that both class-based and gender-based differences are over-determined by race, that their class and gender relations are specific and peculiar to them because of their skin colour. It is possibly in the area of cultural representations that divisions on the basis of colour alone are most apparent.

White feminists may have male partners in their little barred rooms but there is a growing tendency to do coalition work solely with other women. White men are too much implicated in the oppressions – both of gender and race – that white feminists are seeking to overcome. Women of colour, on the other hand, are more likely to accept their menfolk, not only in the 'little barred rooms' but also in coalition work. Two explanations are offered for this – and they are perhaps interrelated. In the cross-classification of race and gender white men are the oppressors and women of colour the oppressed. However men of colour experience the oppression of race and white women the oppression of gender. When Frye argues that white women should forgo their allegiances with white men, forgo their race privilege, she argues that white women should leave the side of the oppressor. When Hooks (1981: 199) argues (not necessarily correctly) that for white women sisterhood does not mean surrendering allegiance to race, class and sexual preference, she is suggesting that for women of colour to leave the side of their men is to leave the side of an oppressed, as well as oppressive, group.

The shared experience of oppression may explain the greater sense of community life among black and ethnic groups, a notion that crops up continually in the literature. Hooks (1984: 28) identifies this issue, Alice Walker (1982) explores the southern black community, based in part, according to Dianne Sadoff (1985: 10), on strong relationships between 'mothers, aunts, and women friends' with 'daughters and nieces'. There is a 'densely interconnected female-affirming community within the coloured community'. Sarah Deutsch (1987: 725) discusses the processes of intercultural relations, assimilation and resistance for Hispanic communities in New Mexico and Colorado, and notes women's 'particular part in constructing the sense of community so vital to the survival of the Hispanic villages'. She also notes, tellingly, that as the immigrants conform more to the isolated nuclear family mode of white society, the sense of community breaks down (Deutsch, 1987: 733). In Australia, migrant women and Aboriginal women have identified the need for community and the fear that participating in the women's movement means 'selling out' (because the participation allowed is so token) and also 'losing touch' with one's community (Boero, 1987: 61). Susan Gardner (1986: 118) discusses the African novelist Bessie Head and describes the widespread rejection of Head's writing as 'un-African'. One reason, according to Gardner, was that Head's individuality was too highly developed to be 'smothered by communal and social demands' (a quotation from one of Head's stories, 'The Lovers' – Gardner, 1986: 118). Both in their common experiences of race oppression and their collective struggles against it (Hooks, 1984: 69), women and men of colour develop links that white women do not have, or, if they do have them, implicate them in the actions of the oppressor. The next section explores Walker's focus on 'community' in her identification of the term 'womanist'.

Race and Gender in Cultural Representations

Cultural politics has sought to expose and remedy the invisibility of women of colour in the canons of what constitutes good literature. This refusal to discuss the works of women of colour persists, as Barbara Smith (1985: 67) reports, in the case of white female literary critics as well known as Elaine Showalter and Ellen Moers. Alternatively, women of colour are presented as stereotypes – 'mammy, bitch or slut' (Hooks, 1981: 80) or 'prostituting Lileth' (O'Neale, 1984: 25). Women writers of colour are seeking to create alternative representations of women of colour – 'womanist' (Walker, 1984: 81–2) for example, or 'strong, humourous, sympathetic' (O'Neale, 1984: 20 in Maya Angelou's work). Additionally, women of colour sometimes invert the place of black people in white stories by making white people the objects of pity or humour (Walker, 1982). And Jean Rhys (1968) reclaims Antoinette from her near invisibility in *Jane Eyre*, making her the central protagonist of *Wide Sargasso Sea*.

Secondly, cultural production by women of colour is an attempt to displace the double marginalization of women in the culture–nature dichotomy. Both women and third world peoples have been identified with nature – as passive and uncreative. This often leads to a representation of women as the bearers of tradition and passivity in texts by third world male authors.

Thirdly women of colour negotiate the relations between colour, class and gender in such a way as to suggest that colour is a significant variable in the lives of such women. Colour realigns their experiences of incest, rape, and white authority, and denotes an alternative cultural tradition that has to be dealt with – either through affirmation (Marshall, 1983; Fauset, 1928) or escape (Riley, 1985) or transformation (Walker, 1982).

On the invisibility of writings by women of colour, most of us have heard of Charlotte Brontë and *Jane Eyre*. But far less of us have heard of *Wide Sargasso Sea* by Jean Rhys, a part-creole West Indian. In this book Rhys retrieves the madwoman in the attic, Antoinette Mason, from her role as mere obstacle to Jane Eyre's happiness. Instead Antoinette, not a coloured women despite Barrett and McIntosh's (1985: 40) claim, but a 'white nigger' (Rhys: 1968: 37,85), proves to be a victim of Rochester's greed and sexual desire (as well as her own dabbling with 'black' magic).

In 'Beyond the Peacock' Alice Walker (1984) implicitly addresses the possibility of her own erasure in comparison with the prominence of Flannery O'Connor. O'Connor's house is preserved and acknowledged, Walker's is half-rotted and unmarked. Additionally, Walker interweaves the themes of women recapturing their female literary tradition with the theme of listening to their mothers. Walker's mother, another unheard voice, plays an authorial role in relation to Flannery O'Connor, suggesting that O'Connor's tale is only half the story.

Both Walker (1984) and Hortense Spillers (1984) point out that limiting culture to literature or art as it is usually understood further erases the cultural production of women of colour. Women of colour often lacked the resources to write, but had the resources and inclination to make gardens, or quilts, or lyrics. Thus Spillers identifies black music and oral history as two major vehicles for passing on women's culture, but which are normally ignored in the academy. The production of a self-affirming culture is essential to escape these white-imposed stereotypes: 'Black women have learned as much (probably more) that is positive about their sexuality through the practising activity of the singer as they have from the polemicist' (Spillers, 1984: 87).

This is why Audre Lorde says, 'Poetry is not a luxury' (Lorde, 1984). It is a means by which black women access their power. Lorde contrasts this intuitive womanly power with the intellectual commands of white knowledge: 'The white fathers told us: I think, therefore I am. The Black mother within each of us – the poet – whispers in our dreams: I feel, therefore I can be free' (Lorde, 1984: 38). Thus Lorde affirms the femaleness of her poetry.

As Ortner's (1974) argument suggested, nature (the site of feeling) is not the site of cultural production. Barbara Christian (1985: 144–5) argues that such phallologocentric oppositions conceal the true nature of white culture. The author is the creator of culture but author means, besides 'begetter, father', 'to enforce obedience'. In this schema, only white fathers are authors. Spillers (1984: 76) further argues that 'black is vestibular to culture' – 'that the blacks mirrored for the society around them what the human being was *not*', a beast. If women of colour respond to the father's command for obedience, they accept that they are natural, non-creative, bestial even, doubly marginalised by colour and gender. This perhaps explains Lorde's inversion: poetry, culture, comes from women's natural assets, dreams and feelings.

Christian (1985a: 145) and Edward Said (1985: 92–5) contrast static third world countries with the dynamic and civilized societies of Europe. Said (1985: 103) calls this process orientalism – an opposition of Occident and Orient. He addresses the construction of the Orient as feminine – its riches as fertile, its main symbol the sensual woman or harem, its despotic but attractive rulers. He suggests these fantasies abroad were related to the suppressed sexuality of Victorian England at home; the imperialist ideology of the late nineteenth century had both its political and its sexual dimensions in the male imagination.

The response of writers in the Orient, and third world countries in general, may be to embrace the traditional values of their culture, to become nativists; or to adopt an oppositional political creed, to become nationalists; or to reaffirm their own religions, to become fundamentalists (Said, 1985: 95). Coloured women, doubly feminized/colonized by this construction (Christian, 1985: 146), are positioned as bearers of traditional culture. This means that they are expected to maintain the cultural or religious traditions of infibulation, wearing the veil and so on, while men in third world countries are freed to enter western occupations and lifestyles.

Women writers from the Arab world (Kilpatrick, 1985: 86), from India (Gupta, 1985) and Indonesia (Hellwig, 1984: 143) explore the relations between western feminism, western lifestyles, traditional cultures and national liberation movements. In Indonesia the most widely read genre, the *poproman* or popular novel, plays out the conflict between western preoccupations and traditional values. The triumph of the latter over the former is also apparent in the submission of women to male authority (Hellwig, 1984: 150–2).

Sometimes tradition provides a space for women's voices, for example in transmission of oral culture (Schipper, 1985: 23-27; Kilpatrick, 1985: 73); more often it confines them to frivolous pursuits, such as 'decorative literature' (Rossi, 1984: 257). Many of these women experience criticism if they deal with male chauvinism (Schipper, 1985: 52) or censorship if they give women active roles (Houwelingen, 1985: 109). Gupta (1985: 63) confirms this: 'I never write down the first word that occurs to me when I feel inspired to write, not even the second word. I always wait until I have sufficiently camouflaged my original thought.'

For these women, writing is often both an act of cultural production and a self-conscious process of political production. Women of colour attempt to transform the meaning of 'nature', the role of dreams, and to replace white-imposed stereotypes with images they have produced.

Women in the third world battle with the identification of women with tradition; they both acknowledge the poignancy and strength of women's anecdotes, songs and sayings, and attempt to deal with the effects of excluding women from the capitalist sectors of their societies. One of the advantages of cultural production is that the result does not have to be 'logical' or 'predictable'; it provides a space for utopian vision; for a working-out or transformation of the contradictions of the societies in which these writers live. The fictional form can encompass a celebration of tradition combined with women's autonomy, or a transcendance of the pain of racism.

Alice Walker's Womanism

Although in Walker's earlier novels her protagonists are scarred by the experiences of racism, in *The Color Purple*, they rise above this to achieve a black feminist utopia. Of course Walker would not call this utopia feminist – she has coined the word 'womanist' to describe a feminist of colour. With this term Walker has attempted to identify what she regards as the special role of black women in American society. Womanist is used by Walker both to distance herself from feminists (who are white in her terms) and to allow her a greater solidarity with black men. Chikwenge Ogunyemi (1985: 64–5) argues that the 'black female aesthetic' points up commonalities between black African and United States women writers as well as the distinctiveness of this tradition from white feminism. The white feminist heroine struggles against patriarchy but the black womanist heroine inherits womanism after a traumatic event that allows her to move beyond the self to a commitment to the 'survival and wholeness of the entire people, male and female'. Thus the womanist, as opposed to the feminist, is concerned with the 'ethics of surviving rather than with the aesthetics of living' (Ogunyemi, 1985: 72). Sadoff (1985: 9), in similar vein, argues that Walker is more at ease with her matrilineage – traced through Zora Neale Hurston – than the white woman writer is with hers, seeing signs of 'inferiorization, self-hatred, and suppressed rebellion' in her foresisters. Walker, it is argued, thus draws on her cultural inheritance to celebrate wholeheartedly the strength of her heroines.

As one would expect from Walker's definition of womanist, and her attempts to rediscover earlier black female writers, some of *The Color Purple* 's concerns are particular to a black writer. Nettie's long struggle to understand the Olinka is a struggle with both the good and bad of the American negroes' origins, and with the imperialist relations out of which slavery grew and which destroyed the magnificent former culture of the Africans (Walker, 1982: 128–9). However, Walker's magic is not the black African magic of finding one's roots in tradition, it is the magic of love, embodied in Shug.

Love and forgiveness are the fictional representations of womanism in *The Color Purple*. Thus love, the womanist perspective, allows both the connection and the transformation of black people that is necessary for their 'survival and wholeness'. On the other hand, hate isolates (white) feminists on the island of Lesbos. Thus in *The Color Purple*, Shug's methods, based on love, are more powerful than Sofia's methods, based on anger. The moral is 'You know meanness kill' (Walker, 1982: 201) but the strength to avoid it is the strength of Jesus (Walker, 1982; 134). Not surprisingly, then, the outcome for Walker's women before she wrote *The Color Purple* was immobilization by guilt and pain. Much of the guilt and pain arose out of the way their menfolk treated them.

Only in *The Color Purple* does love change women's 'economic, political and moral status' (Parker-Smith, 1985: 483) and give them the power also to change their men. What Bettye Parker-Smith does not mention is the additional ingredient of a good dose of economic independence ('idealizing ... economic progress' as Sadoff (1985: 24) describes it). All the 'successful' black women except Sofia ultimately earn their own living – Shug and Mary Agnes sing, Celie makes trousers and inherits a large estate.

Womanism indicates a refusal to forsake black men. However, Walker does not idealize them, either in her other writings or in *The Color Purple*. Both white people and black men 'only listen long enough to be able to tell you what to do' (Walker, 1982: 177). Walker accepts the necessity to be a separatist occasionally 'for health' (Walker, 1984: xi); that is, to retreat sometimes to Reagon's 'little barred room'. The violence perpetuated by black men, particularly 'Mister' and her father, on Celie is not glossed over. Neither does Walker gloss over her own father's behaviour, but feminism has helped explain it, and has allowed Walker to displace its cause onto the society around him (Walker, 1984: 330). Partly Walker wants to be womanist because there are some good 'individual men' (Walker, 1984: xi) in society; for instance her oldest brother who refused the role model offered by his father (Walker, 1984: 329–30). Walker (1984: 331) argues that men 'must represent half the world to me, as I must represent the other half to them'. However, Walker does not merely forgive her father in reality, or Mister in fiction, she loves her father (and perhaps also the transformed Mister): 'I have loved my own parents' faces above all others, and have refused to let them be denied, or myself to let them go' (Walker, 1984: 382). (Of course this is not unusual, even among white feminists. Coran Kaplan (1986: 191) attempted to write of her embattled and loving history with her father but could not, seeing it as an attack or betrayal.)

Womanism gives feminism a coloured inflection; the womanist is a 'black feminist or feminist of color' (Walker, 1984: xi): white women cannot be womanist. Womanist suggests a more outrageous, fun-loving, complete and powerful woman to Walker; it suggests 'round' and 'whole', 'women who love other women, yes, but women who also have concern, in a culture that oppresses all black people (and this would go back very far), for their fathers, brothers, and sons, no matter how they feel about them as males' (Walker, 1983: 81–2). Hence 'womanist is to feminist as purple is to lavender' (Walker, 1983: xii). And hence the title, *The Color Purple*. It is an all-encompassing love that allows Walker's women to become womanist.

However, the path to this liberation is no primrose path. Celie is first the victim of incest at the hands of her presumed father and then the victim of beatings, physical abuse, and isolation from Nettie at the hands of her husband Mister. How does Walker turn this material, so suitable for a feminist novel, into a womanist perspective? One of Walker's strategems is the relationship between Celie and Shug which helps Celie overcome her own doubts. But this intense relationship also has the amazing effect of educating Mister. Mister's treatment of Celie is passed off as 'I wanted to kill you ... and I did slap you around a couple of times'. Shug is 'manly', which means she is 'upright, honest' but has Mister been 'manly' to Celie? Mister's miraculous conversion is explained as 'experience ... everybody bound to git some of that sooner or later' (Walker, 1982: 237).

In *The Color Purple* black men can be made to learn their lessons, and that by women who have somehow escaped the dictates of patriarchal society. To be 'womanist' (round and whole), as opposed to 'feminist' (separated and narrow) only seems possible or desirable if it is worth leaving the island; if the men are going to respond by being manly. Thus it may be argued that the success of a womanist position – one that reconciles attacks on patriarchy with concern for the oppression of black men – is also a form of utopian writing, a genre often used by white feminists such as Marge Piercy or Ursula Le Guinn. This may not be readily apparent in *The Color Purple* because of the epistolary style of the book, the writing of letters which seem to reveal incidents both intimate and real, and thus disguises the improbability of the womanist resolution.

This chapter has focused on relations between women of different colour in the one society. For many women of colour race is more important than gender. It cannot be denied that race is a significant part of these women's identity and experience, an experience white women do not share. It can, however, be questioned whether women of colour should refuse white feminists' arguments as 'frivolous' or merely reflecting a socioeconomic status that most women of colour do not enjoy. Perhaps a more significant criticism, and one that is not really addressed extensively above, is the argument that white women and women of colour can share no common positions at all, that the fear of white women is the fear of the dominant race who know they have been the oppressor: 'You're afraid of the payback, see. You know what you've got coming to you and you certainly don't want it, because you know you deserve it' (Bell in Coleman and Bell, 1986: 75). Feminists, like Rich, have sought to argue against this position by describing white women as 'disloyal to civilization'. If white women are not disloyal to white patriarchal civilization, or cannot be, the chance of a feminist project that treats all women as a category oppressed in particular ways seems remote.

A crucial element of such questioning is the object of political action. Thus Bonnie Dill (1983: 147) argues that 'the women's movement may need to move beyond a limited focus on "women's issues" to ally with groups of women and men who are addressing other aspects of race and class oppression.' In this quotation Dill summarizes many of the arguments which were canvassed above. White feminism, it is suggested, is limited to women's issues and it refuses alliances with women *and* men. Dill also betrays her belief that feminism should be directed against race and class oppression – the women's movement needs to address 'other' aspects of oppression. This implies that feminism should seek to eliminate the structures of racism and class oppression in the whole society, that to be successful it must be a socialist feminism and (perhaps a new word is needed) an anti-racist feminism. On the other hand, those who advocate struggles by 'groups of women and men' united by their shared race or class, often fail to consider whether such struggles can achieve feminist goals of protection from male violence, economic independence for women and so on. Indeed, one needs to ask whether they should attempt to do so. These issues will be explored in relation to third world women in Chapter 4.

4

Colonialism, Imperialism and Development

[T]o listen not to the bark of the guns ... but to the voices of the poets, answering each other, assuring us of a unity that rubs out divisions as if they were chalk marks only; to discuss with you the capacity of the human spirit to overflow boundaries and make unity out of multiplicity (Woolf, 1977: 63)

Chapter 3 attempted to identify some structural bases of racism, for example the 'settlement' of Australia and South Africa by whites, the slave society of the southern American states, British imperialist relations with India and the West Indies. So too should an attempt be made to assess the structural bases of antagonism between so-called first world and third world women. Mirtha Quintanales (1983: 151) warns that 'color' is not the basis. Not all third world women are women of colour (for instance the descendants of the Spanish in South America) while not all first world women are white, for example the Japanese. Third world countries are defined by their relations to the core capitalist countries of the west.

The international expansion of capitalism occurred first in its political cloak of colonialism and then in its economic cloak of imperialism and continues today through the spread of transnational corporations. The exploitation by the core societies of the peripheral societies has allowed many women (and men) of the western world to enjoy a higher standard of living than many women (and men) of the developing countries. Imperialism is etched into the minds of people fighting for national liberation. They fight against soldiers armed by the United States, the USSR and other 'imperialist' powers. However, it is the more subtle economic imperialism that differentiates the west and the third world, whether these other countries are engaged in national liberation struggles or not. The activities of transnational corporations not only provide the valued but body-destroying jobs described below, they also deprive people of land for subsistence by converting it to cash crops. They lend money to developing nations' governments at high interest rates and then seek intervention in the domestic affairs of the debtor nations when their investments appear threatened. No wonder then that many third world women, educated in these evils, find it hard to see North American, European and Australian women as other than the 'imperialist aggressor'.

It is claimed that western women's imperialism has a long history. The suffragists, for example, had pro-imperialist attitudes according to Carby (1982: 22). Western women's contraceptive freedom, which reduced the birth-rate and hence the labour-force, has been gained at the price of third world women becoming guest workers or assemblers in free export zones (Jaggar, 1983: 344). Finally Carby (1982: 220) and Minh-ha (1987: 17) claim that the category 'third world women' collapses a variety of experience, and is yet another sign of western women's imperialist ignorance.

Bourne (1983: 19) argues that third world women have an indigenous history and tradition of struggle from which western feminists could learn. Amos and Parmar (1984: 6) note a tendency to treat pre-capitalist economies as both backward and responsible for women's oppression, while Mama (1984) traces the history of resistance in Africa. Parita Trivedi (1984) discusses the struggles of Indian women, both in autonomous institutions and with men, and both in India and in Britain. Although Mama accepts the need for a united front against the British state by all non-white peoples, she (1984: 24) asserts that 'To generalize for a whole continent borders on the foolish, and in respect of three continents must be the height of folly.'

There are two major points of contention between first and third world women over the universality of feminist politics. First, third world women accuse first world women of ethnocentrism, of uneducated horror at traditional practices such as infibulation or veiling. Secondly, third world women argue that first world women participate in the rewards of imperialism and so their interests must be different. National liberation or socialist revolution is the more pressing agenda item for third world women. The problem is similar to that of black women in relation to white women. Should they ignore the socioeconomic and other structural differences that mark their position, should they desert the political fight alongside their 'brothers', and instead embrace the significance of the similar position they share with white women? It is not for non-participants to decide which political struggle should be uppermost on anyone's agenda; it is however pertinent to ask what goals can be achieved through a national liberation or socialist struggle.

This chapter analyses some of the barriers that apparently stand in the way of a politically unified women's movement around the world, particularly the assertion that first world feminism is ethnocentric. Thus the attempts by first wave feminists to produce a world peace movement or a transnational analysis of women workers seem to be attempts to create a global feminism, attempts which third world women often attack as irrelevant to their needs. Secondly, the potential for feminist outcomes of national liberation and socialist struggles will be explored by analysing the status of women in so-called socialist countries and the attempts of third world women to link feminist goals with national liberation. Finally the International Decade for Women will be analysed, as these meetings of women (and men) from all over the world have thrown light on the prospects for a global feminism.

War, Peace and Labour

Western women's movements have long distanced themselves from war: in 1854 Frederika Brewer formed the first Women's Peace League in Europe (Russell, 1983: 1). The women who attack war often also eschew nationalism. Virginia Woolf (1979: 124–5) wrote in England in 1938:

> And if he says he is fighting to protect England from foreign rule, she will reflect that for her there are no foreigners, since by law if she marries a foreigner she becomes a foreigner ... in fact, as a woman, I have no country. As a woman I want no country. As a woman, my country is the whole world. (Woolf, 1979: 124–5)

Many third world nations are also imperialist constructions, and third world women may not necessarily identify with their nations either. For example, women in contemporary Africa talk about themselves as African Women, not as a 'Luo woman' or a 'Kenyan woman' (Brekke, 1985: 135).

Some women have linked war with the oppression and physical domination of women. Daly (1978: 355), Brownmiller (1975: Ch.3) and the Anzac Day Women Against Rape marches, mourning 'all women of all countries raped in all wars' (Pringle, 1983: 31) link war and rape. 'To the victor belongs the spoils': the rape and murder of women. How close these two are is revealed by the following account by an American soldier in Vietnam:

> We balled these chicks ... they'd rather do that than get shot ... [one yelled out a derogatory remark at her rapist] ... He just reached down for his weapon and blew her away ... [we] picked up our weapons and blew away the other three chicks. (quoted in Pringle, 1983: 32)

There seems to be little differences between the violence of 'balling' and the murders for which a sexual euphemism is used – 'blew'.

Women's groups in a number of western countries have linked opposition to nuclear war to opposition to more widespread male violence, in the United States (Women's Pentagon Action Group for example), Europe (both East and West), Japan, Canada, Australia (especially at Cockburn Sound and Pine Gap), the Pacific (opposition to French nuclear testing), but most notably in England at Greenham Common.

Many women in these peace movements argue that the wider concerns of feminism, such as male violence or competitiveness, also explain war (Buirski, 1983: 63). Their political actions draw on the heritage of suffragists, for example in chaining themselves to the perimeter fence of Greenham Common (Harford and Hopkins, 1985: 19), or other female symbols. The colourful webs woven into the perimeter fence are seen as 'the web of strength through interconnectedness': the web of the ancient spider goddess, is made of the wool of 'homespun inner knowledge' (Harford and Hopkins, 1985: 92). The holes in the fence are filled up with symbols of life and colour: photographs of loved ones, flowers, etc. (Cook and Kirk, 1983: 85; Harford and Hopkins, 1985: 91). The Greenham Common women assert the need for non-hierarchial co-operative decision-making and non-violent resistance (Jones, 1983: 132–6). It is clear then why the Greenham women took the controversial 'women only' decision, although many men disagree with this decision (for example see O'Lincoln, 1984: 88).

Recently some western feminists have affirmed the power of women's links with nature (the neo-maternalists and eco-feminists). Eco-feminists argue that the western dualism of mind and body has led to the armaments-based economy, the shrinking of arable land, the compulsive consumption of non-renewable resources and increased poverty (Griffin, 1983: 1). We are no longer 'connected to the vibrations' of the planet, the rape of which is equivalent to the rape of women (Freer, 1983: 132). Eco-feminists often point to the exemplary non-exploitative relationship traditional societies had with their land (for example, Ngahuia Te Awekotaku (1983) on Maori society or Anita Anand (1983) on the northern Indian Chipko movement).

Does the peace movement live up to its claims to being international? Does it represent women of all colours and nations? Barbara Harford and Sarah Hopkins (1985: 2) say 'It began as a predominantly white, middle-class movement, but as it grew, the barriers of race, class and sexuality began to break down.' In autumn of 1983 women of colour joined the Greenham Common camp. Nevertheless, Connie Mansueto (1983: 118) argues against the relevance of the peace movement to all women:

'These men *could* kill us with their nuclear weapons ... In many parts of the world they are practising non-nuclear warfare, organised torture, and genocide. In Britain ... police brutality, rape, incest, beating.' She argues that these male forms of violence already being perpetrated on third world women and women of colour should be challenged as a first priority.

Critics of the women's peace movement agree with Mansueto but extend the list of forms of violence to include water pollution in India (Amos and Parmar, 1984: 17), rotting in a South African jail (Bryan et al., 1985: 175), or starvation anywhere (Amos and Parmar, 1984: 17). They further argue that the white women's peace movement ignores these more significant forms of violence practised on coloured women. Instead the peace movement displays a parochial preoccupation with 'their own backyards', an identification with 'nationalist' and imperialist sentiments, the 'ideology of Empire' which cannot appeal to coloured women in Britain, who are victims of that very ideology (Amos and Parmar, 1984: 16). As evidence of this parochialism and imperialism is the peace movement's failure to mobilize over uranium mining in Namibia, Pacific land rights, nuclear testing on Australian Aborigines' land, or British occupation of Northern Ireland (Amos and Parmar, 1984: 16). When some peace demonstrators shouted at a black American soldier 'Yanks out', Amos and Parmar (1984: 16) argue they really meant 'Blacks go home.' A group of white women should have been more sensitive than to attack a single black man, because the collective experience of racism is alive in every black individual's conscious and unconscious psyche, as 'is the history of white women's power over black men'.

Dowse and Giles (1984: 67) believe women participate in the anti-nuclear movement as feminists, '*because* we are feminists'. Nevertheless not all women oppose war. In the American Civil War and in the two world wars, some suffragists on both sides of the Atlantic argued that women could win the right to vote by fighting for their country. A similar proposition is endorsed today by many women fighting in national liberation struggles. Women all over the world have, and do, participate in the war industry as prostitutes, wives, widows, social workers, nurses, soldiers, defence workers or even mothers of soldiers (Enloe, 1983a).

Thus few non-western women share the concerns of the largely western women's peace movement. This perhaps is particularly so for women in liberation armies. Cynthia Enloe (1983a: 161–71) suggests that while participation in liberation armies gives women moral authority, and according to Nyasha and Rose (1984: 105) new attitudes to contraception and abortion, liberation armies are not automatically nonsexist because they are non-statist. Hence women are often trained separately because of the sexism of their comrades, and demobilized after victory with the charge to 'go forth and multiply', to add to the country's population (see, for example, Omani Women's Organization in Davies, 1983: 119).

Sara Ruddick (1983) asks whether identifying women with peace and men with war, women as protected and men as protector, merely reinforces gender stereotypes. The women's peace movement's reply is that nonviolent action against war is self-assertion rather than submission while the distinction between combatant and non-combatant disappears with nuclear war (Assiter, 1983: 200).

Again women are apparently confronted with an unpalatable contradiction. Either their identification as peace loving denies them access to some forms of power and political leverage or their role as warriors integrates them into male-defined national liberation struggles.

Exploitation Within International Capitalism

Just as war has become an international affair, so too has production. A number of writers draw links between the activities of transnational corporations and the military economy. Transnational corporations produce military hardware and pressure governments around the world to purchase it (Bertell, 1984: 377). In order to do so, these governments must acquire foreign currency by establishing export zones where transnational corporations take advantage of women's cheap labour to produce, along with other goods, components of the very armaments that are sold to the host government (Enloe, 1983a: 201). A number of third world women declared at Nairobi in 1985 that the majority of casualties of contemporary militarism were third world women, children and the aged. Furthermore:

> peace cannot be separated from development just as equality cannot, because the conditions that breed violence, war, and inequality are themselves often the results of development strategies harmful or irrelevant to the poor and to women. (quoted in Jennett, 1987: 351)

Transnational corporations' offshore relocation of production follows a separation of high-technology, professional and technical work done in the west from low-technology labour-intensive assembly done off shore (Hancock, 1983: 132). Some 90 per cent of workers on offshore plants in the Philippines, Malaysia, Singapore and Thailand are women; the numbers employed in South East Asia have increased from about 15,000 in 1971 to 500,000 in the early 1980s (Hancock, 1983: 134–5). Women's wages are 20–50 per cent lower than men's for comparable jobs, while male productivity is lower (Elson and Pearson, 1981: 148). Often women in developing countries who have such jobs are envied by their female friends. In comparison with non-western employment the wages are higher, and the jobs seem less socially and physically dangerous than that of a hostess or masseuse, who is exposed to the possibility of harassment and violence from clients and employers. Due to the delicacy of the microchip, electronics assembly must be done in air-conditioned buildings, more pleasant surroundings than most worksites offer (Enloe, 1983a: 202).

However in Hong Kong in the 1974–5 recession, for example, one-third of workers for transnational corporations were laid off, in South Korea 34 per cent have an ill-health condition such as deteriorating eyesight. Most will have to leave their jobs before they are 30, and may lose their sight, their livers, their fertility, before they lose their jobs (Hancock, 1983: 141–2). Many have been sexually abused, as for example workers in the Masan Free Export Zone in South Korea are by Japanese supervisors. Women who work in factories are seen as 'not quite respectable' and so are more exposed to the possibility of sexual harassment (Elson and Pearson, 1981: 159).

In the quest for the internationalization of women's oppression, parallels are drawn between assembly workers in western countries and the third world – most are women and most work without union organization (Hancock, 1983: 134). What is not often mentioned is the great disparity in wages (see Table 10). That women in third world countries work for much lower wages than their western counterparts is why transnational capital has relocated production in those countries. Most of these workers suffer a triple burden as women, as migrants (whether from the rural hinterland or another country – Hancock, 1983: 140), and as workers (Phizacklea, 1983: 140). However, the point that United States workers are also black, Hispanic or Asian is not discussed. There is an oft-quoted Malaysian Government brochure's claim – 'The manual dexterity of the oriental female is famous the world over. Her hands are small and she works fast with extreme care' (quoted in Hancock, 1983: 138). Diane Elson and Ruth Pearson (1981: 149) focus on the sexism ('female') of this quotation but ignore its racism ('oriental'). Thus, according to Carby (1982: 220), they fail to highlight the specific position of *Asian* women in these factories in an attempt to claim the universality of female experience in capitalist employment.

Table 10   Wage Rates and Fringe Benefits of Assembly Workers

Country	Hourly Wage Rates ($US)	Wage Plus Fringe ($US)
United States	5.92	8.06
Hong Kong	1.15	1.20
Singapore	0.79	1.25
South Korea	0.63	1.00
Taiwan	0.53	0.80
Malaysia	0.48	0.60
Philippines	0.48	0.50
Indonesia	0.19	0.35

Source: Enloe, 1983a: 202

Another example of western blindness to the significance of culture or race is Elson and Pearson's (1981: 153) description of mass hysteria in Malay assembly plants (in which women see spirits in their microscopes), as 'non-rational forms' of release from 'self-repression'. Parmar (1982: 266) replies that this hysteria is just as effective in closing down the factory as a strike or walk out would be. It is a response more attuned with the women's culture which denies them emotional expression, but does accept the existence of spirits.

The oppositional interests of western female consumers of cheaper clothes produced by the exploited women of the third world is highlighted by Enloe (1983b). Noticing the 'Made in ...' third world country tags on the clothes she shops for she asks 'Does a feminist today have to go naked to live by her principles?' (Enloe, 1983b: 118). The answer is of course that she cannot, and if she is poor must buy the cheapest clothes. Enloe, as trapped in the transnational capitalist web as the Asian worker, can only offer this form of political activity: 'We could try to imagine how in our daily experiences struggling with patriarchy and workplace exploitation we are linked to – and dependent on – other women's daily experiences' (Enloe, 1983b: 119). This will not be very convincing to anyone with a shred of marxist understanding in their theory of the world. It is for this reason that Kate Soper (1987: 111) argues for a 'second level of morality', which comes from an understanding of the wider social structures of oppression. There are some things we cannot change by acting as individuals, by 'being moral'. Such things require 'political activism' and the acceptance of responsibility 'not only for how we act individually within a given system, but for the system itself'. This argument is similar to Jenny Bourne's claim that consciousness-raising will not change racist structures, political intervention is required.

Furthermore, as Joan Robinson, the English economist, is reputed to have said, 'there is only one thing worse than being a third world country exploited by transnational capitalism and that is being a third world country not exploited by transnational capitalism.' If Enloe and other white women refused to consume the clothing produced by third world women, the result would only be the unemployment of these women. Jobs in the export zones often pay better than those in the rest of the economy. Those of a marxist orientation would argue that free trade unions are the appropriate struggle for women in these export zones. But is this just another example of the imperialism of which Parmar accuses Elson and Pearson? Is it really a claim that the struggles of women workers in the west should be duplicated in third world countries? Or is it a recognition that in capitalist enterprises, the most appropriate forms of resistance are western-style methods?

The other alternative that seems to be offered women in the third world is liberation struggle, an attempt to transcend capitalist forms of organization for some form of socialist organization. Such struggles are often a response to the impact of colonization.

The Impact of Colonialism

Chapter 2 traced some of the changes in women's status from hunting, gathering, or horticultural societies to agricultural societies. When societies from either of these two basic types come into contact with capitalist forms of economic organization, the effects on the status of women may be different; in the former lowering women's status, in the latter raising it (see, for example, Giele, 1977: 9–14). However, as Leghorn and Parker warn in their classification of societies, such contrasts are too simple. For one thing the economic effects of capitalism must be separated from other effects, such as those of social practices like the veil or suttee. For another thing, one needs to ask whether all women are advantaged or disadvantaged by the transition to capitalist forms of production.

It was likely that colonial administrators, coming from patriarchal societies as they did, would notice and promote the interests of men rather than women. Indeed the evidence supports this. For instance the colonizers converted communal land traditionally controlled by women into private property vested in men (Carby, 1982: 228); sought out men as leaders of the colonized tribes and groups (Carby, 1982: 224); drew men into wage-labour leaving the women to struggle to meet subsistence needs (Cutrufelli, 1983: 22–3); educated the men for productive labour and the women, if educated at all, for domestic labour (Barnard, 1983: 141; Barthel, 1985); began the process of displacing locally produced goods, often made by women, for imported western goods (Manderson, 1983: 10). Christine Obbo (1980) argues that colonization fed on pre-existing patriarchal forms, but also reinforced and strengthened those forms.

An example of this is the various struggles of the Igbo women of south-eastern Nigeria. Women initiated a three-month protest, in which 53 women were killed, against the rumoured taxation of women by the British colonial rulers. From the 1940s, they also protested against the increased mechanization of palm oil extraction by Pioneer Oil Mills. Formerly the extraction had been done by the women, who were entitled to the kernels, while husbands were entitled to the oils, but both of which products were sold by the women. Mechanization put full responsibility for collection, sale and allocation of the proceeds in male hands. Women were excluded from their economic power base, but again not without resistance – for example a several month long violent demonstration in 1951–2. According to Coleman and Shelly Romalis (1983: 276), the Aba Riots of 1929 were incorporated into the history of the Nationalist Movement, but these histories do not explain why women, not men, were the protestors. The British response was to reinforce the power of the Igbo men, the values of the rulers and missionaries alike asserting the 'subservience and invisibility of women in the political arena' (Romalis and Romalis, 1983: 277). According to Romalis and Romalis (1983: 284, 282) West African men too were uncomfortable with women's economic power, for example levelling accusations of witchcraft at financially successful women. Thus Igbo 'women were also protesting domination by their own Igbo men, and female exclusion from the formal political system.'

Other commentators suggest that third world middle-class women have benefited from colonization but often at the expense of working-class women (Beneria and Sen, 1982: 164), who are the workers in batik factories (Price, 1983), or domestic servants in Equador (Borja, 1984). Kumari Jayawardena (1986), in her analysis of the development of feminism in a number of third world countries early this century, also notes the unequal impact of those changes – it was largely middle-class women who benefited from increased educational opportunities, entry to the professions or changing social customs. This despite the fact that many working-class women were integrated into imperialist development as plantation or factory workers (see Jayawardena, 1986: 131–3). Diane Barthel (1985) notes that it was the daughters of the new entrepreneurial and administrative elite under colonialism, who were given access to Europeanized education. The purpose was clearly to fit them as wives and mothers of this elite, although in an extension of this role many were trained as teachers and health care workers. There was another objective, to make 'less antagonistic to colonial purposes', women who may otherwise have become 'a dangerous, rebellious force: a "Lysistrata under the coconut trees"' (Barthel, 1985: 145):

> The education of the native woman permits the evolution of the family and does not limit to the individual level the action of education received. It will consolidate, finally, in successive generations, the new habits acquired by education and will permanently install our action within the indigenous society. (governor-general of French West Africa in 1937, quoted in Barthel, 1985: 146)

So contemporary nationalist leaders' claims that women should retain their traditional ways may be a legacy from colonial times; development through colonization was a double-edged sword for its participants – and one that nationalist leaders and women's groups handled uneasily.

Today education may remove girls from the labour force and promote their dependence on men while also inculcating subordinate roles (Jennett, 1987: 354). Lourdes Beneria and Gita Sen (1982: 161, 168) also suggest education is a contradictory experience for third world women. Educational programmes mesh well with strategies to integrate third world women into the world capitalist order as cheap workers or as temporary and seasonal labourers. Education also increases women's self-determination, for example their ability and willingness to control their own reproductive strategies.

Although Jayawardena (1986: 2) argues that 'feminism was not imposed on the Third World by the West', it is clear that colonial ties often determined the links between third world feminists and western feminists. For many third world women (and men), the west offered a model of greater independence for women, and this was enthusiastically adopted by most nationalist reformist groups as part of their programme for social change. The 'modernization' strategy produced by the image of more independent western women, as with the other modernization strategies advocated by these reformist movements, yielded contradictory results in most countries. The reformists were also nationalists – they wanted to free their countries from the colonial yoke – but at the same time they wished to obtain the advantages of economic development. As a result nationalist movements were often internally divided. For example, in Indonesia when the colonial government outlawed polygamy, many nationalist groups argued it was an unwanted interference with local customs, some women's groups however supported the legislation (Jayawardena, 1986: 152).

Strobel (1982: 130) identifies the role of missions as both beneficial and harmful to African women – a refuge from the slave trade, an access to (limited) education, a challenge to clitoridectomy, but also repressive of women's rituals, opening the church to men not women, and upholding a sexual double standard. The missions attempted to remake African women in the Christian image, into something like a good white housewife and mother. It has been suggested that in a number of countries the 'modernization' of traditional practices within capitalist relations of production has preserved them – dowry in India, bride-price in Africa, 'machismo' in Latin America (Jennett, 1987: 355).

If exploitation has characterized the colonial development of the east/south by the west/north, there has in the last few decades been a much smaller trickle of resources back the other way. In theory western governments' development programmes are strategies by which western money and personnel increase the self-reliance of third world nations. These programmes are not the altruistic gifts of western benefactors. They are often motivated by a strategy of developing the third world so it can consume more western goods. Much development aid is 'tied', for example, to the purchase of goods from the country 'giving' the aid. In development programmes, too, women have often suffered a loss of economic resources.

Women in Development Programmes

The invisibility of women's labour to the men who designed and executed development programmes has only recently been recognized in the west. Now, however, more development programmes address the 'status of women'. From being seen as external to the productive processes of these countries, women are now more often treated as a resource: 'Developing countries cannot afford to make less than full use of all their resources, including women' (Jackson Committee, 1984: 80). Traditional 'women's crops' (often root crops) have until recently been given lower status than 'men's crops', despite the fact they often yield greater nutritional value; some governments now see the value of training female agricultural extension workers to work with women (Jennett, 1987: 352). Barbara Rogers (1980: 30–3) argues that treating women as a 'resource' dehumanizes and objectifies them; the focus should be on women's control of work relations.

Furthermore, socialist feminists argue that this 'standard developmentalist interest in the problems of third world women ... is motivated by a perception that women are instrumental to programs of population control, increased food production, and the provision of other basic needs' (Beneria and Sen, 1982: 158). Rather than fostering an 'entrepreneurial spirit and achievement orientation' through integration into capitalist accumulation, third world women need to focus on tackling both the class contradictions of development and the special issues of concern to them as women – such as 'control over their environment and their bodies' and the improved health of themselves and their children (Beneria and Sen, 1982: 160, 168). Marjorie Mbilinyi (1984: 290) makes a similar argument for East Africa. Women are already 'integrated' into capitalist production as the most exploited segment of the African labour force, but they are also seen as 'a *problem* in production and reproduction' because they have resisted such integration, seeking alternative parallel markets for their crops and resisting husbands' and others' efforts to make them labour for no foreseeable return. Mbilinyi also endorses the need for revolution rather than the integration that 'bourgeois feminism' calls for – 'There is no middle road to women's liberation' (Mbilinyi, 1984: 293). However, she reveals the ambivalence of this position in a society not yet on the eve of such a revolution. She notes the 'alarming' way in which women entrepreneurs are encouraged but also points out approvingly that despite police opposition entrepreneurial (or at least petty-bourgeois) women 'go right on brewing and selling homebrew beer', they 'assert their own goals and demands against a variety of groups' (Mbilinyi, 1984: 295).

At least the Jackson Committee, established by the federal government to enquire into Australia's aid programme, seeks to redress previous ignorance of women's labour or even its displacement for men's labour (for example, when new technology is introduced) by many development programmes. As a result of women-centred development programmes, however, women often find themselves placed in a new 'aid ghetto'. A common case is handicrafts co-operatives (Dixon, 1978). While women are helped to establish co-operatives relying on traditional skills and the chancy tourist industry (Rogers, 1980: 95), men are trained for the capital-intensive western sector jobs. However, co-operatives do bring women together and provide them with a chance for economic independence. Both Rogers (1980: 104) and the Jackson Committee (1984: 81) suggest that women's enthusiasm for development projects often depends on their prospects for economic gain.

Another departure for aid agencies is the attention to the so-called unproductive domestic labour of women – carrying water, handmilling of corn and so on. In East Africa water carrying consumes 12–27 per cent of the day-time caloric uses of women while it takes three hours to pound enough grain to feed a family for five days (Rogers, 1980: 153, 155). The Jackson Committee (1984: 82) recommends that a water-supply, population planning or health and nutritional services component should be built into every aid programme. Conversely, when women of the Upper Volta were provided with a handmill for grain, family expectations required them to prepare an evening meal while before they had served a cold snack (the cold snack had been 'accepted' by their husbands because of the long hours required to stone-mill grain) (Kelly and Elliott, 1982: 95). The new technology did not reduce women's work, rather it improved nutrition in the diet. Leghorn and Parker (1981: 55) note that digging water wells in Africa saves women water carrying time but it stops them gathering together, a network support activity, as they had done previously.

Population Control
Most development agencies are enthusiastic proponents of population control, whether this is represented in terms of women's health (Jackson Committee, 1984: 78), or as a reason for better education (Cochrane, 1982). Rogers (1980: 108) argues that attempts at coercion actually increased the birth rate in a number of Indian states while the birth-rate continued to fall in those states which did not use coercion. She argues that abortions are the most common method of birth control. Abortions terminate half of all pregnancies in Brazil; complications from abortions account for one-third of all operations in Chile; African women have a 40 per cent chance of admission to hospital due to abortion complications (Rogers, 1980: 110). Botched illegal abortions are the single most common cause of women's hospitalization in Harare (Seidman, 1984: 436). Furthermore, evidence from nineteenth-century observers in both North and South America suggests that the native populations had lower birth rates than contemporary Europeans, due to segregation of husband and wife, polygamy and so on. Rogers (1980: 111) argues that early colonial policy was pro-natalist, requiring labourers for commercial and other colonial ventures. While Rogers recommends contraception projects in the third world, she insists that follow-up care is vital, given the anaemia and malnourishment of many women (Rogers, 1980: 108–9). She asserts that only women should work in delivering contraceptive services, as men are often hostile to contraceptive use.

Heather McRae (1980) analyses the trap for Papua New Guinea

women who under a western legal system, in fact a Criminal Code very similar to Queensland's, are legally denied both their traditional family planning methods and western abortion and sterilization, the latter because of the interpretation given to the Criminal Code. Added to these problems however, contraceptive methods cannot be advertised and the contraceptive pill cannot be prescribed for women under eighteen.

As Rogers' figures suggest, there appears to be little doubt that third world women desire access to safe abortions and contraception, whether it is because traditional methods have been displaced, repressed or forgotten. However, attempts by international agencies, for example the World Bank or the Population Institute, to impose birth control measures on third world nations often pose a dilemma for third world women. There has been a long-term antagonism by white nations towards reproduction by women of colour and third world women. These eugenicist, racist attitudes are widely held, and extend in the west, in muted form, only to white women who are also poor. Third world women do not wish to be seen as the dupes of imperialist institutions, while their own left wing political movements often oppose contraceptive freedom (Prado, 1984: 86). A number of liberation movements exhort women to produce future liberation fighters. A 'common Palestinian saying is that "The Israelis beat us at the borders and we beat them in the bedrooms"' (Anthias and Yuval-Davis, 1983: 70). This 'intensive reproductive "demographic" race' (Anthias and Yuval-Davis, 1983: 71) is obviously not mounted solely in the interests of women, but women perhaps participate willingly, possibly relishing a new positive attitude to the children they bear and their reproductive powers. On the other hand Fahimeh argues that when the Palestinian women attempted to show films from a United Nations family planning office, most women were frightened to attend, partly because 'their husbands would change towards them' even though these women had complained of how tired they became producing so many babies (cited in Al-Hibri, 1981: 189).

The dilemma does not appear to result from ignorance concerning what women want – they desire to control their own reproduction, and that means to be able to choose to *have* babies and choose *not* to have babies. The dilemma is thus a political one, over the strategic alliances women must forge in battles on several fronts, against both nations of the west and men of their own nation. One of the crucial dimensions of this dilemma is the relationship between national liberation and feminism. Thus it will be useful to examine briefly the status of women in so-called socialist countries.

Jayawardena's (1986) analysis of the history of feminist struggles in a number of countries reveals the differential response to women's demands by nationalist reform and nationalist marxist movements. Reform movements often advocated political activism (at least as voters) and education for women, but did so on the grounds that this would improve women as wives and mothers (for example India, Japan, Guomindang China), and that 'liberation' from the yoke of colonialism required the participation of women *in that struggle*. Socialist movements more often advocated the additional role of women as workers in the public sphere, and this sometimes included the demand for collectivized housework (Sukarno in Indonesia – Jayawardena, 1986: 152). Just as the reformist leaders attempted to remake the women's movements in their own image – to struggle for an independent, democratic, developing society – so too, it can be argued, did the socialist movements attempt to integrate women into marxist-inspired definitions of women's liberation.

Women's Work in Socialist Countries

There can be little doubt that women in the USSR, and many other East European countries, are better represented in non-traditional professions like technology and science than in many other western societies (Dodge, 1966: 1). However this may be attributable, in the USSR at least, to the severe shortage of manpower following two world wars and a civil war (Smock, 1977: 45). Indeed workforce participation is a mixed blessing where women retain their domestic duties and there is inadequate child-care and other facilities (Dodge, 1966: 3) while Soviet fathers have generally proved no more willing to share domestic duties than western husbands. So demanding is this double shift that Suzanne Körösi (1984: 291) reports that in Hungary three-quarters of eligible women chose to leave the workforce when they were offered maternity allowances of three years duration. A similar pattern emerges for other socialist societies. For example, Muriel Nazarri (1983: 255) suggests that three-quarters of the Cuban women enlisted to join the labour force in 1969 left their jobs before the year was out, partly because of the 'double shift'. Stress is placed upon access to the workforce, although not necessarily economic equality. In Chinese communes men still control the family's income (Sheridan, 1984: 222) while jobs are divided on the basis of whether they are masculine or feminine with unequal rewards for each (Xioa Lu, 1984: 153).

Similarly, education of women is given a higher priority in socialist countries. This is the official policy in Mozambique, although in the early stages of its implementation some party members beat their wives, so badly they had to be hospitalized, for attending literacy classes (Rodriguez, 1983: 130, 134). Education may help women to avoid traditional roles (Davies, 1983: 119) or allow them to participate in more than sewing and other co-operatives (Rodgriguez, 1983: 127–8).

On the family front, however, far less has been achieved in socialist countries. Elizabeth Croll (1978: 185–212) discusses the Chinese Communist Party's attempts to have women represented in local soviets and to exchange opinions – 'speak bitterness' – about their treatment by men and the marriage laws in the 1930s. These activities provoked hostile reactions from the men in the party. French (1985: 243) suggests that initially 'The Chinese revolution ... seemed the only revolution in history to remain faithful to the feminist principles with which it began ... But so was the Russian at first.' Croll (1978: 302–17) argues that by the 1970s women's liberation in China meant denying romantic love and not seeking attention from husbands; while the women's movement had been incorporated into the party structure.

In Cuba, Germaine Greer (1985: 271–5) attended the fourth congress of the Federation of Cuban Women and was gratified to see Fidel Castro as a member of the audience. Initially a serious observer, then an enthusiastic participant, Castro ordered his ministers to appear the next day to answer the women's charges. Nevertheless, the Family Code, requiring men to share housework, has not reformed the sexual division of labour in Cuba, while heterosexual pairing and women's role as productive labourers are emphasized (La Silenciada, 1984: 171). Nazzari (1983) suggests that the Family Code itself could be seen in regressive terms, that it was Castro's response to the increasing expense of free and collectivized childminding services and maternity allowances. With a retreat to a more incentive-based wage structure to promote economic development, the Family Code 'provided a solution to the woman question that did not need to come out of the national budget' (Nazzari, 1983: 257). Nazzari makes two points here – that treating women workers as different with special needs is incompatible with efficient capitalist-type development and that privatized childcare, or passing the blame and problem to individual husbands, was a strategy based not so much on the desire to re-educate men as to save the state's limited resources for 'more important' projects.

Maxine Molyneux (1985: 250) traces the redistributive policies in Nicaragua, which benefited poor women (by virtue of their class position); and the reformulation of the family as an agent inculcating the new revolutionary values. However she points out that theories of sexual oppression are seen as 'too radical and too threatening to popular solidarity', and that 'women's emancipation' is subordinate to the goal of 'economic development'. Nicaragua's revolution may go the way of Cuba's, if economic development pressures cause a reassessment of the costs of welfare services.

In the USSR, women in the feminist movement suffer KGB harassment, while male alcoholism is widespread and causes considerable domestic violence (Mamonova, 1984: 654). Officially women's organizations do not exist because, officially, sexual inequalities no longer exist. Molyneux, who offers this information, also suggests, perhaps unconvincingly, that the ideology of sexual equality in socialist societies 'influences government policy and ... creates expectations which may induce pressure to see them fulfilled' (Molyneux, 1981: 173). A survey of the last decade's Eastern European documents on women written in English revealed that no Soviet author held out any hopes for the emergence of women's liberation in the USSR. One author explicitly urges western feminists to reject marxism and socialism as strategies for attaining sex equality in western capitalist societies; another believed there was more likelihood of radical departure in female roles and status in the United States (Heitlinger, 1985: 149).

Molyneux (1981: 174–89) lists some of the gains for women in socialist regimes, for example a reduced incidence of female circumcision, polygamy, and child marriages where these have been traditionally practised, less prostitution (with alternative employment provided), greater state acceptance of responsibility for social welfare and the reproduction of labour power, maternity allowances. However, she also notes the iconography of liberation struggles: 'A woman with a gun in one hand and a baby in the other' (Molyneux, 1981: 189). While women are no longer sex objects, but astronauts, professionals, heroines of the revolution, they remain mothers. Men are not represented as working fathers. Symptomatic of this situation is an extract from 'every official handbook from Vietnam to Cuba' (reproduced in Molyneux, 1981: 177):

> Marxists have asserted that the causes of the unequal position of women do not lie in their oppression by men ... rather, their status is inextricably linked to the existence of class society based on the exploitation of man by man [sic] ... the only way to achieve the emancipation of women ... is by pursuing ... the road to revolutionary struggle.

Unsurprisingly then, revolutions founded upon the marxist principles of liberation through labour have enticed women into the workforce but left the remaining social structures largely intact. Körösi (1984) denies the existence of 'women's emancipation through integration into the workforce'. Socialist men have apparently responded with no less hostility than other men to women's attempts at self-education or self-assertion. As a result, socialist regimes either have unenforced legal commitments to women's equality (for example Cuba), or have reasserted the role of women in relation to the family, as in Vietnam (Thidinh, 1984: 429) or Nicaragua (Molyneux, 1985: 249). Although some changes have occurred in the areas of welfare and attitudes to traditional practices such as circumcision, socialist countries appear to be even more hostile to female homosexuality than capitalist regimes.

Jayawardena (1986) traces the mixed attitudes of reformist and women's movements to local cultural practices. Often the colonial governments, backed by Christian missionary advocacy, sought to abolish these practices, for example suttee or polygamy. Sometimes such attempts won the approval of local reform movements, who accepted the ideology of the (western) nuclear family. Often however, local groups reacted with hostility to this imposition of western values. Some women's groups further noted the repression of the vestiges of ancient 'matriarchal' practices, for example in Sri Lanka (Jayawardena, 1986: 115–16). Alternatively local customs sometimes gave women certain resources, for example the political role that harems played in advocating women's rights in Iran (Jayawardena, 1986: 64). In other words, it was not the liberation of women that colonial governments advocated but the remaking of sexual arrangements in a western image.

Female Circumcision and the Veil

Contemporary liberation struggles also affect the incidence and meaning of cultural practices, for example the veil. Accusations of ethnocentrism have been levelled at western women, just as they were at colonial governments, because of their preoccupation with many so-called 'barbaric' traditional cultural practices. Perhaps over no other issue are these debates more acrimonious than over the Muslim practices of female circumcision and the veil. These practices and the debates that surround them reveal the difficulties both for western feminists and for women in Muslim countries in speaking to each other.

There are three types of female circumcision, ranging from the sunna method of partial clitoridectomy, to the excision of the clitoris and labia minora, to excision of clitoris, labia minora and parts of the labia majora. This last type includes infibulation, or the fastening or sewing together of the two sides of the vulva to leave a small opening for urine and later menstrual blood. Some form of female circumcision is common in most of the northern half of Africa as well as some parts of Kenya and

Tanzania, but excluding Morocco, Algeria and the Libyan Arab Republic (Abdalla, 1982: 13). Daly (1978: 155) says in a footnote, 'Lest Westerners feel smugly distant from these rituals, clitoridectomies were inflicted on women in the United States up to the 1930s, while slashing and mutilation of the genitals are common features of gang rapes.' Historically, the chastity belt (with no opening for excrement) or infibulation by means of a ring, buckle or padlock was practised in medieval Christian Europe. So, in terms of barbaric practices, presumably even by western standards, western women are not and have not been immune.

In a survey of attitudes to the practice, Asma El Dareer (1982: 56–7, 84) found that women who had lost their virginity and who were widowed or divorced, for example, often requested recircumcision. Only 17 per cent of women and 12 per cent of men in her sample disapproved of the practice. Both men and women who approved claimed it stopped offensive discharge and beautified women. Maria Cutrufelli (1983: 137) argues that intercourse is often very painful as a consequence of clitoridectomy, quoting one woman who said 'To me, it doesn't make much difference if my husband hits me in the face or has sex with me.' As a result of the practice newly married men often cannot enter their brides without cutting them open, while babies die in childbirth. El Dareer (1982: 23–5) describes a ceremony for female circumcision where the young girl is dressed as a bride, but others suggest the practice is often without ritual in comparison with the boy's initiation rites (Cutrufelli, 1983: 155–6).

Feminists from these African countries do not support female circumcision. What they object to is western feminists' interference which provokes one of three reactions: claims to the right of cultural difference, claims that it is premature to open the matter to public debate, claims that western fanaticism draws attention away from fundamental problems of economic exploitation which 'contribute to the continuation of the practice' (Association of African Women for Research and Development, 1983: 218). Quite how economic exploitation and circumcision are linked is not made clear. The Yemeni Women's Union feel that 'objective processes will destroy the veil' as women enter schools, factories and so on (Moshen and Ba'abad, 1983: 140). Perhaps it is felt that similar 'objective processes' will also cause the practice of female circumcision to wither away. Furthermore, such a claim by an African woman seems to reaffirm western women's argument that circumcision is the practice of a 'backward' society.

Many male third world liberationists endorse circumcision and other practices as 'authentic customs' (Kenyatta quoted in Cutrufelli, 1983:

138). It is easier to eliminate colonial influences than old traditions of lobolo (dowry), initiation rites and polygamy (Rodriguez, 1983: 131). Frantz Fanon, a well-known protagonist of third world liberation, argued that unveiling women led to 'destructuring Algerian culture' (cited in Barry, 1979: 198). A Ngou male sociologist from Cameroon argues that, as opposed to the west, African women have never been oppressed (Cutrufelli, 1983: 12). Samora Machel, later President of the People's Republic of Mozambique, decried 'mechanically dividing the household duties' as a form of emancipation. In the west an 'emancipated woman is one who drinks, smokes, wears trousers and mini skirts, who indulges in sexual promiscuity, who refuses to have children' (quoted in Kimble and Unterhalter, 1982: 13). Not only does this misrepresent the depth of western feminist struggles, but it also asks Mozambique women not only to be different from western feminists but also their menfolk – at least in the case of smoking, trousers, sexual promiscuity and having children. The statement by implication affirms a traditional, certainly a non-westernized, image of women.

The practice of veiling, which often means wearing a hot and clumsy covering garment, a *burqua* as it is called in India, limits a woman's freedom of movement and visibility (Jeffery, 1979: 123–52). Mai Ghoussoub (1986: 5) warns against imposing western constructions of the inferiority of women on Islamic practices. She suggests that Islam does not advance the proposition of women's inherent inferiority. It is rather because of her potential equality that she must be 'clamped down on ... [in] ... a fearful seclusion', in the practice of veiling and segregated spaces for women. Al-Hibri (1981: 184) also notes that Islam treated women as 'dangerous beings' and it is because of this they must be restrained. She suggests that not until she came to the United States did she experience her capabilities being questioned *because* she was a woman (Al-Hibri, 1981: 185).

Leila Ahmed (1982: 523) condemns the ignorance that passes for knowledge among Americans that the 'harem, the veil, polygamy', are synonymous with barbaric oppression. In relation to the harem, she says that it produces a women's space to which men are denied access (while women veiled and as servants of men can enter the male domain) and in which women assert and teach their female children disrespect for 'male pomposity and power' (Ahmed, 1982: 531). She admits that women *are* confined and constrained in the harem – but it *is* a source of strong female support. It is western women's model of heterosexual coupling and access to male worlds of power that refuses to see these advantages. Indeed some western feminists, for example Leghorn and Parker (1981) do now argue for the advantages of women's networks.

Ahmed (1982: 525) identifies, in passing, the long tradition of western women's feelings of superiority. Lady Mary Nortley Montagu in 1716 noted with surprise that Muslim women controlled their own property and were 'wonderfully liberated' (Ahmed's term). On the other hand (and in counterpoint to contemporary western women's criticism of the veil), a Muslim woman exclaimed at the Lady's stays: 'Come hither and see how cruelly the poor English ladies are used by their husbands. You need boast indeed of the superior liberties allowed you, when they lock you thus up in a box' (quoting Montagu).

On a different note, Gurji (quoted in London Iranian Women's Liberation Group, 1983: 151) argues that the veil is the female aspect of appropriate dress, a standard which applies also to men. The veil is a sign of self-respect, and a request not to be treated as a sex object. Nevertheless the veiled women of Delhi were often taunted in the streets; they could be identified despite the claims of anonymity, while they could not always see their taunters (Jeffery, 1979: 154). Ahmed (1982: 523), however, argues that the veil is not experienced as an oppressive custom by those who habitually wear it. When 15,000 unveiled women in Iran protested Khomeini's reintroduction of the veil on International Women's Day, they were assaulted with 'You want to be prostitutes? ... come on, I'll fuck you!' (London Iranian Women's Liberation Group, 1983: 153). When it is remembered that prostitutes are executed under Khomeini's regime, this was both a sexual and a death threat.

Thus the cultural meaning of the veil is of a chaste woman, a woman who is not a prostitute. To be chaste however, a woman has to be blinkered and hobbled. Despite the claims of anonymity, the veil is not indifferent between the sexes. In India at least, men *can* see in, while the veiled woman cannot as easily see out; neither does the veil deliver the promise of respect for its wearers. These are some of the meanings of the veil at the level of sexual politics. The sexual meanings and practical effects of female dress customs are not unconnected. As with the veil, most modes of female dress seek to restrict a woman's mobility.

The veil also underwent changes in political meaning with the emergence of liberation struggles. When the French sought to 'liberate' Algerian women from the veil, perhaps because they used it to carry hidden bombs and so on in their resistance struggles (French, 1985: 226), wearing the veil became a symbol of nationalism. This meaning was also established during the Shah of Iran's reign; the Shah attempted 'cultural change' and 'modernization' without redressing the 'foreign exploitation of resources' (El Saadawi, 1980: i). Women who identified with western feminism by going unveiled were seen as helpmates of the

Shah's oppression; particularly his oppression of the struggle against American intervention (El Saadawi, 1980: v). However, the common media image of the Iranian revolution, a veiled woman carrying a gun, was to have all its contradictions realized.

Khomeini's Iran is, in some respects at least, a worse place for women by western feminists' criteria than the Shah's was. Apart from compulsory veiling and execution of prostitutes, Khomeini has allowed fathers to marry off their daughters at birth (the age was 16 under the Shah), while if a man kills a woman he can only be executed if her guardians can afford the blood money for his life. There is no blood money on women's lives (Afshar, 1982: 83 and 87). But according to Haleh Afshar (1982: 86), women have more rights under Qur'anic (Koranic) law than they are actually granted by most Muslim governments, including Iran.

The evidence shows that to discard the veil today in Iran, besides being mortally dangerous, now has the meaning of resistance to Khomeini's oppression of women. Western feminists and their Iranian supporters, in this at least, have been vindicated. The political function of the veil has apparently come full circle. The veil was at first the sign of resistance to French rule. It then became, in its absence, the sign of westernizing under the Shah, while wearing the veil represented resistance to the Shah. Today the absence of the veil represents resistance to Khomeini's fundamentalism. However, it has been argued (Tabari, 1980) that some middle-class (westerners would perhaps say more emancipated) women remained opposed to the wearing of the veil throughout these political vicissitudes. None the less, in the resistance to the Shah, they donned veils to express solidarity with other women who habitually wore veils. The veil wearers brought spare scarves and veils to meetings for this purpose. For some women, then, wearing the veil was an expression of solidarity concerning a more urgent priority. If they had any doubts about women's future under Khomeini, they repressed them at this time.

The story of the veil is the story of the conflict between national (perhaps read 'nativist' or 'fundamentalist' in Said's 1985: 95 sense) and feminist struggles. Their goals are not the same, and there is no reason why they should be. For women living in third world countries, trained in anti-imperialist rhetoric, surrounded by men as well as women in poverty, the choice between the two may be so agonizing, or so obvious, that they argue that the one (feminism) can be achieved with the other (socialism or national liberation). Such arguments are central to the antagonisms that erupted in the three conferences held during the United Nations Decade for Women.

Feminist and Other Strategies

Basically third world women fall into three camps on the relationship between feminist and other political struggles. First, there are the feminists who separate the particular issues of women's oppression from other political and economic issues (for example, writers for *Manushi* in India). Secondly, there are the women who seek to combine the struggle for women's liberation with the struggle for national liberation (for example, the Association of El Salvadorean Women, 1983: 94). Finally there are the women who argue that 'feminism is a luxury', a western plot of no relevance, and indeed threatening to third world political struggles. Thus June Nash and Helen Safa (1980: x–xi) identify the 'problems of uneven development and the global political issues resulting from this' as more significant than western 'women's issues exclusively defined'. It is not men who keep women at home, they argue, but the structure of the capitalist system.

In that the first and third positions clearly separate the concerns of either national liberation or sexual liberation, a definite political choice can be made. The second position, however, in like manner to the protagonists of capitalist patriarchy, attempts to combine the two programmes. It is an analysis of this position that throws light on the reasons for the other two choices, as well as the possibility for double-edged political action.

This second position has many parallels with the position of women of colour *vis-à-vis* their menfolk and white women discussed in Chapter 3. First it is argued that the effects of imperialism oppress men in third world countries, as well as women. Then it is argued that because of this women must seek to educate or transform their menfolk but not oppose them in outright feminist struggle. Finally, this means that these women often find themselves in hostile relations with western feminists who attack patriarchal practices regardless of race or creed, but who are seen to represent the imperialist exploiter of both third world women and their comrades in armed or political struggle.

Thus the Association of El Salvadorean Women (1983: 94) argues that issues like forced sterilization, free childcare and safe family planning must be fought for, but not by women losing sight of their common struggle with men for the basic necessities of life and a changed power structure (Galdamez, 1983: 224). Obbo (1980: 157) argues that African women on the whole do not wish to antagonize men, a point that Cutrufelli (1983: 172) repeats in relation to African women's organizations, as do Aisha Moshen and Noor Ba'abad (1983: 134) for South Yemen and an Angolan women's organization (Cutrufelli, 1983: 7).

On the other hand Judy Kimble (1981: 109) suggests that women in the Guinean liberation movement could see the 'two colonialisms' – of Portuguese and husbands – and resolved the prospects for a disunited struggle by seeing that the 'enemy was not the Portuguese people, any more than it is the men: rather it is the system of oppression which must be fought and transformed in both cases'.

Bolivia's Domitilia Barrios de la Chungara (1983: 56) says 'We, compañeras, are man's other half. If this half does nothing it would mean there's no fight, because man has so many problems.' They stress that women must not separate from their husbands but make them understand. In South America the machismo-mariamismo dichotomy constructs women as conformist, unimaginative, timid and incapable of education and decision-making and bonds men throughout life to their mothers rather than their wives (Smock, 1977: 391). South Americans have differing responses to this. Jorge Bustos (1980: 37) says machismo is related to men's insecurity and fear, while Miriam Galdamez (1983: 92) from El Salvador says 'machismo is a real problem, but nothing's ever going to change until we have the basic necessities of life ... we must join with our men who suffer too ... as well as fight for our specific rights.'

Generally where women's issues are recognized, they are seen as lesser, as projects within the wider struggle. Thus women in the ex-colonial world believe that 'western women represent a privileged middle-class elite fighting for sectarian aims, while women in national liberation struggles are fighting on behalf of their *whole* people' (Kimble and Ulterhalter, 1982: 13 – emphasis added). Nazzari (1983: 247) suggests that 'the changing position of women will be analysed in the context of the *larger* struggle surrounding the economic strategies adopted during Cuba's transition from capitalism to socialism' (emphasis added). This perspective reveals the marxist base of most of these analyses – in the end it is economic struggle that is paramount, and the feminist struggle must be subordinate to it, contained within it. A hierarchies-of-oppression argument is also clear from these statements – the *whole* people's liberation, the *larger* struggle as opposed to the sectarian smaller struggle of feminists/women. By substituting different, separate, distinct for these notions of hierarchies and connectedness, perhaps the whole analysis would shift ground. But those who argue that the position of third world women depends on their race *and* their class *and* their gender would argue that such different ground would misunderstand the position of third world women.

Others argue that there is little difference between the incidence of 'malnutrition, disease, unemployment' between men and women (Borja,

1984: 191). As the World Report on Women (Davis et al., 1985) indicates, this is simply not true, although there may be greater differences between western women and third world women than between third world women and men. And indeed it may be this – the benefits of imperialism and transnational capitalism – that divide western and non-western women.

Third world women argue, as do the women of colour, that western feminists are also eurocentric within their own movement. While western feminists may not be responsible for all the problems of imperialism and colonialism, they *are* accused of endorsing a 'supremicist colonial pattern', of refusing to listen to women from the third world and trying to command the conversation (Mernissi, 1984: 449). An exchange between the Persian Women's Society and the British suffragists in 1911 reveals both the attempted communication across national boundaries and the unwitting ethnocentric response of the British women:

> *Persian Women's Society*: The ears of the men of Europe are deaf to our cries; could you women not come to our help?
> *The British suffragists*: Unhappily, we cannot make the British government give political freedom *even* to us, their country women. (quoted in Jayawardena, 1986: 65, emphasis added)

Additionally, western feminists are accused of imposing their trajectory of freedom on third world women, of recommending birth control, education, political participation in national forums for third world women.

Fatima Mernissi (1984: 450) argues that western women should try to grasp and to decode women's rebellion whether voiced in an oral culture, or practices considered 'marginal, criminal or erratic'. Sisterhood, she suggests, will exist when we cut through class and culture, focusing on what we share, rather than jockeying for position as the most liberated. Mernissi attacks western women's ethnocentrism, which assumes that women's traditional practices are necessarily conservative. This is not always the case: women in Ethiopia and the Caribbean use church membership to sustain their women's networks (Leghorn and Parker, 1981: 261). Devaki Jain (1984: 309) reports Indian women's turning of a traditional chant from ceremonial to political purposes. The prayers are normally chanted on the sacred day by women rubbing the elephants' legs, at which the elephants kneel down. On this day of political action, when the elephants were brought in to trample the squatters' huts, the elephants responded with 'customary grace' and the demolition was halted.

In Papua New Guinea, Diane Johnson argues that the articulate highly talented women in the bureaucracy stress the significance of retaining traditional customs, which include wife-beating or wife-sale in some areas (Johnson, 1979: 19) and kin resistance to family planning (McRae, 1980: 15). Furthermore, these women argue, to be concerned with women's rights is to be seen as divisive, and opposed to development. Instead, violence towards women is attributed to colonial influences (Johnson, 1984: 35–6). However, not all Papua New Guinean women have accepted the mores of custom. Barbara Sullivan's (1985) analysis of articles in the *Papua New Guinea Post Courier* from July to December 1984 revealed that many women, aware of the problems of sexual violence, marched in Lae and Port Moresby calling for tougher penalties for rapists, rape crisis centres, and the banning of pornographic videos. (These demands have a western flavour to them.) The government's response was to meet the first and third demands but ignore the second, the one that would increase women's autonomy and link rape victims through a women's network.

These two contrasting analyses of Papua New Guinea suggest alternative explanations. Women in any third world country, as is the case in western nations, may not all share the one set of political strategies; observers may see different aspects of a culture or interpret those aspects differently; women's political struggles may change their nature over time.

Conflict at the Decade for Women Conferences

A political rapprochement or at least a greater dialogue between women of the third world and the west may have been made possible by the forums of the International Decade for Women. The actual outcome of this project reveals the great difficulties faced by a global feminist project.

From 1935 to 1937 women's organizations made representations to the predecessor of the United Nations, the League of Nations, for an international body to examine the problems of improving the status of women and eliminating discrimination against them. The League of Nations Status of Women Committee was established, four of its seven members being leading women lawyers, jurists or members of parliament. Its work was discontinued with the dissolution of the League of Nations in 1946. Despite these early moves for international anti-discrimination legislation, Boserup (1970: 194–5) reports that throughout the 1960s the United Nations Conferences, notwithstanding the occasional protesting voice, opposed the expansion of employment opportunities for women, arguing that third world men would lose jobs as a result. The United Nations Decade for Women (1975–85) then, promised a break from its own past for the United Nations, as well as an international forum for all women to discuss the prospects for international feminism.

The Decade for Women was subtitled Equality, Development and Peace. Some argued that these goals could be achieved through national liberation struggles, opposition to apartheid, racism, zionism and colonialism. Others argued that the New International Economic Order, an attempt by 'non-aligned developing countries' to identify and redress the systematic exploitation of the South by the North, would be achieved through non-aggressive nationalism, sovereign control of natural resources, income-sharing between nations, control of transnational corporations. Others argued that at the very least these issues should be related to the specific position of women, and that more importantly sexism should be added to 'apartheid, racism, zionism and colonialism' in the list of 'isms' that oppress women. Additionally, as the decade proceeded, the effects of worldwide economic exploitation specifically on women were investigated, so that it was argued that women were the 'shock absorbers' for IMF and World Bank austerity measures, providing by their own labour services no longer provided by their governments, or earning money to pay for services such as health and education which were formerly free (Jennett, 1987: 349).

On the whole it was women from western nations who advocated specific attention to women's issues, and it was women, or at least as often the men leading these delegations, from the third world who focused on the international economic and political issues. However, through the three conferences, Mexico (1975), Copenhagen (1980), Nairobi (1985), issues of specific concern to women (for example, international prostitution, contraceptive freedom) gained more prominence.

Laurie Bebbington (1975: 375) suggested that the woman and child logo of the Mexico Conference was reflected in the World Plan of Action, a 'paternalistic and jargonist document which foists a compulsory parenthood on all women'. Perhaps this interpretation is suggested by an ungenerous reading of the following, resolution 142:

While States have a sovereign right to determine their own population policies, individuals and couples should have access, through an institutionalized system, to the information and means that will enable them to determine freely and responsibly the number and spacing of their children and to overcome sterility. (Resolution 142 passed by 1975 Conference: in Sipila, 1975: 86)

(A similar resolution was passed at the Nairobi Conference – although 'couples and individuals' now had the right to 'decide freely and informedly' – quoted in Jennett, 1987: 353.)

The resolution does not focus explicitly on the rights of women, and it asserts national sovereignty, potentially in opposition to women's rights. The resolution apparently endorses the right to be 'child-free', though only if the 'number' of children can mean no children, but lays more stress on the right to have a family. The resolution attempts to negotiate both the needs of nations (the needs of men *and* women) *and* the rights of women; to be responsive to the inequality of the world economic system *and* recognize women's particularly economically and politically exploited position. It remains silent on sexual and social exploitation of women within this system.

Such an ambivalence characterizes the tenor of many of the resolutions. The World Plan of Action covered the issues of international co-operation and peace, political participation of women, education and training of women, employment and related economic roles, health and nutrition, housing, services for migrants, the elderly and criminal women (Sipila, 1975: 70 89). An indication that sexuality issues were not seen as paramount came with the booing and hissing of lesbian women. While women from the west stressed personal relations of self-confidence and power, that is individual freedoms, women from poor countries put more stress on survival of the whole family unit (Papanek, 1975: 221). Bourne (1983: 21) suggests that the 'idea of individualism is alien to third world countries, where familial, caste, tribal or national interests are often dominant'.

The Mexico Conference battled over issues such as contraceptive choice, and fears that women and men would become divided as a result of western feminists' programmes (Sipila, 1975: 14–15). Thus Egypt objected to the reference in the plan to 'consensual unions' because 'it negated the traditions ... of the country' and India objected to co-educational primary schooling because of India's cultural conditions (Sipila, 1975: 31). Betty Friedan was accused by South American feminists of manipulating the Tribune, while Yasser Arafat claimed that for Palestinian women liberation of their homeland was the key issue (*Sydney Morning Herald*, 30 June 1975: 14). Western feminists, it was argued:

> were not aware of the class struggle, of economic problems, of social problems, of the real suffering of the majority of men and women struggling for their livelihood every day. They concentrated solely on

issues of sexuality and male domination. And that was the major difference between us and them. Our position is that we must not merely fight against patriarchy but against the patriarchal *class* system. (Nawal El Sadaawi, quoted in Jennett, 1987: 349)

At the Copenhagan Conference Nawal El Sadaawi asked how women in Beirut, subjected to daily bombardment by Israeli planes, could be expected to worry about their orgasms (Bourne, 1983: 20).

A woman from the United States asked of the Latin American women: 'Have I been put down by the men of my country for 52 years only to be put down again here by all of you?' (Papanek, 1975: 217). A Japanese woman delegate, in a kind of reply, argued that western women should oppose their governments' imperialist policies (Papanek, 1975: 217).

Thus the two points of division at Mexico City echo the previous analysis of third world women's responses to western feminism. For many delegates liberation struggles were the more significant battle while attempts to place sexuality issues, for instance governing marriage customs, on the agenda were seen as attacks on the traditions and customs of third world nations.

According to Pat Eatock (an Australian Aboriginal feminist who attended the Conference at Mexico City), the dispute between feminists from the United States and the third world was not so much a result of imperialist-based divisions of resources as the supremicist attitudes these engendered in the United States feminists:

the great news from Mexico in 1975, was that Australian feminist theory was leading the world. Liz Reid, Laurie Bebbington (the radical lesbian activist from the Australian Union of Students), Pat Giles (trade unionist and now ALP senator from Western Australia) and other Australian women caught and held the centre stage of world interest as their theory of feminism related to practice in their fields. At the same conference, American feminists were booed from the stage when, with chauvinistic arrogance, they attempted to align the might of the international conference on one side or the other of their internal schisms and disputes. (Eatock, 1987: 27)

Most of the issues were hotly debated again at Copenhagen. Some delegates argued that the battle for the New International Economic Order (NIEO) was an essential precondition for raising the economic status of third world women. Others used the forum to attack 'imperialist aggressors', particularly the United States. Delegates from the United States were enraged at the equating of zionism with racism and colonialism, arguing that 'in the din of political polemics ... women's true interest in political affairs had been ignored' (United Nations, 1980: 196-7). (Canada and Australia had also rejected the condemnation of zionism.)

Tinker (1981: 534) attempts to draw a sharp distinction between 'issues relating to women' – fertility control, shortage of firewood, the 'double day' – and the impact of the spread of multinationals as realized in debates around the NIEO. She argues that these other issues turned 'a unity trip into an international debating society'. But how separate are these issues in reality? Tinker herself admits that women's issues can be readily represented within the framework of the NIEO debate, but some western feminists resisted this. If so, doesn't that mean that women's issues can also divide women as the NIEO divides men, that one woman's economic loss may be another woman's economic gain? On the whole, western women called for unity (Tinker, 1981: McIntosh, 1981: Izraeli, 1981). Third world women wondered whether this was at the cost of their own special needs (Wong, 1981: 776), or involved ignoring the role of western women's oppressive governments (Cagalay and Funk, 1981: 778) or was an expression of cultural superiority by western women (Ahmed, 1981: 480). However, Charlotte Bunch (1981), a western feminist, argues that the NIEO *is* significant for third world women. Western women must take their own political and economic implication in the global economy seriously, while also working to enlarge the definition of politics and economics so women are not duped by 'patriarchal governments'.

Besides a reaffirmation of economic, educational and other developmental goals, the Copenhagen Conference's Plan of Action, adopted only after acrimonious debate, also contained a number of sections on 'women-specific' issues. One such issue was battered women and violence in the family, which was condemned, not so much because of the harmful effects on women, but because it was 'a grave problem for the physical and mental health of the family as well as for society' (United Nations, 1980: 67). Another section deplored the traffic in women and children, the Conference calling on governments around the world to take appropriate legal action against procurers and traffickers.

By Nairobi, according to Pat Giles (1985: 112) and Christine Jennett (1987: 348, 353) the position of women *qua* women rather than as participants in international political struggles was more prominent. The Conference recognized systematic violence against women; African women recognized the barbarity of female circumcision; while Sally Mugabe, who headed the Zimbabwean delegation, argued that women must control their own fertility, as this formed the basis of their enjoyment of other rights. African women attacked 'religious, cultural and political fundamentalism' as 'authoritarian' and 'militaristic', because it questions the rights women have acquired during this decade, while 'scapegoating' women (quoted in Jennett, 1987: 384–5). Nevertheless, political antagonisms still erupted, for example, between the Palestinian and Jewish delegates, or the United States and some third world delegates. The following three extracts, reflections by a white Australian delegate, offer some reasons why:

> but sadly the Palestinian women, who seemed to have male 'minders', were not in a listening/exchanging frame of mind. (Ryan, 1985: 119) (The Palestinian women are here being defined in a patronising way, restricted by their male 'minders'.)

> Cathy, an Aboriginal speaks about 40,000 years of culture smashed by 200 years of white occupation. She demands land rights saying the land already held is inadequate. (Ryan, 1985: 120) (The interests of Aboriginal and white women are divided and perhaps unalterably opposed by 200 years of white domination.)

> on returning to Nairobi I spent twenty-four hours in an old colonial house with my two Sydney friends ... we had the run of the place, with four servants. (Ryan, 1985: 121) (Ryan happily accepts and enjoys her 'run of' the colonial house and its servants.)

In an international evaluation of the United Nations Decade for Women, women in the third world reported patchy results. Most countries had been forced into appointing women's bureaux or encouraging some development programmes for women (usually small-scale self-employment rural based activities) (Velasco, 1985; Goonatilake, 1985). In most countries some women had become active in promoting women's issues. For black women in the United States and for women in India, although the lives of very few poor and rural women have changed, media coverage and sympathy for women's issues appear to have expanded (Lewis, 1985; Butalia, 1985).

The major gains have perhaps been the growth in awareness, first by women in different countries of each other, and secondly by men of women's issues. As a result there has been a flood of small-scale development projects for women. No doubt, these development projects will quickly cease without continued action by women around the world.

The United Nations Decade for Women was not a women-only affair. Men were present and argued strenuously for the same political programmes they argue for in the United Nations (men's) assembly. Western women particularly resisted this mode of politicization of the debates, that is, the displacement from women's issues to those of third world development, zionism and so on. Third world women argued that this resistance merely revealed the implication of western women in their own countries' international politics.

Western women may refuse to support national liberation struggles for eurocentric reasons and still claim to be feminists. It may be legitimate for feminists to argue that specific forms of domination – men over women – can be isolated from the impact of colonialism or imperialism as the focus of their political movement. The questions third world women ask of this position are several. Can sexual domination be separated from domination based on race or imperialism, for instance the American soldiers who raped Vietnamese women or the American and Australian citizens who go to Bangkok for a 'sex holiday'? Should women's specific oppression be put ahead of struggles that will unite women in the third world with their husbands, fathers, male comrades in arms? As no country appears to be free of patriarchal practices, third world women in political struggle do have to make choices, even if temporary and reversible, between alliances for national political and economic liberation or struggles specifically for women.

Ultimately, then, there will be debates about whether the position of, say, South African, Aboriginal, Asian and other 'doubly exploited' women can be better improved by the abolition of apartheid or sexism. It may well be the case that apartheid has the greatest impact on women's economic, social and political status. But what the feminists say, and so far no history contradicts them, is that only a feminist struggle will significantly change relations between men and women that concern issues such as sexuality, violence, control of women's bodies by women, the cultural politics of dress, other representations of gender and so on. What then are the prospects for a global feminist struggle over these issues?

5

Women in One World

> Freedom from hunger, from dictatorship, from foreign domination – struggles which by necessity challenge fundamental power structures and benefit whole classes or nations – define *their* priorities. But they in turn should tell us about our own and shape our feminism – and point us, once again, towards the holism of which we are legatees and to which we aspire. (Bourne, 1983: 21)

Some common themes run through the critiques of western feminism, arguments concerning the eurocentric experiences that have created feminist theory, the consequent unidimensionality of the categories that white feminist theory works with, the partiality of the political programmes that have been fought for. Beyond this, beyond the need to correct feminist theory so it hears and responds to the voices of women of colour and third world women and thus comes to speak of all women, there is another more fundamental argument. Some women of colour and the third world argue that not only must white feminists take account of the experiences of all women, but they must make 'black women *central* to their political analyses' (Bhavnani and Coulson, 1986: 83). 'Few white feminists in Britain and elsewhere have elevated the question of racism to the level of primacy' (Amos and Parmar, 1984: 5). At this point, some white feminists and women of colour will part company. For many feminists the project of feminism, both politically and theoretically, is to make women and gender oppression central. The patriarchy debate revealed the difficulties of integrating class and gender oppression under the categories of marxist analysis. Should feminists seek now to integrate race and gender within the rubric of analyses of imperialism and racism? Some black women claim they should, and offer interesting arguments as to why. Some white feminists would claim that such a project is not only theoretically impossible, it will shift the object of analysis so that we are no longer engaged in a feminist project.

Women of colour argue for this shift in emphasis because they feel that racial oppression is the primary experience in their lives. This is the most keenly felt basis of differential treatment, therefore this must be the major locus of political battle. Debates over strategies will also be reviewed in this chapter. A coward's solution, perhaps, is to argue for a 'rainbow politics' for different groups of women to choose their own battles, intersecting and drawing strength from each other as appropriate – Bernice Reagon's 'coalition politics'. An impediment to this strategy, so it is argued, is that women's issues and women's subordination (unless one is a white middle-class woman) cannot be separated from race and class oppression. To argue for the autonomy of feminist movements is to argue for continuing oppression of some women (black, working-class, third world) for the benefit of others (privileged, western, white, middle-class).

Experience and Feminist Theory

Feminism in the academy has been uneasy about the role of experience in the development of feminist theory. Male-dominated science condemns categories such as 'experience' as prejudice, empiricism, the particular, and contrasts them unfavourably with the pure abstract categories of theory. Feminists have replied in a variety of ways. Those who engaged in the patriarchy debate sought to clothe the discoveries of women in theoretical garb and thereby admit them to the halls of structural analysis. Those who claimed that western feminism had learned its lessons from the experiences of women, for example, Catherine MacKinnon (1982), argued that all theory is based on experience. Male-dominated theories in the academy, described as knowledge, confined themselves to male experience for their raw data. Western knowledge pretends to uncouple the culture–nature, reason–passions, objectivity–subjectivity, mind–body dichotomy (Harding, 1986: 661) and claim for itself the superior categories, the pure categories of reason and objectivity. Some feminists have laid claim to, and celebrated, the other side of the couplet. We are embodied creatures; we have passions and lived experience; we have seen the male academy's refusal of these, and the intellectual oppression and aridity to which it leads – 'his life and body are always the same ... He knows nothing' (an Abyssinian women quoted in Al-Hibri, 1981: 171).

Many black feminists however, while arguing for the need to take account of the experiences of the majority of women on the globe, resist the move towards a celebration of women's otherness. Trinh Minh-ha (1987: 18) argues that the difference that is constructed for women is a difference of biology. To celebrate our difference will give back to the enemy its weapon; will imprison women in their bodies. This has resonances with the 'difference' of racist ideologies – the biological differences of the inferior race that has been used to justify oppression by whites for so long (Anthias and Yuval-Davis, 1983: 67). But the difference of women's bodies also suggests a 'sisterhood' based on common oppression, and many women of colour deny that women's oppression is common. Both black and white feminists, then, walk the uneasy line between knowing that their experiences are different and that these experiences have been excluded from theoretical analyses, while also realizing that those experiences result in some way from the identification of women with their bodies, as contaminated by their nature. Black women writers often seek to escape the tension between their different experiences and shared biology with arguments about structures of oppression, the role of transnational capitalism and the nationalist–racist state; such constructions seek to displace the biologism of racism and sexism.

Sandra Harding (1986: 647) warns that western feminists must not replicate the 'patriarchal association between knowledge and power' 'to the detriment of women whose experiences have not yet been fully voiced'. The warning is apt, and the writings of women of colour and third world women, if listened to by western feminism, can only enrich feminism's understandings of the position of women. That these voices have not been listened to before is no doubt true, and it has only been because third world and black women have come to speak on our stage – at conferences, at meetings, in universities, journals, books – that we have paid attention to their voices. This reflects our eurocentrism and our race privilege, but it also reveals that someone had to do the translation. Women in the third world and black women in the west have been the *objects* of study for a long time. Their position has also been of concern to feminists as far back as Olive Schreiner and the American suffragists. Women of colour argue that these studies and references have been ethnocentric, or undertaken only for the purpose of explaining and exploring white society: white feminism 'does not speak to the experiences of black women and where it attempts to do so it is often from a racist perspective or reasoning' (Amos and Parmar, 1984: 4). Many western feminists baulk at translating feminism for men, seeing it as another ploy by the oppressor to divert their energies. Women of colour also ask how often and to what effect they will be asked to speak. The embeddedness of theory in experience, however, means that translation is necessary if women of colour are to be heard by those with different experiences.

Furthermore, women of colour complain that western feminists appropriate the experiences of black and third world women for their own ends. Their project, to save feminism by enriching it with the experiences of a wider diversity of women, is not a project shared by all women. Thus to use those experiences for 'other ends', not to argue for the centrality of racism but to expand the categories of feminist analysis, would be seen as an appropriation by those who believe feminism is, and must remain, politically bankrupt. Examination of the experiences of black and third world women can expand feminist theory's understanding of the role of the family in the oppression of women, of the state's differential treatment of white women and women of colour, strategies for equality in a man's world and the role of 'women's worlds'. However, because we assess the different against the familiar, it may seem that these analyses, outlined below, only use the experiences of women of colour to increase understanding of white women's experiences. I, too, may be accused of appropriating non-western women's experiences for my own ends.

The Family as the Site of Oppression

Second wave white feminists responded to the 'cult of domesticity', which Sylvia Hewlett (1987: Part Three) argues rose to its fiercest pitch in the 1950s, with interpretations of the family as the central institution oppressing women. The 'problem with no name' was experienced by women isolated in the suburbs. The family cordonned off from external interference, because it was 'private', was the site of incest, violence, the appropriation of women's love and labour. These analyses found voice in the patriarchy debate where the site of patriarchal oppression was the institution of the family, just as the factory was the site of class oppression. Michèle Barrett and Mary McIntosh (1982) captured feminist concerns with their title *The Anti-Social Family*. Not all feminists, including Barrett and McIntosh, described families as oppressive and violent through and through; some, like Sheila Rowbotham (1981), reminded feminists that men can be loving and supporting. None the less the 'family is the institution that has been consistently singled out as central for any understanding of patterns of sexual domination and subordination' (Caldwell, 1984: 88).

These astonishing discoveries – that the white middle-class nuclear family was not a 'haven in a heartless world' but one of the most violent institutions in society – were implicitly assumed to describe other family forms. Within the patriarchy debate, the concept of 'the family' or the 'family under capitalism', substituted for the variety of family forms and familial experiences. Alternatively feminists sought the same signs of oppression and subordination in non-white families: arranged marriages and the passivity of wives in Asian families; clitoridectomy and infibulation as preparation for marriage in South

African families; the sexism of the Afro-Caribbean male (Amos and Parmar, 1984: 9). White feminists saw other family forms, so black women claimed, as equivalent to their own much despised family form. Moreover, white feminists described some 'other' family forms as *more* oppressive than their own. The Asian wife did not even choose her oppressor; the African woman was subject to 'barbaric' practices to make her a satisfactory sexual commodity. Hence the charges by black feminists of eurocentrism. As Sylvia Walby (1986: 49) notes, the 'arrangement of marriages by parents may be no worse a method of selection of a women's husband than either rating and dating or romantic fantasy'. If patriarchal oppression of women occurs in families, does it really matter how women get there? Some white feminists responded, as Walby (1986: 49) does, with 'but it is not clear that it [arrangement of marriage] is better, or that it tackles the problems inherent in marriage for women.' The point white feminists make is that all family forms oppress women: and indeed all social forms – thus Mary Daly's (1978) linking of infibulation and psychoanalysis, footbinding and pack rape, as variations on the common theme of women's oppression.

Women of colour respond that such universalization of oppression misses the point of both the specific empirical forms of non-white families and their particular political place in black people's struggles. The family is not a universal form with unvarying effects. It requires the gaze of race-based analysis to see this. For example, a far greater percentage of black families than white families in the United States and Britain are and have been female-headed. This has led to the myth of the 'black matriarch', a myth which Angela Davis and Bell Hooks both affirm and deny. They affirm the resourcefulness, strength and struggles of black women – their 'womanism' as Alice Walker would describe it. But they point out that the black female household head is often poor, works in a demeaning job, and would happily enter the 'gilded cage' in which white bourgeois women have so much leisure and access to material resources. None the less, it could be argued that Hooks' (1986) insight that 'sisterhood' derives from the shared weakness of white women's oppression, hardly an appropriate basis for struggle, is an insight made possible through her knowledge of the strength of black women.

Secondly, where the state affirms and supports the white nuclear family, it often seeks to dismantle the black or Asian family. In South Africa apartheid's employment policies separate husbands and wives for weeks or years; in Britain harassment and humiliating medical examinations are the lot of Asian women seeking to immigrate to join their husbands; Asian wives are deported following separation from their husbands; black families are raided by the police; psychologists propound theories of the 'pathological' black family. Amos and Parmar (1984: 13–14) argue that only deployment of the category of imperialism explains the different responses of the state to white and black families. Eugenics encourages white women to stay at home and have children while it discourages women of colour from doing the very same thing. It is race then, and not gender, that is essential to understanding women's experiences in different family forms. Furthermore, because the state is seeking to destroy Asian and black families, these become a site of resistance and solidarity: 'The goal of the state is the control of the Asian community through repression and attack on one of its strongest institutions, the family, with its wide network of ties' (Trivedi, 1984: 47).

Women of colour who put race-based struggles first claim that white feminists should not only recognize the specificity of the Asian and black family, but they should also refrain from attacking it. By attacking such family forms as 'backward', their comments, whether wittingly or otherwise, strengthen the racist rhetoric of society at large and give support to the state's racist practices. It is not up to white feminists to discuss these families; that is for women of colour to do: 'on our own terms and in our own culturally specific ways' (Amos and Parmar, 1984: 15). On the other hand, Walby (1986: 49) argues that 'while a husband and wife may form a mutually supportive alliance against certain features of racism, it has not been shown that the partnership is one of equality.' Women of colour do not necessarily deny this, although they suggest that white feminists do not understand the internal dynamics of non-white families and so should remain silent.

Similar differences concerning the significance of the family emerged at the United Nations Decade for Women Conference. Laurie Bebbington deplored the mother and child logo at the Mexico Conference, while the resolutions passed affirmed the right of couples to make reproductive decisions and the needs of the family unit for survival. Western feminism appears to reflect western liberalism in its demands that individual freedom and equality be extended to women. Western feminists have perhaps failed to understand both the status of motherhood and the greater difficulties of childbearing in many non-western societies (Rowbotham, 1981: 75). The differential impact of eugenics and poverty on women's lives which limits the ability to have healthy children has blinded white women, who focus on the right *not to have* children, to the fact that many women do not have the right *to have* healthy children.

The debate between white western feminists and women of colour and the third world over birth control is a classic example of the charges of ethnocentrism made against western feminism. Speaking as a group of women that had long battled with states seeking the reproduction and expansion of the white race by 'fit' middle-class mothers, the freedom from birth seemed more elusive than the freedom to give birth. The experiences of black women in the west, and more recently third world women under pressure from the World Bank or the IMF, is just the reverse. Ironically, motherhood brings little status and few rewards to women in the west (Hewlett, 1987). For example, data on the United States reveal that the effects of being a female-headed household with children (average income = $11,689) is far more devastating than the effects of being a female-headed household (average income = $18,528). (The average income of male-headed households without children was $23,473 and of all households $24,656 in 1980 – Mann, 1986: 54.) In some of those countries where motherhood does enhance the status and material security of women, it is discouraged with programmes of the sort Picard (1986: 3) advocates; prevented with sterilizations without women's consent; attended by the hazards of Depo-Provera, malnutrition and inadequate health care. As Petchesky points out, abortions have become the privilege of white middle-class women; cheaper, more brutal methods are practised on other women. And, as Amos and Parmar (1984: 13–14) argue, only the goals of white imperialist expansion, not feminism *per se*, can explain this differential treatment of women.

However, and here the feminists may point to some commonalities in all women's experiences, while white supremicist states promote the birth of white children, other states are no less implicated in the 'demographic race'. The PLO urge their women to have children, to beat the Israelis 'in the bedrooms'. Newly liberated socialist states sometimes encourage women to leave the workforce and the liberation armies to expand the population. Black revolutionaries in the United States attack lesbianism because 'homosexuality does not birth new warriors for liberation' (Clarke, 1983: 198). The difference is only a matter of colour – the strategy of the state or the male-dominated movement is the same: to develop population policies irrespective of the desires of women to control their own reproductive capacities. Of course the *experiences* of women of different colours in these various states remains quite different.

The Racist State

The racist state, rather than the patriarchal state, is also seen as a prime mover in the oppression of black people as a whole – for example the discussions of the 'myth of the black rapist'. The stereotyping of the black woman as a sexed being and the white woman as a pure moral being placed the white woman above the black woman, beyond reach on her pedestal. However, both white women and black women are oppressed by these stereotypes. Is it preferable to be seen as strong, resourceful, as a sexually available person or 'submissive' (Sadoff, 1985: 10), 'juvenile' (davenport, 1983: 86), 'powerless' (Palmer, 1983: 159)? In being placed out of sight and beyond reach, the white woman was denied agency just as much as the black woman; more so perhaps in some ways because it was deemed she needed the protection of men. As Petchesky (1986: 148–61) notes, white girls have lived up to this stereotype, seeking a husband as soon as they become pregnant, perhaps because they do not have the experience of female-headed households that so many black girls have.

However, argue the women of colour, this stereotyping gave the white woman the protection of the state when she 'cried rape', a protection that black women were denied. If the white women cried rape against a black man, all the better – she was 'lionized' (Joseph, 1981: 100) by a racist judicial system which accepted uncontrolled male sexuality as readily as it accepted the myth of the highly sexed black woman. It may be that a white woman crying rape against a black man is likely to be heard (although one doubts that she is very often lionized, given Brownmiller's (1975) discussions). None the less it is well documented that a claim of rape against white acquaintances has little chance of success, while in many jurisdictions it is legally impossible for a wife to be raped by her husband. The operations of the law construct white women's sexuality in different ways to black women's sexuality, but the point remains that neither black women nor white women have the freedom to determine who will have access to their bodies and when. It is not the protection of the white rape victim as an autonomous woman that brings the full force of the law against her black attacker, it is the protection of white men's property. This is obvious when one considers the wife has no protection from her husband, as she is his property.

But if this analysis is correct, if the racist state seizes on the white rape victim as a pawn for its own purposes, should not white women show solidarity with the other pawn – the black rapist – by maintaining silence? If both white women and black men are 'movable pawns' (Brownmiller, 1975: 233) in the state's policing, why do white women turn to the state demanding more policing of male violence? Why do white women attempt to derive benefits from a state that is demonstrably patriarchal as well as racist? It would seem more appropriate that white women listen to the claims made by women of colour that the state is part of the enemy, and that alternative female networks – like women's refuges, kin support – can make up the deficit when the state refuses to intervene. It is no doubt because white women do have a leverage with the state that is denied women of colour that white feminists have developed a variety of political strategies directed at state intervention. This has perhaps been taken furthest in Australia where the term 'femocrat' (feminist bureaucrat) was coined. Femocrats have worked in government agencies to introduce and implement equal employment opportunity and anti-discrimination legislation, to restructure the welfare benefits system to minimize its gender-biases, to remodel the laws to give greater protection to women from domestic violence and rape.

No doubt such strategies look bizarre to women of colour for whom the state is both racist and patriarchal. Whether white feminists can avoid the charge of racism by claiming that such protection and benefits are available to all women is debatable, although Bobbi Sykes claims some benefits for Aboriginal women's groups (Black Women's Action Newsletter, September 1987: 3). The very benefits that the femocrats struggle for, and the likelihood of winning them, are a function of their position in society, a position more completely described if one takes account of its racial as well as its gender location. If white women demand protection from *all* male violence, the state, if it responds at all, will in all likelihood respond with greater policing of black men. If white women demand state-provided economic support for all supporting mothers, the British state is unlikely to stop deporting Asian women who have separated from their husbands. If white women demand the cessation of nuclear build-up in Britain, the state is unlikely to spend more money on aid to the third world. If white women demand equal employment opportunities, neither the state nor employers will convert this into equal opportunity irrespective of skin colour, unless this is also struggled for. White women's struggles around the state thus reflect their own race and class position and will not automatically improve the position of women of colour. These struggles may additionally bring about a further deterioration in the position of some black men. White feminists should therefore consider the likely effects of their struggles in a state that is both racist and patriarchal. This does not necessarily mean that they would cease to be feminists if they continued with a struggle likely to disadvantage men of colour. But it does mean that such struggles are less likely to attract women of colour to the feminist movement.

In a symptomatic passage Hester Eisenstein outlines three possible political strategies for women: to compete in the male world on its terms; to withdraw 'creating instead an otherworld of female *retreat*'; or to enter the world to change it 'in the image of woman-centred values of nurturance and intimacy' (Eisenstein, 1984: 144–5, emphasis added). Clearly the 'real' world described by Eisenstein as '*the* world', is the public world where the men are, and although Eisenstein argues that this world must be changed, it is still the place where women must go to do their politics. As Rowbotham (1985: 55) comments (somewhat unfairly given Eisenstein's emphasis on nurturance and intimacy): 'Western feminism with its strong radical–liberal heritage, tends to emphasize individual autonomy, personal freedom. It has greater difficulty with the other side of the coin, the human need for close association.' The centrality of struggles for equality in western feminism reflect both its development within the milieu of liberalism and the experiences that white women therefore have as isolated, autonomous individuals.

Women of colour have attacked white feminists' claims that equality – for example equality of employment opportunity – can be the grounds for the liberation of all women. Hooks (1984: 18) says equality is a bourgeois goal, women are demanding participation in the 'white supremicist, capitalist, patriarchal class structure'. When white women ask for equality they mean equality with white middle-class men – and nothing less. Would it be an improvement, in feminist terms, if the earnings and occupations of women when compared with men revealed no differences, when women are placed equally with men throughout the occupational structure? Black women, like Hooks, answer no; they believe that under affirmative action white women climb the occupational ladder at the expense of black men. Equality by gender, if it were achieved, would reveal stark inequalities by race. White women and men would be in the top jobs, black women and men in the bottom jobs. To say, in this scenario, that women had achieved equality with men would be to ignore the blatant race oppression by which it was achieved.

Furthermore, there is a debate within western feminism itself as to whether equality is a suitable goal for women: 'whether equality in a man's world is really what women should be aiming at' (Hoskyns, 1985: 72). Marxist feminists share with women of colour a belief that this strategy will lead only to the advancement of a few white middle-class women – that indeed this outcome is explicitly what white liberal feminists are attempting. On the other hand, feminists soon discover that the struggle for genderless equality is impossible. Women do have primary childcare functions, women are seen by men both at work and at home as sexed beings with particular appropriate roles. The struggle for equality requires a transformation of both family and work relations and obligations. It is this transformation that 'state feminism' – both in capitalist and socialist societies – resists: in Europe (Hoskyns, 1985); in Nicaragua (Molyneaux, 1985); in Cuba (Nazzari, 1983). Equality of employment legislation is one thing; the practices necessary to support equal employment opportunities are quite another.

On the other hand, one would think that women of colour who attack the racist legislation and practices of the British, American, Australian or South African state, may see the advantages of legislation that was gender-neutral or even provided some protection for women. They certainly see the disadvantages of racist legislation. They argue, however, that white feminism has misplaced its energies. The state is racist before it is sexist. As an example, to achieve equality of the sexes in terms of immigration laws, the British state further oppressed Asian men (Bhavnani and Coulson, 1986: 85). On the other hand, it could be argued that the formal equality, at least, of black and white people could be achieved relatively easily. The formal equality of women cannot be so easily legislated when women are everywhere defined and treated as wives and mothers, as singularly different from men. As Sue Lees (1986: 95) argues, racial inequality can be 'eradicated within the existing social structure inasmuch as it would require people to be treated equally irrespective of their race but would not require a fundamental redefinition of their social roles'. Both arguments have force: our society and our state are shot through with gender differentiation, but that differentiation *is* further divided, so that white women and women of colour are also treated differently. Working-class and middle-class white women may have formal equality before the law, but non-nationals and nationals of Britain, white and black women in South Africa, do not. Furthermore, formal equality may seem like a thin measure when it is brutal police practices or systematic discrimination in employment or a worldwide system of economic exploitation that most threatens the lives of black women in Australia, South Africa, Britain, the United States, and third world women.

The Female World of Love and Ritual

The claim to equality is a claim by women who regard their menfolk and then ask for the same rights. In these terms, revolutionary men too have spoken of the need for equality of women. Oliver Tambo of the ANC (African National Congress) argues that men must regard women as 'equals', help emancipate them in the home so they can be politically active (quoted in Kimble and Unterhalter, 1982: 25). 'The PLO charter talks of the equality of men and women and the elevation [*tarqia*] of women's role in revolution' (May Sayegh quoted in Al-Hibri, 1981: 186). Whatever the purpose of equality, the notion of equality between men and women within *both* economically or racially oppressed *and* dominant groups has some currency. Possibly the stark opposition of liberal-individual freedom to collective struggle misses some of the nuances of the term 'equality.'

White western feminists' struggles for equality are often associated with the denial of biologism as a necessary source of women's oppression, while many liberal and marxist feminists express a continuing concern that the glorification of 'female' capacities and reassertion of 'separate spheres' has many 'dangers' (Barrett, 1980: 13; see also Segal, 1987). On the other hand, the recent reassessment of the 'separate spheres' argument draws on both white women's, and more particularly third world women's experiences, to investigate the historical specificity and narrowness of contemporary western feminist understandings.

Carroll Smith-Rosenberg's (1983) evaluation of the 'female world of love and ritual' pointed to the quite recent isolation of western women from extensive female kin networks and close female friendships. It was the triumph of both capitalism and Freudian psychoanalysis that reoriented women towards men, towards husbands, as their prime emotional as well as economic targets (see also Jeffreys, 1985). Measuring themselves against their boyfriends, lovers or husbands, white feminists demanded the same rights – to go out into the world and earn their own public place in it. Schooled in the 'suspicious, defensive, competitive behaviour' (Hooks, 1986: 129) of 'rating and dating' and then of job-seeking and promotion, western feminists attacked polygamy, harems, women's communities from the perspective of their own experiences. Joint wives must be as jealous and competitive of each other as white wives are of other women; household communities full of women must be just as isolated and powerless as the white suburban housewife; the woman who does not work for wages must be dependent on her husband's goodwill for any money and resources. The 'female world' had been so emasculated, so masculinized, that white feminists had little experience of its potential strengths. Thus Ellen DuBois (1980: 31) suggests that the women's culture Smith-Rosenberg describes has little to do with 'classical women's rights feminism, with its focus on political *equality*' (italics added). As women are subordinated within society, their own culture must reinforce that oppression. Only a political struggle on the same terms and in the same forms as men have struggled will achieve a transformation in women's power. Smith-Rosenberg (1980: 63) replies that the demise of the 'world of women-identified women' was coterminous with the demise of first-wave feminism in the 1920s and 1930s. For her the two events are not unconnected: 'The world of women does not automatically produce feminism. But can feminism develop outside a female world?' (Smith- Rosenberg, 1980: 62).

Lisa Leghorn and Catherine Parker (1981) argue that women have the greatest status and resources in negotiating power societies, in societies where they have a separate respected sphere of influence, where women's networks are dense and supportive, where women spend much of their time with each other. Leila Ahmed (1982) and Patricia Jeffery (1979) describe the rich women's culture of the harem. However, Ahmed (1982: 53) does not deny that women are confined in the harem – she is making the point that, in contrast with the isolated white middle-class household, that confinement affirms women's sense of worth.

The emptying out of western women's worlds of their love and ritual has left us ill-placed to assess the value of female culture. However, the fact that many white feminists turned to 'sisterhood', 'consciousness-raising' and 'separatism', strategies which sought to rebuild female worlds, suggests that we had a lesson to learn about the sources of female strength, a lesson we might have learned sooner had we not cast such a prejudicial eye over the experiences of women of colour.

Although 'sisterhood' might be a strategy for rebuilding a white feminist culture, many women of colour are suspicious of 'sisterhood'. While they point to the strength women derive from female kin in black American households or the importance of women's networks, rituals and communities in various third world cultures, they also assert the importance of the whole black community, the whole Asian family, the whole Aboriginal people, as the basis for struggle. Because individualism is alien to third world values, the 'separation of women's freedom from other freedoms becomes impossible' (Bourne, 1983: 21). Sisterhood seeks to separate women from men, join them together against men. Some white feminists may have little trouble separating from white men, although marxist feminists would argue that only bourgeois feminists can do this with equanimity. But when the men are also oppressed, because of race or class, it is neither easy to separate from their struggles nor see them as the 'enemy', the prime beneficiaries of the system.

Arguments about sisterhood are based on the notion of women's 'common oppression' (Hooks, 1986: 127). This ignores both the fact that black women must base their struggles on 'shared strength and resources', cannot afford to see themselves as victims, and that women are so divided in terms of their outlooks and conditions that they do not share a common oppression. Where sisterhood describes for white women the common oppression of women, the notion of 'community' seems to perform a similar function for black and third world women. It denotes the shared experience of race or imperialist oppression; and it is because of this experience that third world women and women of colour feel they cannot desert their menfolk: 'We *compañeras*, are man's other half' (Domitilia Barrios de la Chungara, 1983: 56). Lesbian denotes separation and isolation while womanism denotes the generosity that can embrace the needs of fathers and brothers, the survival of the 'entire people' (Ogunyemi, 1985: 65). Moreover, because white women and white society participate in the oppression of black men, some black women argue not only for the needs of the 'entire people' but more strenuously for the needs of black men. Black men 'particularly' must receive '*real* power and control' in our society (Bobbi Sykes quoted in Jennett, 1987: 369). In almost an inversion of white feminists' demands for equality based on their weak position *vis-à-vis* white men, some black women deny the strengths of their own position and demand the superiority of black men, a reversal of their emasculation at the hands of white society. It is this trigonometry of comparisons that has provoked both the hierarchies of oppression and the debate over the political strategies that are argued to flow from it.

Differences are More Than Skin Deep

There has been a tendency among white western feminists to reduce the debate with women of colour and third world feminists to a question of attitude – to prejudice, ethnocentrism, or 'ignorance' (Frye, 1983: 119). Sometimes white feminists have responded to black women's rage with guilty breastbeating, to which women of colour make replies such as: 'the [Barrett and McIntosh, 1985] paper's sole purpose seemed to be a self-indulgent exercise, excising the guilt socialist feminists feel about the myopia of their past analyses' (Mirza, 1986: 103). For such critics, theoretical or analytical corrections, even attempts to eliminate racism in the women's movement, are misplaced. They ignore the structures of racist oppression, structures in which white women often participate, and whether they actively engage or not they are among the beneficiaries.

Working with Differences
None the less some women of colour, for example Gayatri Spivak (in Gunew and Spivak, 1986: 139) not only assert that white women must do their 'homework', learn about other women's experiences, but that their

responses to other experiences will allow white feminists to interrogate
their own speaking positions. Such exchanges, when *all* women, rather
than just white women, can speak from their own positions with
authority about each other's oppression and be heard (Minh-ha, 1987:
14) cannot but enrich feminist analysis. For the moment, however, when
third world women are asked to speak, they are asked to speak only of
their own differences and not to challenge western women's
self-constructions:

> I try my best to offer my benefactors and benefactresses what they
> most anxiously yearn for: the possibility of a difference, yet, a
> difference or an otherness that will not go so far as to question the
> foundation of their beings and makings. (Minh-ha, 1987: 14)

Similarly Jane Flax (1987: 633) warns against our entanglement with
patriarchal knowledge that leads us to suppress the 'discomforting
voices' in an attempt to maintain the '(apparent) authority, coherence
and universality of our own'. Bourne (1983: 17) describes the recent cult of
the 'black female experience' as the mindless celebration of such women
as 'odd', an example of something different (like the older woman or the
disabled woman) against which we (white middle-class hale and
hearty feminists) can measure our 'normal' experience.

Women of colour do not deny their difference, in fact they wish that
white feminists would see the differences among them – not
'homogenize' their experiences by asking the one 'token' woman of colour
to represent the bulk of women in this world, who are neither white nor
western nor middle-class. The diversity of black women's and third
world women's experiences is seen as a basis of strength in their political
movement. This is another reason why women of colour oppose the
celebration of sisterhood: it represses their differences. Furthermore, it
suggests a biological basis for unity, and it posits the struggle for
women's emancipation as paramount.

Amos and Parmar (1984: 6) describe sisterhood as the 'implicit
assumption that women *qua* women has a necessary basis for unity and
solidarity'. Floya Anthias and Nira Yuval-Davis (1983: 63) talk of the
mystification of the category of sisterhood. A speaker at the second
Women and Labour Conference in Australia said the 'associated
differences between women of class, race, ethnicity and region were such
that women may never really constitute a definable political group'
(Levy, 1984: 106).

Because the only thing that all women share is their gender,
sisterhood also slides into a kind of biologism:

While claiming to liberate women from biological determinism, it has denied women an existence outside that determined by their sex. And behind the idea that every woman is equally oppressed biologically is the idea that gender per se, rather than a particular system or set of relations, is the primary enemy of women. (Bourne, 1983: 19)

Indeed there is a kind of biologism in some of white feminists' arguments. Robin Morgan (1984: 1–2) argues that the centrality of women's right to reproductive choice is inextricable from every other issue facing women, a point which Sally Mugabe (quoted in Jennett, 1987: 353) also made at the Nairobi Conference. Sexuality is constructed on biology: white western women seek control over both the effects of their biology and the constructions of sexuality that are built on it. This may explain the shift to issues of sexuality among some western feminists recently. It is not the denial of economic and public-political struggles, born of middle-class women's comfortable material circumstances as Bourne (1983: 18) suggests, but the sharpening of a focus on what it is about women that singles them out as a category for oppression. On the other hand, even on sexuality issues, Kum-Kum Bhavnani and Margaret Coulson (1986: 84) say:

The problem with the concept of gender is that it is rooted in an apparently simple and 'real' material base of biological difference between women and men. But what is constructed on that base is not one femininity in relation to one masculinity, but *several*. It is not only that there are *differences* between different groups of women but that these differences are often also *conflicts of interest*.

Lees (1986: 84) suggests that the hierarchies of oppression debate is fruitless, we should not focus on empirical generalizations about who dominates who. She then goes on to say, in an empirical generalization par excellence: 'in Britain sexual oppression is more ubiquitous than racial oppression for the simple reason that women are not, and cannot be, a minority.'

Because gender is constructed on sex, feminism which seeks explanations for women's shared oppression has been required to come to terms with biologism. Apart from a celebration of biological differences, feminists have argued for the shared experiences that are built on these differences. But the one obvious shared experience is gender-based oppression, and this suggests that a unique women's perspective arises out of our subordinate position. Clearly such an argument – the special nurturant or supportive or flexible world-views of women are a result of oppression – is not politically strategic. It condemns women for ever to oppression if they are to maintain their superior culture. Just to take two examples, on the one hand, Lynne Segal (1987: 148) notes the bifurcated vision of the oppressed: 'greater attentiveness, watchfulness, and desire to please in their relations with others'. On the other hand, Jane Flax (1987: 642) suggests that the notion of *one* feminist standpoint

> assumes that the oppressed are not in fundamental ways damaged by their social experiences ... [but rather] ... have a privileged (and not just different) relation and ability to comprehend a reality that is 'out there' waiting for our representation.

If neither shared biology nor shared oppression can be said to define the category of women, it is difficult to think of another candidate. Of course, an obvious solution is to deny that there is a single category of women, but this would ignore the widespread, possibly universal, practices of gender-based differentiation in human society.

Some feminists thus clearly believe that the struggle for women's emancipation is paramount. Patriarchy came first and seems to be the prior condition. Mary Daly (quoted in Gardner, 1985: 84) argues that gynocide gives rise to genocide and that rapism has spawned racism. On the whole, however, western feminists don't argue for the priority of feminist struggles, just their specificity. They argue that there are some forms of oppression based on gender, which although they differ in their empirical realization across societies, are unique to women and can only be addressed in a feminist struggle.

Many women of colour and third world women argue that race or class issues are paramount. As was discussed in Chapter 3, Hooks tends to run issues of race- and class-based oppression together without separating the effects of the two. Just as some marxist feminists decried bourgeois women's struggles for 'equal rights within capitalist society' (Vogel, 1983: 168), so third world women seem to measure women's progress against the template of capitalist transformation. Development programmes which integrate women into capitalist production or encourage them to be entrepreneurs are viewed as 'alarming' (Mbilingi, 1984: 293). 'Alarming' or not, third world women clearly wish to have access to economic rewards for their labours, as the experience of aid agencies attests. As Chapter 4 suggested, women in socialist regimes participate more extensively and equally in paid work. However, this is often against their wishes as Körösi (1984) reveals for Hungary; given the chance, these women will abandon the double shift. Thus it can be argued that socialist revolution goes only so far, only far enough to create women as productive workers but not to change family relations, the status of women, sexual freedom and protection from male violence. Can it not also be argued that white western feminism that seeks only to transform the status of women within capitalist society can go only so far, only as far as its demands are compatible with capitalist production?

This is indeed the claim that black feminists like Hooks and Amos and Parmar make. As long as the patriarchal and racist structures remain untouched, only some women can benefit; and it will probably be white middle-class women. These women's claims for the autonomy of feminism thus become self-serving pleas to perpetuate their own privileged position. As long as there are hierarchies of occupations, power, privilege, even if men and women are distributed evenly throughout them, some women will be better placed than other women. It is the logic of this assessment that commends to women of colour the struggle for 'human emancipation' or at least that of all women: 'Feminism is the political theory and practice that struggles to free *all* women ... Anything less than this vision of total freedom is not feminism, but merely female self-aggrandizement' (Barbara Smith quoted in Minh-ha, 1987: 12).

It would appear then, that some women at least are oppressed by their race and class as well as their gender: 'only a synthesis of class, race, gender and sexuality can lead us forward, as these form the matrix of black women's lives' (Amos and Parmar, 1984: 18). This might suggest that we must struggle to end transnational capitalist exploitation of Asian women; redirect our national budgets from warfare to international aid; end racist employment, policing and legislation; that women must struggle on all fronts to achieve a global feminism. For the woman in Asia starving because she is Asian as well as because she is a woman, a struggle on all fronts would seem necessary. For all women of colour who speak on this issue, race and class cannot be quarantined from gender as a basis of their oppression. While none of the writers provides a systematic critique of how these elements are interrelated, they assert that they are and that serious consideration of the issues of race 'involves a fundamental and radical *transformation* of socialist-feminism' (Anthias and Yuval-Davis, 1983: 85).

But it was exactly this fundamental redrawing of patriarchy that the marxist feminists attempted in the 1970s. The attempt failed: 'The relationship between struggles around sex and class has never been resolved at the level of theory. Nor can it be' (Lees, 1986: 96). So while these structures of oppression are interrelated, while they impact on women as interconnected and inextricable, they may also be to some degree autonomous. Thus socialist revolution improves the position of women in some respects only; women's role in resisting colonial oppression was often conditioned by whether the nationalist movement was liberal or marxist (Jayawardena, 1986); liberal feminism meets opposition precisely when it seeks to gain recognition and specific compensation for women's role as mothers. We can put on men's clothes and go to work – although even the chance of full-scale success along these lines seems limited, given Game and Pringle's (1983) and Walby's (1986) interpretations of gender-based struggles at work, and the experiences of women in socialist societies. But when it comes to changing power relations between men and women as men and women, specific struggles are necessary. Feminists have argued not only for the *necessity* of these struggles – which seems incontrovertible in the face of the evidence – but also their *autonomy*.

Compromises

It is the autonomy of feminism that is the sticking-point for third world and black women, just as it was for marxist feminists engaged in the patriarchy debate. Autonomous feminism is tempted to turn a blind eye to the implication of some women in racist domination. White women 'dominated' black men in colonial societies of the ante-bellum south; western women buy cheap clothes made by poorly paid women in free export zones in Asia; middle-class women hire domestic servants so they can pursue professional careers. Western women refused to discuss the New International Economic Order at the United Nations Decade of Women Conferences, yet participate in a standard of living based on the present terms of trade between the west and the third world. White Australian women live on land that rightfully belongs to Aboriginal people. White women experience the 'second-hand superiority' (Frye, 1983: 126) of being a member of the master race. Whether white women directly oppress black people, or are merely beneficiaries of racism, or are even occasionally 'disloyal to civilization' (Rich, 1984: 282), seems not to matter if they keep their tongues and hands tied over issues of race. On the other hand, if racism is a set of structural practices, and most women of colour argue that it is:

> even male feminists receive benefits from an institutionalized sexism they actively struggle to eliminate. Objectively, no individual man can succeed in renouncing sexist privilege any more than individual whites can succeed in renouncing racist privilege – the benefits of gender and race accrue regardless of the wishes of the individuals who bear them. Gender, like race and class, is not a voluntarily

disposable individual characteristic. After all, fundamentally our feminisms address the extraction and transfer of social benefits from women to men *as groups* of humans, on a worldwide scale. Thus the standpoint theorists, in identifying the common aspects of women's social experiences cross-cuturally, contribute something important to our work. (Harding, 1986: 658)

This statement may give some comfort to white feminists. But there are things we are urged to do as individuals, activities that fall far short of agitating for the transition of capitalism or the demise of imperialism. We are asked not to march through black neighbourhoods demanding 'better policing'; we are asked to transform our whole understanding of feminism to include the oppression of black men and white working-class men; we are asked to keep silent about veiling, infibulation, harems and arranged marriages. We are asked to abandon affirmative action legislation, the struggle for political representation and public visibility for women; we are asked not to campaign for the expansion of state powers that could lead to the loss of autonomy and power for black men. We are asked to rewrite history to include 'the fundamental ways in which white women have benefited from the oppression of black people' (Amos and Parmar, 1984: 5); we are asked to make space for and listen attentively to the many voices of women of colour and third world women – to recognize their variegated experiences, politics and viewpoints.

With some of these requests I have no argument; with some, others possibly, you might have no argument. Of course it all comes back to what feminism means for you and me. As Anthias and Yuval-Davis (1983: 72) ask, once we accept that western feminism (leaving aside for the moment its internal diversity) no longer provides the criteria for defining the contents of feminism, because it has been shown to be culture and class specific, then does that mean that whatever women do is feminist? Surely not, because we have 'Women Who Want to be Women', Margaret Thatcher, and a host of other conservative females seeking to reaffirm the dependence of women on men in society. Neither does it seem that Anthias and Yuval-Davis's (1983: 72) distinction will get us very far: feminism challenges traditional gender divisions while other women merely use them in pursuit of nationalist, anti-racist and other struggles. It will not be so easy to separate feminist struggles from those of other women given the proclivity of feminists everywhere to measure the struggles of others in their own terms:

Many African women felt they had more in common with women from other third world countries than with black American women. They felt that they were being patronized and told how to run their movement by black American women who have never experienced their oppression. (Hendessi, 1986: 149)

Many third world women could have told western feminists about the strengths derived from networking, controlling the products of one's own labour, separate spheres and other 'traditional gender divisions' long before these things occurred to second wave feminists. Perhaps not all traditional gender divisions should be challenged; it may be that gender divisions should be enhanced and western women should turn away from the struggle to be equal with men in the public spheres of work and politics. The 'battle of the genders', as Bourne (1983: 19) says, may not hold 'the key to women's liberation everywhere'. These issues are not settled, either inside or outside western feminism.

Accepting then our differences, must these become divisions? Do western women and third world women have conflicts of interest rather than merely differences of opinion? For those of a marxist persuasion we do – we are irreconcilably divided by class. For those who see race oppression as primary, we do – both black women in some limited respects and certainly white women have more autonomy and resources than black men. For other women of colour, there is the prospect of 'coalition work' as Bernice Reagon (1984) calls it. Rather than the misty-eyed transculturalism of sisterhood, we accept that our interests intersect and overlap – that we can share the road on occasions, but must go our separate ways on others (Watson, 1987: 51); but we do not forget that our coalition partners are not family. They are not our sisters and they cannot, finally, understand us. Hooks (1986: 138) too argues that we 'do not need to eradicate difference to ... fight equally to end oppression'. On the other hand, however, Adrienne Rich (1984: 308) warns that we must not lose sight of the importance of women's issues. Postponement of our concerns for the 'larger' struggle – to end capitalism, to end racism, to end imperialism – is merely a prioritizing that reproduces the 'mass psychology of male supremicism'. Furthermore, just as white feminists must accept that the structures of racism cannot be overcome with the eradication of their own ethnocentric values, so does it seem reasonable to argue that patriarchal practices are more than mere prejudices, more than mere sexual preferences, more than lifestyle issues. This does not seem to be widely accepted by third world women and women of colour who (understandably enough) put the struggle for economic survival ahead of the needs of women in relation to men: 'In our country [South Africa] white racism and apartheid coupled with economic exploitation have degraded the African woman more than any male prejudices' (quoted in Kimble and Unterhalter, 1982: 14).

Put in this way, the need to fight apartheid first seems obvious. But when we remember that 'male prejudices' cover clitoridectomies, domestic violence, rape, lack of choice over childbirth and so on, it is not so easy to say that one struggle must necessarily have priority. Can we hierarchize the various threats to bodily integrity these women face – starvation because of the class system, forced removal, relocation, death in riots or prison because of apartheid, genital mutilation, unwanted childbearing with its risk of death because of patriarchal practices? We can surely understand why the struggle against apartheid is paramount, but this is not to say that African women suffer only male 'prejudice'.

Reviewers choose how to represent the voices of others. The telling of this story has left us at a point where the possibility, at least, of a global feminism is not unthinkable.

One World Women's Movement?

The major problem that women of colour see in joining with western feminists is that they will be asked to break ranks with their male comrades in political struggle, their menfolk, their male workmates. They feel they will be asked to forgo the struggles against racism or imperialism or capitalism and instead be asked to struggle against male violence or state control of women's bodies or husbands' control of the products of women's labour. Being asked to 'forgo' particular struggles in favour of others implies that men do participate in the oppression of women; otherwise a choice would not be required. Jayawardena (1986: 260), on the strength of her multi-nation study of nationalist and feminist politics, accepts 'the male domination that underlies all Asian social practice'. She feels, however, that contemporary women's movements in Asia are opposing it.

One needs to consider whether a global feminism must necessarily put the oppositions starkly, as an 'either' (national liberation) 'or' (feminist struggles) choice. There are perhaps three possible scenarios for describing a global feminism. A global feminist movement might consist of women around the world united under a homogeneous political banner with its enemy being men and patriarchal structures. Or it might be a movement that acknowledges the variations and complexities in the condition of women around the world, accepts the struggles over racism and imperialism but says the major struggle must be the one against male domination. Or it might be a constellation of different localized movements, which movements engage now in a struggle for higher wages for all workers, now in a struggle for freedom from a political regime, now in a struggle for women's control of reproductive choice, and whose members are united by only one belief – that there are forms of oppression based on gender differences and that these must ultimately be addressed if women are to achieve satisfactory autonomy in society. Must the members of any of these suggested movements hate men, be separatists, or can they decide to work with sympathetic men to change their condition?

The potential for a global feminism lies in the apparent similarities of women's position around the world – gender-based mutilation, unequal access to economic, legal and political resources compared with men in each country, and evaluation of women, at least by official culture and most men, as of lesser status, whether by identification with nature, emotion, or some other pollutant of reason or religion. As Elsa Atkin (1987: 96), an immigrant to Australia from Baghdad says: 'It frightens me still that in spite of hundreds of years of different cultural traditions in so many different countries, the issues concerning women are virtually universal and therefore so much harder to change or eradicate.'

The impediments to an international feminism are the differences between women. The results of colonialism, slavery, racism, and imperialism seem to create hierarchies of oppression, hierarchies in which some women benefit from the oppression of others. Ngahuia Te Awekotuku and Marilyn Waring (1984: 480) combine the two structures of patriarchy and colonialism to identify fourth world women, women who are an oppressed group within an oppressed group: Maoris, Aborigines, black women in the west, and women in the poor countries, or at least the poorer classes, of the third world. For many fourth world women the oppressions of race and class seem more urgent than the oppressions of gender. They are more immediately preoccupied with economic survival, keeping families together, or national liberation, than they are with violence to women or other gender-based differences within their societies.

Questions arise then for the possibility of a global feminism. What should be the first priority for women of colour and the third world? Must they consider their interests *qua* women as excluding the possibility of alliances with men? A number of women whose positions were discussed above do not see the interests of women as pre-eminent. By some western definitions this would deny them a definition as feminist. But in the third scenario for global feminism posited above, women do not have to choose to fight only for the specific concerns of women; they may also pursue in addition and sometimes as a priority other objectives they consider more pressing.

The first scenario, that of a homogeneous women's movement, perhaps accords most nearly with the project of international socialism. Marx urged the workers of the world to unite because, he argued, they had more in common with each other in their exploitation through capitalist relations, than they had with national compatriots who were capitalists. However, just as third world women accuse first world women of benefiting from the oppression of their sisters – as consumers of cheaper goods, as beneficiaries of higher wages or better jobs – so did such divisions emerge among the brotherhood of working men. Lenin identified the 'aristocracy of labour', better paid workers in Britain and other imperialist countries, who benefited from the exploitation of cheaper labour in the colonies. In the First World War, working men of the world did not unite but rather enlisted in national armies to kill each other.

Many reasons have been advanced for the failure of international socialism, among them the salience of national identities and the hegemony of conservative or populist ideologies. Others have argued that different living standards and different relations with capital (for example, the so-called 'new middle class') mean that the working class are so internally divided and fractured that they do not recognize the features of their shared exploitation.

While Virginia Woolf claims (perhaps to some extent in the way that Marx and Engels urged the workers of the world to unite) that nationalism has less appeal to women – 'as a woman I have no country' – the struggle of third world women for national liberation shows that many women want a country they can call their own. Similarly, just as there have always been some conservative working men, so are many women deeply conservative. Such women include the marchers of the pots and pans against Allende's regime in Chile (Agosin, 1984: 139), the government-sponsored women's movement in Indonesia (Sullivan, 1983: 151), and the revival of Hindu mythological women in India as part of an anti-Muslim and anti-Sikh rhetoric (Patel, 1985: 85). Conservative women in Sri Lanka claim that women should be wives and mothers (Goonatilake, 1985: 441), even though Sri Lanka had the first female prime minister in the world, and women have long been able to enter the Buddhist order.

Fanny Tabak (1984: 108–11) points out that in some countries less than 30 per cent of the female population is in the workforce, while those that are employed often do backbreaking low paid work. In such situations, leftwing movements' advocacy of freedom through labour often sounds hollow in comparison with authoritarian regimes' elevation of motherhood. Furthermore, just as first wave feminists were sometimes attacked out of context by postwar feminists as reactionary prudes, so too does the elevation of motherhood make sense – at least as a rhetoric – in societies where husbands desert, or refuse their traditional obligations as a result of the upheavals of 'modernization'. Thus while feminists may argue that conservative women's attempts to make individual husbands support their wives and children are misplaced, they no doubt agree that the position of women in societies where they are dependent on men's support makes this policy attractive.

The experience may be shared, but the responses vary. While conservative women may demand that the family be further entrenched by reinforcing the distinct roles of husband and wife, some feminists argue that marriage is an unequal bargain that should be eschewed. Discussions of the relationship between women's experience and their political strategies may appear to reproduce arguments about workers' 'false consciousness' to explain working-class conservatism. The notion of 'false consciousness', of necessity, is measured against an externally imposed standard, whether it be a 'scientific' analysis of capitalism or patriarchy.

Towards a Diversity of Feminism
Instead of searching for the 'correct line', Morgan (1984: 26) argues that global feminism should not reproduce the strategies of male-dominated politics. Rather we should attempt to draw flexible and open lines between experience and political action. For instance:

> To say that women share a common culture, similar values and responses to their environment, is not to say that all women in all cultures identify with each other ... their biology, their relationship to the economies in which they live and perhaps even their history, structures their experience in similar ways. Women can only know and understand this underlying structure of similarities in their lives if they explore the differences in these experiences. (Leghorn and Parker, 1981: 252)

In the same vein, Barbara Engel (1984: 2) asks if the personal is political how can we define the political of someone whose personal circumstances are utterly different from our own? Is the refusal to accept as 'feminist' women's movements with goals opposed to our own another form of imperialism? What would global feminism look like? The simplicity but also limited nature of her answer – dialogue is perhaps our best and only strategy (Engel, 1984: 3) – reveals how little real work has been done in coming to terms with women's unity in diversity.

Those who seek to save the project of feminism argue that women must learn to exploit their differences, to build on them as a basis for political action, not to erase them in the pursuit of a common united front. To marxists or other hard-headed materialists, the differences of class and race may seem insurmountable. The dream of global feminism as a kaleidoscope of looseknit networks may seem utopian. Certainly none of the writers who discuss the potential of global feminism gives a clear political programme for its realization. But perhaps they would argue that this must be produced collectively in the course of its practice. Perhaps they would argue that there can be no single political programme, but that the way forward is through many different and localized struggles. Such an argument would reflect the theoretical movement of patriarchy into its 'adjectival phase'; 'patriarchal' indicates both the commonalities and the specific differences of the instances.

The spirit of much of the argument in the foregoing pages commends a catholic global feminism, the last scenario rather than the first. As such, women as political actors have the freedom to choose their priorities, to choose their battles. However, most feminists would argue that some struggles – for example, the struggle for reproductive freedom or freedom from male violence – require specifically feminist struggles. This is not to say that women united with men in unions have not achieved higher wages for women as well as men, or that national liberation struggles will not improve the position of women in terms of labour force participation and welfare services. It is to say that such struggles must usually run in tandem with other struggles which are specifically feminist if 'sexuality' issues are to be addressed. Women's workforce participation under socialism is not accompanied by extensive childcare facilities or husbands who share the housework; it is premised on the notion that everyone should participate in productive labour. Similarly, and quite naturally, female suffragists could only share platforms with men when they aligned the demand for votes for women with the demand for votes for the working class or votes for negroes. Sometimes they were asked to subordinate the demand for votes for women to the demand for votes for (male) workers or negroes. It is this point, the point when women are asked to choose between a campaign for (some) women and a campaign for (some) men, or a campaign for women which opposes the interests of male comrades (for example, reproductive freedom), that some western feminists would say marks the litmus test of feminist politics. However, to choose on this day, in this struggle, to fight by the side of the men, should not condemn a woman. To fail to see that the choice has been made against some specifically feminist goals, for whatever reason, may perhaps be evidence of ignorance of the feminist project.

Women of colour and the third world have rightly charged western feminism of ignorance of their specific problems. One goal at least of western feminist movements can be to put a broom through their own house, to gain knowledge of the positions and needs of other women and to excise racism and eurocentrism from their own movement. Not only is this a necessary antidote to the partiality of western feminism that pretends to speak for all women, but it will strengthen and enrich feminism. It will give women more models of action to consider, more puzzles to ponder, more strengths to draw on. Many would argue that this process should not be at the cost of turning a blind eye to patriarchal practices, whoever perpetrates them. Even this will be a political and theoretical struggle: the definition of patriarchal practices or appropriate forms of resistance is rarely immediately obvious.

Such a minimalist demand – a new broom – will not meet the claims of some women of colour and the third world that the whole house needs rebuilding. In the process of spring-cleaning, however, it would seem that some structural changes will be made if white women really engage with the 'colour-blindness' of their own work. But the argument that feminists need to change their address, to place the liberation of all oppressed people at the head of their political agenda, is the hardest to incorporate into a feminist project. Admittedly none of us can be free – can enjoy personal, emotional and physical security – until this world is rid of the excesses of capitalism and imperialism. But those struggles are not specifically feminist struggles, and the fight against capitalism will not make women free as women. Similarly it must be accepted that the fight against patriarchal practices focuses on the relations between men and women, and so has specific goals that will not necessarily guarantee all women the same economic and social resources. Nevertheless, when one considers the broad sweep of struggles that call themselves feminist – anti-war and pro-conservation, in unions for better wages and conditions for women, within the state for anti-discrimination legislation, better welfare services, pornography legislation – it is clear many of these do challenge the logic of capitalism and imperialism. Socialist feminists might argue that in failing to see this challenge, or to put it at centre-stage, such feminist opposition is doomed to failure when it meets the limits of capitalism's reformism.

But the point should also be made that much specifically feminist struggle, unlike much socialist struggle, does not focus on a 'big bang' theory of change, but *localized* and targeted gains. Even Lynne Segal (1987: 220ff.), who mourns the decomposition of socialist feminism, points to the 'practical campaigns and projects', the small-scale strategies, which she believes mark the possibilities of socialist feminism's resurgence.

The title of this book, *One World Women's Movement*, identifies the deep ambiguities for the global project. If there is only one world, if there are underlying structures of sexual oppression, then a global project should be possible. But this project should not ape the unitary goals of men's political movements. Women, on the whole, can live with more ambivalence and uncertainty than men. Women are trained in the necessity to hear the voices of men, while also experiencing the desire to listen to their own voices. Their subordinate position should make them wary of singular answers, all-pervasive solutions that deny openness to other viewpoints. Thus the world's women's movement need not be 'one', but can be many, modelled on the female symbols of the web or the patchwork quilt. The web and the quilt are made of threads that by themselves are not strong. When stitched together, however, the web and quilt are strong, integrated and eye-pleasing wholes. On the other hand, both the web and quilt are usually created by a single author or to a predetermined pattern. The greatest challenge for all women will be to allow the patchwork to grow, to accommodate one's own work to the shape of other contributions, to allow for the jarring of patterns and colours, but never to lose sight of the project which, as a utopian dream, must be pleasing to the mind's eye, to the eyes of women seeking their strength.

Some recent writings by feminists support both the possibility of a multi-faceted political and theoretical project, and the *value* of such a diversity of feminisms:

> I would argue instead that it is a positive aspect of the difference between feminisms that it has not easily produced a set of alternative definitions, but instead, secured a public hearing in government, civil service, courts, schools, workplace, theatre, unions and media for challenges to those meanings and the practices that flow from them. (Kaplan, 1986: 6–7)

or

> If we do our work well, 'reality' will appear even more unstable, complex, and disorderly than it does now. In this sense, perhaps Freud

was right when he declared that women are the enemies of civilization. (Flax, 1987: 643)

The strength of feminism lies in its ability not to ape the unitary categories and Archimedean points of male theory, philosophy and politics; not to search for the one position from which the 'truth' of all women can be seen, nor the one lever that will transform the whole female world, but to abandon the privileges of hierarchies for the multiple connections of the web and the quilt.

As Ti-Grace Atkinson said, 'sisterhood is powerful – it can kill, sisters mostly', and as Joan Russell (1987: 144) replies, 'Sisterhood can save, and not only sisters, either.' To focus on saving and not killing as the mark of a powerful movement calls for a generosity and flexibility outside the parameters of any political movement devised by men.

Bibliography

Abdalla, Raqiha Haji Dwaleh (1982) *Sisters in Affliction: Circumcision and Infibulation of Women in Africa*, London: Zed Books Ltd.

Adlam, Diana (1979) 'The Case Against Capitalist Patriarchy', *m/f*, no. 3, pp. 83–102.

Afshar, Haleh C. (1982) 'Khomeini's Teachings and their Implications for Iranian Women' in Azar Tabari and Nahid Yeganeh (compilers) *In the Shadow of Islam: The Women's Movement in Iran*, London: Zed Books Ltd.

Agosin, Marjorie (1984) 'Chile: Women of Smoke', in Robin Morgan (ed.) *Sisterhood is Global*, New York: Anchor Press/Doubleday.

Ahmed, Leila (1981) 'Comments on Tinker's "A Feminist View of Copenhagen"', *Signs*, vol. 6, no. 4, pp. 780–3.

Ahmed, Leila (1982) 'Western Ethnocentrism and Perceptions of the Harem', *Feminist Studies*, vol. 8, no. 2, pp. 521–34.

Alexander, Sally and Taylor, Barbara (1981) 'In Defence of "Patriarchy"' in Feminist Anthology Collective (eds) *No Turning Back: Writings from the Women's Liberation Movement 1975–80*, London: Women's Press.

Al-Hibri, Azizah (1981) 'Capitalism is an Advanced Stage of Patriarchy: But Marxism is not Feminism' in Lydia Sargent (ed.) *Women and Revolution: A Discussion of the Unhappy Marriage of Marxism and Feminism*, Boston: South End Press.

Allaghi, Farida (1984) 'Libya: the Wave of Consciousness cannot be Reversed' in Robin Morgan (ed.) *Sisterhood is Global*, New York: Anchor Press/Doubleday.

Allen, Judith (1983) 'Marxism and the Man Question: Some Implications of the Patriarchy Debate' in Judith Allen and Paul Patton (eds) *Beyond Marxism? Interventions after Marx*, Leichhardt: Intervention Publications.

Allen, Judith (1987) *Postwar Feminism*, Nathan: School of Humanities, Griffith University.

Amos, Valerie and Parmar, Pratibha (1984) 'Challenging Imperial Feminism', *Feminist Review*, 17, Autumn, pp. 3–20.

Anand, Anita (1983) 'Saving Trees, Saving Lives: Third World Women and the Issue of Survival' in Leonie Caldecott and Stephanie Leland (eds) *Reclaim the Earth: Women Speak Out for Life on Earth,* London: Women's Press.

Anthias, Floya and Yuval-Davis, Nira (1983) 'Contextualizing Feminism – Gender, Ethnic and Class Divisions', *Feminist Review,* no.15, pp. 62–75.

Arena, Franca (1987) 'No More Crumbs' in Jocelynne A. Scutt (ed.) *Different Lives: Reflections on the Women's Movement and Visions of its Future,* Ringwood: Penguin.

Ashworth, Georgina (1985) 'Editorial', *Women's Studies International Forum,* vol. 8, no. 2, pp. 93–9.

Assiter, Alison (1983) 'Woman Power and Nuclear Politics: Women and the Peace Movement' in Dorothy Thompson (ed.) *Over Our Dead Bodies: Women Against the Bomb,* London: Virago.

Association of African Women for Research and Development (AAWARD) (1983) 'A statement on genital mutilation' in Miranda Davies (compiler) *Third World Second Sex: Women's Struggles and National Liberation,* London: Zed Books Ltd.

Atkin, Elsa (1987) ' In Retrospect' in Jocelynne A. Scutt (ed.) *Different Lives: Reflections on the Women's Movement and Visions of its Future,* Ringwood: Penguin.

Barnard, Rosemary (1983) 'Housewives and Farmers: Malay Women in the Muda Irrigation Scheme' in Lenore Manderson (ed.) *Women's Work and Women's Roles: Economics and Everyday Life in Indonesia, Malaysia and Singapore,* Canberra: Development Studies Centre, Australian National University Press.

Barrett, Michèle (1980) *Women's Oppression Today: Problems in Marxist Feminist Analysis,* London: Verso.

Barrett, Michèle (1982) 'Feminism and the Definition of Cultural Politics' in Rosalind Brant and Caroline Rowan (eds) *Feminism, Culture and Politics,* London: Lawrence & Wishart.

Barrett, Michèle and McIntosh, Mary (1982) *The Anti-Social Family,* London: Verso.

Barrett, Michèle and McIntosh, Mary (1985) 'Ethnocentrism and Socialist Feminist Theory', *Feminist Review,* 20, Summer: 23.47.

Barrios De La Chungara, Domitilia (Bolivia) (1963) 'Women and Organization' in Miranda Davies (compiler) *Third World Second Sex: Women's Struggles and National Liberation,* London: Zed Books Ltd.

Barry, Kathleen (1979) *Female Sexual Slavery,* New York: Avon.

Bartel, Diane (1985) 'Women's Educational Experience under Colonialism: Towards a Diachronic Model', *Signs,* vol. 11, no. 1, pp. 137–54.

Bebbington, Laurie (1975) 'The Mexico IWY Conference', *Meanjin Quarterly*, 34, December 1975, pp. 373–9.

Beechey, Veronica (1979) 'On Patriarchy', *Feminist Review*, no. 3, pp. 66–82.

Bell, Diane (1980) 'Desert Politics: Choices in the Marriage Market' in Mona Etienne and Eleanor Leacock (eds) *Women and Colonization*, New York: Praeger.

Bell, Diane and Ditton, Pam (1980) *Law: the Old and the New: Aboriginal Women in Central Australia Speak Out*, Canberra: Aboriginal History.

Bell, Diane (1983) *Daughters of the Dreaming*, Sydney: McPhee Gribble and George Allen & Unwin.

Beneria, Lourdes and Sen, Gita (1982) 'Class and Gender Inequalities and Women's Role in Economic Development – Theoretical and Practical Implications', *Feminist Studies*, vol. 8, no. 1, pp. 157–75.

Berg, Barbara J. (1979) *The Remembered Gate: Origins of American Feminism*, New York: Oxford University Press.

Berndt, Catherine H. (1983) 'Mythical Women Past and Present' in Faye Gale (ed.) *We are Bosses Ourselves: The Status and Role of Aboriginal Women Today*, Canberra: Australian Institute of Aboriginal Studies.

Bertell, Rosalie (1984) *No Immediate Danger: Diagnosis for a Radioactive Earth*, London: Women's Press.

Bhavnani, Kum-Kum and Coulson, Margaret (1986) 'Transforming Socialist-Feminism: The Challenge of Racism', *Feminist Review*, no. 23, pp. 81–92.

Black Women's Action Group (1987) 'Tribute Paid to Black Male Members of BWA', *Newsletter*, September, p. 3.

Bligh, Vivian (1983) 'A Study of the Needs of Aboriginal Women who have been Raped or Sexually Assaulted' in Faye Gale (ed.) *We are Bosses Ourselves: The Status and Role of Aboriginal Women Today*, Canberra: Australian Institute of Aboriginal Studies.

Bocquet-Siek, Margaret (1983) 'The Peranakan Chinese Women at a Crossroad' in Lenore Manderson (ed.) *Women's Work and Women's Roles: Economic and Everyday Life in Indonesia, Malaysia and Singapore*, Canberra: Development Studies Centre, Australia National University.

Boero, Patricia (1987) 'The Double Burden: A Woman and a Wog' in Jocelynne A. Scutt (ed.) *Different Lives: Reflections on the Women's Movement and Visions of its Future*, Ringwood: Penguin.

Borja, Carda (1984) 'Ecuador: Needed a Revolution in Attitude' in Robin Morgan (ed.) *Sisterhood is Global*, New York: Anchor Press/ Doubleday.

Boserup, Ester (1970) *Women's Role in Economic Development*, London: George Allen & Unwin.

Boserup, Ester (1975) *Integration of Women in Development: Why, When, How*, New York: United Nations Development Program.

Bourne, Jenny (1983) 'Towards an Anti-racist Feminism', *Race and Class*, vol. 25, no. 1, pp. 1–22.

Brekke, Torill (1985) 'The Family – Kenya' in Angela Davis et al. *Women: A World Report: A New Internationalist Book*, London: Methuen.

Brennar, Johanna and Ramas, Maria (1984) 'Rethinking Women's Oppression', *New Left Review*, no. 144, March–April, pp. 33–71.

Brown, Wilmette (1983) 'Roots: Black Ghetto Ecology' in Leonie Caldecott and Stephanie Leland (eds) *Reclaim the Earth: Women Speak Out for Life on Earth*, London: Women's Press.

Brownmiller, Susan (1975) *Against Our Will: Men, Women and Rape*, New York: Simon & Schuster.

Bryan, Beverley, Dadze, Stella and Scafe, Suzanne (1985) *The Heart of the Race: Black Women's Lives in Britain*, London: Virago.

Buirski, Jeannette (1983) 'How I Learned to Start Worrying and Hate the Bomb: the Effects of a Nuclear Bombardment' in Dorothy Thompson (ed.) *Over Our Dead Bodies: Women Against the Bomb*, London: Virago.

Bunch, Charlotte (1981) 'Comments on Tinker's "A Feminist View of Copehenhagen"', *Signs*, vol. 6, no. 4, pp. 787–90.

Burgmann, Meredith (1984) 'Black Sisterhood: the Situation of Urban Aboriginal Women and their Relationship to the White Women's Movement' in Marian Simms (ed.) *Australian Women and the Political System*, Melbourne: Longman Cheshire.

Bustos, Jorge Gissi (1980) 'Mythology about Women, with Special Reference to Chile' in June Nash and Helen Icken Safa (eds) *Sex and Class in Latin America*, Massachussetts: Bergin & Garvey.

Butalia, Urvashi (1985) 'Indian Women and the New Movement', *Women's Studies International Forum*, vol. 18, no. 2, pp. 131–4.

Cagalay, Nilüfer and Funk, Ursula (1981) 'Comments in Tinker's "A Feminist View of Copenhagen"', *Signs*, vol. 6, no. 4, pp. 776–8.

Caldecott, Leonie and Leland, Stephanie (1983) 'Introduction' in Leonie Caldecott and Stephanie Leland (eds) *Reclaim the Earth: Women Speak Out for Life on Earth*, London: Women's Press.

Caldwell, Lesley (1984) 'Feminism and "The Family"', *Feminist Review*, no. 16, April, pp. 88–97.

Cambridge Women's Peace Collective, The (ed.) (1983) *My Country is the Whole World: An Anthology of Women's Work on Peace and War*, London: Pandora.

Cameron, Anne (1983) *Daughters of Copper Women*, Vancouver: Press Gang Publishers.

Cameron, Barbara (1983) 'Gee, you don't seem like an Indian from the reservation' in Cherríe Moraga and Gloria Anzaldúa (eds) *This Bridge Called My Back*, New York: Kitchen Table, Women of Color Press.

Carby, Hazel V. (1982) 'White Woman Listen! Black Feminism and the Boundaries of Sisterhood' in Centre for Contemporary Studies, *The Empire Strikes Back: Race and Racism in 70s Britain*, London: Hutchinson.

Carmen et al. (1984) 'Becoming Visible: Black Lesbian Discussions', *Feminist Review*, no. 17, pp. 53–72.

Carter, Angela (1983) 'Anger in a Black Landscape' in Dorothy Thompson (ed.) *Over Our Dead Bodies: Women Against the Bomb*, London: Virago.

Chaney, Elsa M. and Schmink, Marianne (1980) 'Women and Modernization: Access to Tools' in June Nash and Helen Icker Safa, *Sex and Class in Latin America*, Massachusetts: Bergin & Garvey.

Christian, Barbara (1985a) *Black Feminist Criticism*, New York: Pergamon Press.

Christian, Barbara (1985b) 'Alice Walker: The Black Woman Artist as Wayward' in Mari Evans (ed.) *Black Women Writers (1950–1980) A Critical Evaluation*, New York: Anchor Press/Doubleday; London: Pluto Press.

Chrystos (1983) 'I don't understand those who have turned away from me' in Cherrie Moraga and Gloria Anzaldua (eds) *This Bridge Called My Back*, New York: Kitchen Table, Women of Color Press.

Clarke, Cheryl (1983) 'The Failure to Transform: Homophobia in the Black Community' in Barbara Smith (ed.) *Home Girls: A Black Feminist Anthology*, New York: Kitchen Table, Women of Color Press.

Cochrane, Susan H. (1982) 'Education and Fertility: an Expanded Examination of the Evidence', in Gail P. Kelly and Carolyn M. Elliott (eds) *Women's Education in the Third World: Comparative Perspectives*, Albany: State University of New York Press.

Cockburn, Cynthia (1983) *Brothers: Male Dominance and Technological Change*, London: Pluto Press.

Coleman, Wanda and Bell, Jeanie (1986) 'An Interview', *Hecate*, vol. 12, nos. 1–2, pp. 64–75.

Collier, Eugenia (1985) 'The Closing of the Circle: Movement from Division to Wholeness in Paule Marshall's Fiction' in Mari Evans (ed.) *Black Women Writers (1950–1980) A Critical Evaluation*, New York: Anchor Press/Doubleday; London: Pluto Press.

Collier, Jane F. and Rosaldo, Michelle Z. (1981) 'Politics and Gender in Simple Societies' in Sherry Ortner and Harriet Whitehead, *Sexual Meanings: The Cultural Construction of Gender and Sexuality*, Cambridge: Cambridge University Press.

Combahee River Collective (1983) 'A Black Feminist Statement' in Cherríe Moraga and Gloria Anzaldúa (eds), *This Bridge Called My Back*, New York: Kitchen Table, Women of Color Press.

Connolly, Clara et al. (1986) 'Feminism and Class Politics: A Round-Table Discussion', *Feminist Review*, no. 23, pp. 13–29.

Connor, Linda H. (1983) 'Healing as Women's Work in Bali' in Lenore Manderson (ed.) *Women's Work and Women's Roles: Economic and Everyday Life in Indonesia, Malaysia and Singapore*, Canberra: Development Studies Centre, Australian National University.

Cook, Alice and Kirk, Gwyn (1985) *Greenham Women Everywhere: Dreams, Ideas and Actions from the Women's Peace Movement*, London: Pluto Press.

Coward, Rosalind (1981) 'Socialism, Feminism and Socialist Feminism', in Feminist Anthology Collective (eds) *No Turning Back: Writings from the Women's Liberation Movement 1975–80*, London: Women's Press.

Coward, Rosalind (1983) *Patriarchal Precedents: Sexuality and Social Relations*, London: Routledge & Kegan Paul.

Croll, Elisabeth (1978) *Feminism and Socialism in China*, London: Routledge & Kegan Paul.

Crompton, Rosemary and Mann, Michael (1986) 'Introduction' in Rosemary Crompton and Michael Mann (eds) *Gender and Stratification*, Oxford: Polity Press.

Cutrufelli, Maria Rosa (1983) *Women of Africa. Roots of Oppression*, London: Zed Books Ltd.

Daly, Mary (1978) *Gyn/Ecology: The Metaethics of Radical Feminism*, London: Women's Press.

davenport, doris (1983) 'The Pathology of Racism: a Conversation with Third World Women' in Cherríe Moraga and Gloria Anzaldúa (eds) *This Bridge Called My Back*, New York: Kitchen Table, Women of Color Press.

Davies, Miranda (1983) 'Preface' in Miranda Davies (compiler), *Third World Second Sex: Women's Struggles and National Liberation*, London: Zed Books Ltd.

Davis, Angela (1981) *Women, Race and Class*, London: Women's Press.

Davis, Angela et al. (1985) *Women: A World Report: A New Internationalist Book*, Methuen: London.

Delphy, Christine and Leonard, Diana (1986) 'Class Analysis, Gender

Analysis, and the Family' in Rosemary Crompton and Michael Mann (eds) *Gender and Stratification*, Oxford: Polity Press.

Deutsch, Sarah (1987) 'Women and International Relations: The Case of Hispanic New Mexico and Colorado', *Signs*, vol. 12, no. 4, Summer, pp. 719–39.

Dill, Bonnie Thornton (1983) 'Race, Class and Gender: Prospects for an All-Inclusive Sisterhood', *Feminist Studies*, vol. 9, no. 1, pp. 131–50.

Dixon, Ruth B. (1978) *Rural Women at Work: Strategies for Development in South Asia*, Baltimore: Johns Hopkins Press.

Dodge, Norton T. (1966) *Women in the Soviet Economy*, Westport, Connecticut: Greenwood Press.

Dowse, Sara and Giles, Patricia (1984) 'Australia: Women in a Warrior Society' in Robin Morgan (ed.) *Sisterhood is Global*, New York: Anchor Press/Doubleday.

Dubois, Ellen Carol (1978) *Feminism and Suffrage: the Emergence of an Independent Women's Movement in America 1848–1869*, Ithaca: Cornell University Press.

Dubois, Ellen (1980) 'Politics and Culture in Women's History: A Symposium', *Feminist Studies*, vol. 6, no. 1, pp. 28–36.

Dworkin, Susan (1985) 'The Making of *The Color Purple*', *Ms*, December, pp. 66–70; 94–5.

Eatock, Pat (1987) 'There's a Snake in My Caravan' in Jocelynne A. Scutt (ed.) *Different Lives: Reflections on the Women's Movement and Visions of its Future*, Ringwood: Penguin.

Eisenstein, Hester (1984) *Contemporary Feminist Thought*, London: Unwin.

Eisenstein, Zillah (1979a) 'Developing a Theory of Capitalist Patriarchy and Socialist Feminism' in Zillah Eisenstein (ed.) *Capitalist Patriarchy and Socialist Feminism*, New York: Monthly Review Press.

Eisenstein, Zillah (1979b) 'Some Notes on the Relations of "Capitalist Patriarchy"' in Zillah Eisenstein (ed.) *Capitalist Patriarchy and Socialist Feminism*, New York: Monthly Review Press.

Ehrlich, Carol (1981) 'The Unhappy Marriage of Marxism and Feminism: Can it be Saved?' in Lydia Sargent (ed.) *Women and Revolution: A Discussion of the Unhappy Marriage of Marxism and Feminism*, Boston: South End Press.

El Dareer, Asma (1982) *Women, Why do you Weep?*, London: Zed Books Ltd.

El Saadawi, Nawal (1980) *The Hidden Face of Eve: Women in the Arab World*, London: Zed Press.

Elson, Diane and Pearson, Ruth (1981) 'The Subordination of Women and the Internationalisation of Factory Production', in Kate Young, Carol Wolkowitz and Roslyn McCullagh (eds), *Of Marriage and the Market: Women's Subordination in International Perspective*, London: CSE Books.

Engel, Barbara Alporn (1984) 'Introduction: Feminism and the Non-Western World', *Frontiers*, vol. 7, no. 2, pp. 1–3.

Engels, Frederick (1972) *The Origin of the Family, Private Property and the State*, New York: International Publishers.

Enloe, Cynthia (1983a) *Does Khaki Become You? The Militarization of Women's Lives*, London: Pluto Press.

Enloe, Cynthia (1983b) 'We Are What We Wear: the Dilemma of the Feminist Consumer' in Wendy Chapkis and Cynthia Enloe (eds) *Of Common Cloth: Women in the Transnational Textile Industry*, Amsterdam: Transnational Institute.

Evans, Mari (ed.) (1984) *Black Women Writers (1950–1980) A Critical Evaluation*, New York: Anchor Press/Doubleday.

Fauset, Jessie Redman (1928) *Plumball*, repr. London: Routledge & Kegan Paul, 1985.

Feuchtwang, Stephen (1980) 'Socialist, Feminist and Anti-racist Struggles', *m/f: A Feminist Journal*, no. 4, pp. 41–56.

Firestone, Shulamith (1972) *The Dialectic of Sex: The Case for Feminist Revolution*, London: Paladin.

Flax, Jane (1987) 'Postmodernism and Gender Relations in Feminist Theory', *Signs*, vol. 12, no. 4, pp. 621–43.

Freer, Jean (1983) 'Gaea: the Earth as our Spiritual Heritage' in Leonie Caldecott and Stephanie Leland (eds) *Reclaim the Earth: Women Speak out for Life on Earth*, London: Women's Press.

French, Marilyn (1985) *Beyond Power: Women, Men and Morals*, London: Jonathan Cape.

Frye, Marilyn (1983) *The Politics of Reality: Essays in Feminist Theory*, New York: Crossing Press.

Galdamez, Miriam (1983) 'Women's Lives in El Salvador' in Miranda Davies (compiler) *Third World Second Sex: Women's Struggles and National Liberation*, London: Zed Books Ltd.

Gale, Faye (ed.) (1983) *We are Bosses Ourselves: The Status and Role of Aboriginal Women Today*, Canberra: Australian Institute of Aboriginal Studies.

Game, Ann and Pringle, Rosemary (1983) *Gender at Work*, Sydney: George Allen & Unwin.

Gardner Susan (1985) 'Is Racism "Sexism Extended?". Feminist Criticism, "Moral Panics" and *The Grass is Singing*', *Hecate*, vol. 11, no. 1, pp. 75–97.

Gardner, Susan (1986) '"Don't Ask for the True Story": A Memoir of Bessie Head', *Hecate*, vol. 12, Nos.1–2, pp. 110–29.

Ghoussoub, Mai (1986) 'Feminism – or the Eternal Masculine – in the Arab World', *New Left Review*, no. 161, pp. 3–19.

Giddings, Paula (1984) *When and Where I Enter: The Impact of Black Women On Race and Sex in America*, Toronto: Bantam.

Giele, Janet Zollinger (1977) 'Introduction' in Janet Zollinger Giele and Audrey Chapman Smock (eds) *Women's Roles and Status in Eight Countries*, New York: John Wiley & Sons.

Giles, Patricia (1985) 'Nairobi Conference: the End of a Decade', *Australian Feminist Studies*, no. 1, Summer, pp. 111–16.

Goonatilake, Hema (1984) 'Sri Lanka: the Voice of Women', in Robin Morgan (ed.) *Sisterhood is Global*, New York: Anchor Press/Doubleday.

Goonatilake, Hema (1985) 'The Impact of the Women's Decade in Women of Sri Lanka', *Women's Studies International Forum*, vol. 8, no. 2, pp. 127–30.

Greer, Germaine (1985) 'Politics – Cuba' in Angela Davis et al. *Women: A World Report: A New Internationalist Book*, London: Methuen.

Griffen, Vanessa (1984) 'The Pacific Islands: All it Requires is Ourselves', in Robin Morgan (ed.) *Sisterhood is Global*, New York: Anchor Press/Doubleday.

Griffin, Susan (1983) 'Foreword' in Leonie Caldecott and Stephanie Leland (eds) *Reclaim the Earth: Women Speak out for Life on Earth*, London: Women's Press.

Gross, Elizabeth (1986) 'What is Feminist Theory?' in Carole Pateman and Elizabeth Gross (eds) *Feminist Challenges*, Sydney: George Allen & Unwin.

Gunew, Sneja and Spivak, Gayatri Chakrovorty (1986) 'Questions of Multiculturalism', *Hecate*, vol. 12, nos. 1–2, pp. 136–42.

Gupta, Sanjukta (1985) 'An interview with Nabaneeta Deb-Sen' in Mineke Schipper (ed.) *Unheard Words: Women and Literature in Africa, the Arab World, Asia, the Caribbean and Latin America*, London: Allison & Busby.

Hall, Jacquelyn Dowd (1983) 'The Mind that Burns in each Body: Women, Rape and Racial Violence' in Ann Snitow, Christine Stansell and Sharon Thompson (eds) *Desire: The Politics of Sexuality*, London: Virago.

Hancock, Mary (1983) 'Transnational Production and Women Workers' in Annie Phizacklea (ed.) *One Way Ticket: Migration and Female Labour*, London: Routledge & Kegan Paul.

Hamilton, Cicely (1981) *Marriage as a Trade*, London: Women's Press.

Harding, Sandra (1986) 'The Instability of Analytical Categories of

Feminist Theory', *Signs*, vol. 11, no. 4, pp. 645–64.

Harford, Barbara and Hopkins, Sarah (1985) *Greenham Common: Women at the Wire*, London: Women's Press.

Hartmann, Heidi (1981) 'The Unhappy Marriage of Marxism and Feminism: Towards a More Progressive Union' in Lydia Sargent (ed.) *Women and Revolution: A Discussion of the Unhappy Marriage of Marxism and Feminism*, Boston: South End Press.

Hartsock, Nancy C.M. (1985) *Money, Sex and Power: Toward a Feminist Historical Materialism*, Boston: North Eastern University Press, first published 1983.

Heitlinger, Alena (1985) 'Women in Eastern Europe: Survey of Literature', *Women's Studies International Forum*, vol. 8, no. 2, pp. 147–52.

Hellwig, Tineke (1984) 'South-east Asia' in Mineke Schipper (ed.) *Unheard Words: Women and Literature in Africa, the Arab World, Asia, the Caribbean and Latin America*, London: Allison & Busby.

Henderson, Hazel (1983) 'The Warp and the Weft. The Coming Synthesis of Eco-philosophy and Eco-feminism' in Leonie Caldecott and Stephanie Leland (eds) *Reclaim the Earth: Women Speak Out for Life on Earth*, London: Women's Press.

Hendessi, Mandana (1986) 'Fourteen Thousand Women Meet: Report from Nairobi, July 1985', *Feminist Review*, no. 23, pp. 147–56.

Hewlett, Sylvia Ann (1987) *A Lesser Life: The Myth of Women's Liberation*, London: Michael Joseph.

Hooks, Bell (1981) *Ain't I a Woman: Black Women and Feminism*, Boston: South End Press.

Hooks, Bell (1984) *Feminist Theory from Margin to Center*, Boston: South End Press.

Hooks, Bell (1986) 'Sisterhood: Political Solidarity Between Women', *Feminist Review*, no. 23, pp. 125–38.

van Houwelingen, Flora (1985) 'Francophone Literature in North Africa' in Mineke Schipper (ed.) *Unheard Words: Women and Literature in Africa, the Arab World, Asia, the Caribbean and Latin America*, London: Allison & Busby.

Hoskyns, Catherine (1985) 'Women's Equality and the European Community', *Feminist Review*, no. 20, pp. 71–88.

Hughes, Psiche (1985) 'Women and Literature in Latin America' in Mineke Schipper (ed.) *Unheard Words: Women and Literature in Africa, the Arab World, Asia, the Caribbean and Latin America*, London: Allison & Busby.

Hull, Gloria T., Scott, Bell and Smith, Barbara (eds) (1982) *All the Women are White, All the Blacks are Men, But Some of Us are Brave*, New York: The Feminist Press.

Izraeli, Dafa N. (1981) 'Comments on Tinker's "A Feminist View of Copenhagen"', *Signs*, vol. 6, no. 4, pp. 783–4.

Jackson, R. Gordon (1984) Report of the Committee to Review the Australian Overseas Aid Program, Canberra: Australian Government Publishing Service.

Jaggar, Alison M. (1983) *Feminist Politics and Human Nature*, New Jersey: Rowman & Allanheld.

Jain, Devaki (1984) 'India: a Condition across Class and Caste' in Morgan, Robin (ed.) *Sisterhood is Global*, New York: Anchor Press/Doubleday.

Jayawardena, Kumari (1986) *Feminism and Nationalism in the Third World*, London: Zed Books Ltd.

Jeffery, Patricia (1979) *Frogs in a Well: Indian Women in Purdah*, London: Zed Books Ltd.

Jeffreys, Sheila (1985) *The Spinster and her Enemies: Feminism and Sexuality* 1880–1930, London: Pandora.

Jennett, Christine (1987) 'The Feminist Enterprise' in Christine Jennett and Randall G. Stewart (eds) *Three Worlds of Inequality: Race, Class and Gender*, Melbourne: Macmillan.

Johnson, Diane (1979) 'Aspects of the Legal Status of Women in Papua New Guinea: a Working Paper', *Melanesian Law Journal*, vol. 7, no. 1, pp. 5–81.

Johnson, Diane (1984) 'Gender and Ideology: Women in the Papua New Guinea Bureaucracy', *Refractory Girl*, May, pp. 34–7.

Johnson, Elizabeth L. (1984) 'Hakka Women', in Mary Sheridan and Janet W. Salaff, *Lives: Chinese Working Women*, Bloomington: Indiana University Press.

Jones, Lynne (1983) *Keeping the Peace*, London: Women's Press.

Joseph, Gloria (1981) 'The Incompatible Menage A Trois: Marxism, Feminism and Racism' in Lydia Sargent (ed.) *Women and Revolution: A Discussion of the Unhappy Marriage of Marxism and Feminism*, Boston: South End Press.

Kaplan, Cora (1986) *Sea Changes: Culture and Feminism*, London: Verso.

Kappeler, Suzanne (1986) *The Pornography of Representation*, Oxford: Polity Press.

Kelly, Gail P. and Elliott, Carolyn (1982) *Women's Education in the Third World: Comparative Perspectives*, Albany: State University of New York.

Kilpatrick, Hilary (1985) 'The Arab East' in Mineke Schipper (ed.) *Unheard Words: Women and Literature in Africa, the Arab World, Asia, the Caribbean and Latin America*, London: Allison & Busby.

Kimble, Judy (1981) 'The Struggle within the Struggle', *Feminist*

Review, no. 8, p. 107–11.

Kimble, Judy and Unterhalter, Elaine (1982) '"We opened the road for you, you must go forward": ANC Women's Struggles, 1912–1982', *Feminist Review*, no. 2, pp. 11–35.

Körösi, Suzanne (1984) 'Hungary: the non-existence of "Women's Emancipation"' in Robin Morgan (ed.) *Sisterhood is Global*, New York: Anchor Press/Doubleday.

Kuhn, Annette (1978) 'Structures of Patriarchy and Capital in the Family' in Annette Kuhn and Ann Marie Wolpe (eds) *Feminism and Materialism*, London: Routledge & Kegan Paul.

Kuhn, Annette and Wolpe, Ann Marie (1978) 'Feminism and Materialism' in Annette Kuhn and Ann Marie Wolpe (eds) *Feminism and Materialism*, London: Routledge & Kegan Paul.

Kung, Lydia (1984) 'Taiwan garment workers', in Mary Sheridan and Janet W. Salaff, *Lives: Chinese Working Women*, Bloomington: Indiana University Press.

La Silenciada (1984) 'Cuba: Paradise Gained, Paradise Lost – the Price of "Integration"' in Robin Morgan (ed.) *Sisterhood is Global*, New York: Anchor Press/Doubleday.

Lees, Sue (1986) 'Sex, Race and Culture: Feminism and the Limits of Cultural Pluralism', *Feminist Review*, no. 22, pp. 92–102.

Leghorn, Lisa and Parker, Catherine (1981) *Woman's Worth: Sexual Economics and the World of Women*, Boston: Routledge & Kegan Paul.

Levy, Bronwen (1984) 'Sisterhood in Trouble: The Fourth Women and Labour Conference, Brisbane 1984', *Hecate*, vol. 10, no. 2, pp. 105–9.

Lewis, Shelby (1985) 'The Meaning and Effects of the U.N. Decade for Women on Black Women in America', *Women's Studies International Forum*, vol. 8, no. 2, pp. 117–20.

Lipman, Beata (1984) *We Make Freedom: Women in South Africa*, London: Pandora.

Lockwood, David (1986) 'Class, Status and Gender' in Rosemary Crompton and Michael Mann (eds) *Gender and Stratification*, Oxford: Polity Press.

London Iranian Women's Liberation Group (1983) 'Iranian Women: the Struggle since the Revolution' in Miranda Davies (compiler) *Third World Second Sex: Women's Struggles and National Liberation*, London: Zed Books.

Lorde, Audre (1983) 'An Open Letter to Mary Daly' in Cherríe Moraga and Gloria Anzaldúa (eds) *This Bridge Called My Back. Writings by Radical Women of Color*, New York: Kitchen Table, Women of Color Press.

Lorde, Audre (1984) *Sister Outsider*, New York: Crossing Press.

McCluskey (jr.), John (1985) 'And Called Every Generation Blessed: Theme, Setting and Ritual in the Words of Paule Marshall' in Mari Evans (ed.) *Black Women Writers (1950–1980) A Critical Evaluation*, New York: Anchor Press/Doubleday; London: Pluto Press.

McDinny, Eileen and Isaac, Annie (1983) 'Borroloola Community and Land Rights' in Faye Gale (ed.) *We are Bosses Ourselves: The Status and Role of Aboriginal Women Today*, Canberra: Australian Institute of Aboriginal Studies.

McDonagh, Celia (1985) 'The Women's Peace Movement in Britain', *Frontiers*, vol. 8, no. 2 (Special Issue: Women and Peace).

McDonough, Roison and Harrison, Rachel (1978) 'Patriarchy and Relations of Production' in Annette Kuhn and Ann Marie Wolpe (eds) *Feminism and Materialism*, London: Routledge and Kegan Paul.

McIntosh, Mary (1981) 'Comments on Tinker's "A Feminist View of Copenhagen"', *Signs*, vol. 6, no. 4, pp. 771–5.

MacKinnon, Catharine A. (1982) 'Feminism, Marxism, Method and the State: An Agenda for Theory' in Nannerl O. Keohane et al. (eds) *Feminist Theory: A Critique of Ideology*, Brighton: Harvester Press.

McRae, Heather (1980) 'Laws Relating to Fertility Control and Family Planning in Papua New Guinea', *Melanesian Law Journal*, vol. 8, no. 1, pp. 5–53.

MacCormack, Carol P. and Strathern, Marilyn (eds) (1980) *Nature, Culture and Gender*, Cambridge: Cambridge University Press.

Maher, Vanessa (1981) 'Work, Consumption and Authority within the Household: a Moroccan Case' in Kate Young, Carol Wolkowitz and Roslyn McCullagh (eds) *Of Marriage and the Market: Women's Subordination in International Perspective*, London: CSE Books.

Mama, Amina (1984) 'Black Women, the Economic Crisis and the British State', *Feminist Review*, no. 17, Autumn, pp. 21–36.

Mamonova, Tatyana (1984) 'The Union of Soviet Socialist Republics: It's Time we Began with Ourselves' in Robin Morgan (ed.) *Sisterhood is Global*, New York: Anchor Press/Doubleday.

Manderson, Lenore (1983) 'Introduction' in Lenore Manderson (ed.) *Women's Work and Women's Roles: Economics and Everyday Life in Indonesia, Malaysia and Singapore*, Canberra: Development Studies Centre, Australian National University.

Mann, Michael (1986) 'A Crisis in Stratification Theory? Persons, Households/Families/Lineages, Genders, Classes and Nations' in Rosemary Crompton and Michael Mann (eds) *Gender and Stratification*, Oxford: Polity Press.

Mansueto, Connie (1983) 'Take the Toys from the Boys: Competition and the Nuclear Arms Race' in Dorothy Thompson (ed.) *Over our Dead*

Bodies: Women Against the Bomb, London: Virago.

Manushi (1983) 'Indian Women Speak Out against Dowry' in Miranda Davies (compiler) *Third World Second Sex: Women's Struggles and National Liberation*, London: Zed Books Ltd.

Marshall, Paula (1983) *Praisesong for the Widow*, London: Virago.

Martin, Joan (1984) 'The Unicorn is Black: Audre Lorde in Retrospect' in Mari Evans (ed.) *Black Women Writers (1950–1980) A Critical Evaluation*, New York: Anchor Press/Doubleday; London: Pluto Press.

Mbilinyi, Marjorie (1984) 'Research Priorities in Women's Studies in Eastern Africa', *Women's Studies International Forum*, vol. 7, no. 4, pp. 289–300.

Mernissi, Fatima (1984) 'Morocco: the Merchant's Daughter and the Son of the Sultan' in Robin Morgan (ed.) *Sisterhood is Global*, New York: Anchor Press/Doubleday.

Minh-ha, Trinh T. (1987) 'Difference: "A Special Third World Women Issue"', *Feminist Review*, no. 25, pp. 5–22.

Mirza, Heidi Safia (1986) 'The Dilemma of Socialist Feminism: A Case for Black Feminism', *Feminist Review*, no. 22, pp. 103–5.

Molyneux, Maxine (1981) 'Women in Socialist Societies: Problems of Theory and Practice' in Kate Young, Carol Walkowitz and Roslyn McCullagh (eds) *Of Marriage and the Market: Women's Subordination in International Perspective*, London: CSE Books.

Molyneux, Maxine (1985) 'Mobilization Without Emancipation? Women's Interests, The State, and Revolution in Nicaragua', *Feminist Studies*, vol. 11, no. 2, pp. 227–54.

Moraga, Cherríe and Anzaldúa, Gloria (eds) (1983) *This Bridge Called My Back*, New York: Kitchen Table, Women of Color Press.

Moraga, Cherríe (1983) 'Foreword to the second edition', in Cherríe Moraga and Gloria Anzaldúa (eds) *This Bridge Called My Back*, New York: Kitchen Table, Women of Color Press.

Morgan, Elaine (1972) *The Descent of Woman*, London: Souvenir Press.

Morgan, Robin (ed.) (1970) *Sisterhood is Powerful*, New York: Vintage.

Morgan, Robin (1984) 'Introduction: Planetary Feminism: the Politics of the 21st Century' in Robin Morgan (ed.) *Sisterhood is Global*, New York: Anchor Press/Doubleday.

Moschkovich, Judit (1983) '– But I Know You American Woman' in Cherríe Moraga and Gloria Anzaldúa (eds) *This Bridge Called My Back*, New York: Kitchen Table, Women of Color Press.

Moshen, Aisha and Ba'Abad, Noor (1983) 'Building a New Life for Women in South Yemen' in Miranda Davies (compiler) *Third World Second Sex: Women's Struggles and National Liberation*, London: Zed Books Ltd.

Nash, June and Safa, Helen Icken, 'Introduction' in June Nash and Helen Icken Safa (eds) *Sex and Class in Latin America*, Massachusetts: Bergin & Garvey.

Nazzari, Muriel (1983) 'The "Woman Question" in Cuba: An Analysis of Material Constraints on its Solution', *Signs*, vol. 9, no. 2, pp. 246–63.

Newby, Liza (1987) 'A Sense of Place' in Jocelynne A. Scutt (ed) *Different Lives: Reflections on the Women's Movement and Visions of its Future*, Ringwood: Penguin.

Nemiroff, Greta Hofmann (1984) 'Canada: the Empowerment of Women' in Robin Morgan (ed.) *Sisterhood is Global*, New York: Anchor Press/ Doubleday.

Nyasha and Rose (1984) 'Four Years of Armed Struggle in Zimbabwe' in Miranda Davies (compiler) *Third World Second Sex: Women's Struggles and National Liberation*, London: Zed Books Ltd.

Oakley, Ann (1981) *Subject Women*, Oxford: Martin Robertson.

Obbo, Christine (1980) *African Women: Their Struggle for Economic Independence*, London: Zed Books Ltd.

O'Brien, Mary (1981) *The Politics of Reproduction*, Boston: Routledge & Kegan Paul.

Ogundipe-Leslie, Molara (1984) 'Nigeria: not Spinning on the Axis of Maleness' in Robin Morgan (ed.) *Sisterhood is Global*, New York: Anchor Press/Doubleday.

Ogunyemi, Chikwenge Okanja (1985) 'Womanism: the Dynamics of the Contemporary Black Female Novel in English', *Signs*, vol. 11, no. 1, pp. 63–80.

O'Lincoln, Tom (1984) 'What's Wrong with "Disarmament Feminism"', *Hecate*, vol. X, no. 1, pp. 86–97.

O'Neale, Sandra (1984) 'Reconstruction of the Composite Self: New Images of Black Women in Maya Angelou's Continuing Autobiography', in Mari Evans (ed.) *Black Women Writers (1950–1980) A Critical Evaluation*, New York: Anchor Press/Doubleday; London: Pluto Press.

Ortner, Sherry (1974) 'Is Female to Male as Nature is to Culture?' in Michelle Rosaldo (ed.) *Woman Culture and Society*, Stanford: Stanford University Press.

Ortner, Sherry and Whitehead, Harriet (eds) (1981) *Sexual Meanings: The Social Construction of Gender and Sexuality*, Cambridge: Cambridge University Press.

O'Shane, Pat (1976) 'Is there any Relevance in the Women's Movement for Aboriginal Women?', *Refractory Girl*, September, pp. 31–4.

OWAARD, (1981) 'Black Women and Health' in Feminist Anthology Collective (eds) *No Turning Back: Writings from the Women's Liberation Movement 1975–80*, London: Women's Press.

Palmer, Phyllis Marynick (1983) 'White Women/Black Women: The Dualism of Female Identity and Experience in the United States', *Feminist Studies*, vol. 9, no. 1, pp. 151–70.

Papanek, Hanna (1975) 'The Work of Women: Postscript from Mexico City', *Signs*, vol. 1, no. 1, Autumn, pp. 215–26.

Parker-Smith, Bettye J. (1985) 'Alice Walker's Women: in Search of Some Peace of Mind' in Mari Evans (ed.) *Black Women Writers (1950–1980) A Critical Evaluation*, New York: Anchor Press/Doubleday; London: Pluto Press.

Parmar, Pratibha (1982) 'Gender Race and Class: Asian Women in Resistance' in Centre for Contemporary Cultural Studies, *The Empire Strikes Back: Race and Racism in 70s Britain*, London: Hutchinson.

Patel, Vibhati (1985) 'Women's Liberation in India', *New Left Review*, no. 153, September/October, pp. 75–86.

Petchesky, Rosalind Pollack (1986) *Abortion and Woman's Choice: The State, Sexuality and Reproductive Freedom*, London: Verso.

Phaf, Ineke (1985) 'Women and Literature in the Caribbean', in Mineke Schipper (ed.) *Unheard Words: Women and Literature in Africa, the Arab World, Asia, the Caribbean and Latin America*, London: Allison & Busby.

Phillips, Anne (1981) 'Marxism and Feminism' in Feminist Anthology Collective (eds) *No Turning Back: Writings from the Women's Liberation Movement 1975–80*, London: Women's Press.

Phizacklea, Annie (1983) 'Introduction' in Annie Phizacklea (ed.) *One Way Ticket: Migration and Female Labour*, London: Routledge & Kegan Paul.

Picard, Andre (1986) 'Of JR and Condoms', *New Internationalist*, no. 156, February, p. 3.

Prado, Danda (1984) 'Brazil: a Fertile but Ambiguous Feminist Terrain' in Robin Morgan (ed.) *Sisterhood is Global*, New York: Anchor Press/Doubleday.

Price, Susanna (1983) 'Rich Woman, Poor Woman: Occupation Differences in a Textile Producing Village in Central Java' in Lenore Manderson (ed.) *Women's Work and Women's Roles: Economics and Everyday Life in Indonesia, Malaysia and Singapore*, Canberra: Development Studies Centre, Australian National University.

Pringle, Rosemary (1983) 'Rape: the Other Side of Anzac Day', *Refractory Girl*, no. 26, June, pp. 31–5.

Quintanales, Mirtha (1983) 'I Paid very Hard for my Immigrant "Ignorance"' in Cherríe Moraga and Gloria Anzaldúa (eds) *This Bridge Called My Back*, New York: Kitchen Table, Women of Color Press.

Radl, Shirley Rogers (1983) *The Invisible Women: Target of the Religious Right*, Laurence: Delta.

Reagon, Bernice Johnson (1984) 'Coalition Politics: Turning the Century' in Barbara Smith (ed.) *Home Girls: A Black Feminist Anthology*, New York: Kitchen Table, Women of Color Press.

Reid, Elizabeth (1975) 'The World Conference for International Women's Year, Mexico, 19 June–2 July, 1975', *Dyason Home Papers*, no. 2, August, pp. 3–5.

Rendall, Jane (1985) *The Origins of Modern Feminism: Women in Britain, France and the United States, 1780–1860*, London: Macmillan.

Rich, Adrienne (1984) *On Lies, Secrets and Silence: Selected Prose 1966–1978*, London: Virago.

Riley, Joan (1985) *The Unbelonging*, London: Women's Press.

Rhys, Jean (1966) *Wide Sargasso Sea*, Harmondsworth: Penguin.

Robinson, Kathy (1983) 'Women and Work in an Indonesian Mining Town' in Leonore Manderson (ed.) *Women's Work and Women's Roles: Economics and Everyday Life in Indonesia, Malaysia and Singapore*, Canberra: Development Studies Centre, Australian National University.

Rodriguez, Anabella (1983) 'Mozambican Women after the Revolution' in Miranda Davies (compiler) *Third World Second Sex: Women's Struggles and National Liberation*, London: Zed Books Ltd.

Rogers, Barbara (1980) *The Domestication of Women: Discrimination in Developing Societies*, London: Kogan Page.

Romain, Patsy (1983) 'Women in New Grenada' in Miranda Davies (compiler) *Third World Second Sex: Women's Struggles and National Liberation*, London: Zed Books Ltd.

Romalis, Coleman and Romalis, Shelly (1983) 'Sexism, Racism and Technological Change: Two Cases of Minority Protest', *International Journal of Women's Studies*, vol. 6, no. 3, pp. 270–87.

Rosaldo, Michelle Zimbalist (1980) 'The Use and Abuse of Anthropology: Reflections on Feminism and Cross-cultural Understanding', *Signs*, vol. 5, no. 3, pp. 389–417.

Rossi, Christina Peri (1984) 'Interview with Cristina Peni Rossi by Psiche Hughes' in Mineke Schipper (ed.) *Unheard Words: Women and Literature in Africa, The Arab World, Asia, the Carribbean and Latin America*, London: Allison & Busby.

Rowbotham, Sheila (1981) 'The Trouble with "Patriarchy"' in Feminist Anthology Collective (eds) *No Turning Back: Writings from the Women's Liberation Movement 1975–80*, London: Women's Press.

Rowbotham, Sheila (1985) 'What do Women Want? Women-Centred Values and the World as it is', *Feminist Review*, no. 20, pp. 49–69.

Rubin, Gayle (1975) 'The Traffic in Women: Notes on the "Political Economy" of Sex' in Rayna R. Reiter (ed.) *Towards an Anthropology of Women*, New York: Monthly Review Press.

Ruddick, Sara (1983) 'Pacifying the Forces: Drafting Women in the Interests of Peace', *Signs*, vol. 8, no. 3, pp. 471–89.

Russell, Dora (1983) 'Foreword' to Lynne Jones, *Keeping the Peace*, London: Women's Press.

Russell, Diana E.H. and Van de Ven, Nicole (1976) *Crimes Against Women: Proceedings of the International Tribunal*, Millbrae, California: Les Femmes.

Russell, Joan (1987) 'I am a daughter, I am a mother, I am a woman, I am a feminist', in Jocelynne A. Scutt (ed.) *Different Lives: Reflections on the Women's Movement and Visions of its Future*, Ringwood: Penguin.

Ryan, Julia (1985) 'Nairobi Conference: Letter to Pamela in India', *Australian Feminist Studies*, no. 1, Summer, pp. 116–22.

Sachs, Albie (1978) 'The Myth of Male Protectiveness and the Legal Subordination of Women' in Carol Smart and Barry Smart (eds) *Women, Sexuality and Social Control*, London: Routledge & Kegan Paul.

Sadoff, Dianne F. (1985) 'Black Matrilineage: the Case of Alice Walker and Zora Neale Hurston', *Signs*, vol. 11, no. 1, pp. 4–26.

Safa, Helen I. (1980) 'Class Consciousness among Working Class Women in Latin America: Puerto Rico' in June Nash and Helen Icken Safa (eds) *Sex and Class in Latin America*, Massachusetts: Bergin & Garvey.

Said, Edward W. (1985) 'Orientalism Reconsidered', *Cultural Critique*, vol. 1, Fall, pp. 89–107.

Salaff, Janet W. (1984) 'Wage Earners in Hong Kong' in Mary Sheridan and Janet W. Salaff, Lives: *Chinese Working Women*, Bloomington: Indiana University Press.

Salazar, Gloria Gonzalez (1980) 'Participation of Women in the Mexican Labor Force' in June Nash and Helen Icken Safa (eds) *Sex and Class in Latin America*, Massachusetts: Bergin & Garvey.

Sankar, Andrea (1984) 'Spinster Sisterhoods' in Mary Sheridan and Janet W. Salaff, Lives: *Chinese Working Women*, Bloomington: Indiana University Press.

Sargent, Lydia (1981) 'New Left Women and Men: The Honeymoon is Over' in Lydia Sargent (ed.) *Women and Revolution: A Discussion of the Unhappy Marriage of Marxism and Feminism*, Boston: South End Press.

Schipper, Mineke (1985) 'Women and Literature in Africa' in Mineke Schipper (ed.) *Unheard Words: Women and Literature in Africa, the*

Arab World, Asia, the Caribbean and Latin America, London: Allison & Busby.

Schreiner, Olive (1978) *Woman and Labour*, London: Virago.

Seidman, Gay W. (1984) 'Women in Zimbabwe: Post-independence Struggles', *Feminist Studies*, vol. 10, no. 3, pp. 419–40.

Segal, Lynne (1987) *Is the Future Female? Troubled Thoughts on Contemporary Feminism*, London: Virago.

Sharara, Yolla Polity (1983) 'Women and Politics in Lebanon' in Miranda Davies (compiler) *Third World Second Sex: Women's Struggles and National Liberation*, London: Zed Books Ltd.

Sharma, Ursula (1980) *Women, Work and Property in North West India*, London: Tavistock.

Sheridan, Mary (1984) 'Contemporary Generations' in Mary Sheridan and Janet W. Salaff, *Lives: Chinese Working Women*, Bloomington: Indiana University Press.

Sheridan, Mary and Salaff, Janet W. (1984) 'Conclusion' in Mary Sheridan and Janet W. Salaff, *Lives: Chinese Working Women*, Bloomington: Indiana University Press.

Sipila, Helvi (1975) *Meeting in Mexico: The Story of the World Conference of the International Women's Year*, New York: United Nations.

Smith, Barbara (1983) 'Introduction' in Barbara Smith (ed.) *Home Girls: A Black Feminist Anthology*, New York: Kitchen Table, Women of Color Press.

Smith, Barbara (1985) 'Toward a Black Feminist Criticism' in Judith Newton and Deborah Rosenfelt (eds) *Feminist Criticism and Social Change*, New York: Methuen.

Smith-Rosenberg, Carroll (1980) 'Politics and Culture in Women's History: A Symposium', *Feminist Studies*, vol. 6, no. 1, pp. 55–64.

Smith-Rosenberg, Carroll (1983) 'The Female World of Love and Ritual: Relations between Women in Nineteenth-Century America' in Elizabeth Abel and Emily K. Abel (eds) *The Signs Reader: Women, Gender and Scholarship*, Chicago: University of Chicago Press, article first published 1975.

Smock, Audrey Chapman (1977) 'Conclusion' in Janet Zollinger Giele and Audrey Chapman Smock (eds) *Women Roles and Status in Eight Countries*, New York: John Wiley & Sons.

Soper, Kate (1987) 'Marxism and Morality', *New Left Review*, no. 163, pp. 101–13.

Spender, Dale C. (1982) *Women of Ideas*, London: Routledge & Kegan Paul.

Spillers, Hortense J. (1984) 'Interstices: a Small Drama of Words' in Carol S. Vance (ed.) *Pleasure and Danger: Exploring Female*

Sexuality, Boston: Routledge & Kegan Paul.

Stone, Janey (1985) '"Iron Ladies": Women in the 1984–5 British Miners' Strike' *Hecate*, vol. 11, no. 2, pp. 7–32.

Strobel, Margaret (1982) 'Review Essay: African Women', *Signs*, vol. 8, no. 6, pp. 109–131.

Sullivan, Barbara (1985) 'Decolonization, Dependency and Development: Papua New Guinea and Micronesia', unpublished paper.

Sullivan, Norma (1983) 'Indonesian Women in Development: State Theory and Urban Kampung Practice', in Lenore Manderson (ed.) *Women's Work and Women's Roles: Economics and Everyday Life in Indonesia, Malaysia and Singapore*, Canberra: Development Studies Centre, Australian National University.

Tabak, Fanny (1984) 'Women and Authoritarian Regimes' in Judith Wicks Stiehm (ed.) *Women's View of the Political World of Men*, New York: Transnational Publishers.

Tabari, Azar (1980) 'The Origins of the Veiled Iranian Women', *Feminist Review*, no. 5, pp. 19–32.

Tabari, Azar and Yeganeh, Nahid (1982) *In the Shadows of Islam: The Women's Movement in Iran*, London: Zed Books Ltd.

Tanner, Nancy (1974) 'Matrifocality in Indonesia and Africa and among Black Americans' in Michelle Zimbalest Rosaldo, *Woman, Culture and Society*, Stanford: Stanford University Press.

Te Awekotuku, Ngahuia (1983) 'He Wahine, He Whenua: Maori Women and the Environment' in Leonie Caldecott and Stephanie Leland (eds) *Reclaim the Earth: Women Speak Out For Life on Earth*, London: Women's Press.

Te Awekotuku, Ngahuia and Waring, Marilyn J. (1984) 'New Zealand: Foreigners in Our Own Land' in Robin Morgan (ed.) *Sisterhood is Global*, New York: Anchor Press/Doubleday.

Thidinh, Nguhen Thi (1984) 'Vietnam: "the Braided Army"' in Robin Morgan (ed.) *Sisterhood is Global*, New York: Anchor Press/ Doubleday.

Tinker, Irene (1981) 'A Feminist View of Copenhagen', *Signs*, vol.6, no. 3, pp. 531–5.

Trivedi, Parita (1984) 'To Deny Our Fullness: Asian Women in the Making of History', *Feminist Review*, no. 17, pp. 37–50.

United Nations (1980) *Report of the World Conference of the United Nations Decade for Women: Equality, Development and Peace*, New York: United Nations.

Vajrathon, Mallica (1984) 'Thailand: We Superwomen Must Allow the Men to Grow Up' in Robin Morgan (ed.) *Sisterhood is Global*, New York: Anchor Press/Doubleday.

Valerio, Anita (1983) 'It's in my blood, my face – my mother's voice, the way I sweat' in Cherríe Moraga and Gloria Anzaldúa (eds) *This Bridge Called My Back*, New York: Kitchen Table, Women of Color Press.

Velasco, Jeannie Anderson (1985) 'The UN Decade for Women in Peru', *Women's Studies International Forum*, vol. 8, no. 2, pp. 107–10.

Vidal, Isabel Pico (1980) 'The History of Women's Struggle for Equality in Puerto Rico', in June Nash and Helen Icken Safa, *Sex and Class in Latin America*, Mass.: Bergin & Garvey.

Vogel, Lise (1983) *Marxism and the Oppression of Women: Toward a Unitary Theory*, London: Pluto Press.

van Vuuren, Nancy (1979) *Women Against Apartheid: The Fight for Freedom in South Africa 1920–1975*, Palo Alto, California: R & E Research Associates Inc.

Walby, Sylvia (1986) *Patriarchy at Work*, Oxford: Polity Press.

Walker, Alice (1982) *The Color Purple*, New York: Washington Square Press.

Walker, Alice (1984) *In Search of Our Mothers' Gardens: Womanist Prose*, London: Women's Press.

Walker, Alice (1985) 'Writing *The Color Purple*' in Mari Evans (ed.) *Black Women Writers (1950–1980) A Critical Evaluation*, New York: Anchor Press/Doubleday; London: Pluto Press.

Watson, Lilla (1987) 'Sister, Black is the Colour of my Soul' in Jocelynne A. Scutt (ed.) *Different Lives: Reflections on the Women's Movement and Visions of its Future*, Ringwood: Penguin.

Weems, Renita (1983) '"Artists without Art Form": a Look at the Black Woman's World of Unrevered Black Women' in Barbara Smith (ed.) *Home Girls: A Black Feminist Anthology*, New York: Kitchen Table, Women of Color Press.

Williams, Elizabeth (1987) 'Aboriginal First, Woman Second' in Jocelynne A. Scutt (ed.) *Different Lives: Reflections on the Women's Movement and Visions of its Future*, Ringwood: Penguin.

Wong, Aline K. (1981) 'Comments on Tinker's "A Feminist View of Copenhagen"', *Signs*, vol. 6, no. 4, pp. 775–6.

Woo, Merle (1983) 'Letter to Ma' in Cherríe Moraga and Gloria Anzaldúa (eds) *This Bridge Called My Back*, New York: Kitchen Table, Women of Color Press.

Woolf, Virginia (1977) *Three Guineas*, Harmondsworth: Penguin.

Xiao, Lu (1984) 'China: Feudal Attitudes, Party Control and Half the Sky' in Robin Morgan (ed.) *Sisterhood is Global*, New York: Anchor Press/Doubleday.

Yamada, Mitsuye (1983) 'Asian Pacific American Women and Feminism' in Cherríe Moraga and Gloria Anzaldúa (eds) *This Bridge Called My Back*, New York: Kitchen Table, Women of Color Press.

Yeganeh, Nahid (1982) 'Women's Struggles in the Islamic Republic of Iran' in Azar Tabari and Nahid Yeganeh (compilers) *In the Shadow of Islam: the Women's Movement in Iran*, London: Zed Books Ltd.

Index